Modernizing Schools

Also available from Continuum

Analysing Underachievement in Schools, Emma Smith
Education and Community, Dianne Gereluk

Modernizing Schools

People, Learning and Organizations

Edited by Graham Butt and Helen Gunter

continuum

CONTINUUM International Publishing Group
The Tower Building
11 York Road
London SE1 7NX

80 Maiden Lane
Suite 704
New York
NY 10038

www.continuumbooks.com

British Library Cataloguing-in-Publication Data
A catalogue record for this book is available from the British Library.

ISBN-10: 0826490379 (hardcover) ISBN-13: 978-0-8264-9037-7 (hardcover)

Library of Congress Cataloging-in-Publication Data
A catalog record for this book is available from the Library of Congress.

Typeset by Servis Filmsetting Ltd, Manchester
Printed and bound in Great Britain by Biddles Ltd, King's Lynn, Norfolk

Contents

Acknowledgements

The editors and authors would like to express their gratitude to a number of people who have helped in the production of this book.

The editors owe a special debt of thanks to the team at Continuum who have been supportive during the writing, editing and production process. Anthony Haynes, as previous Commissioning Editor for Education, is worthy of a special mention for being so encouraging about the project from the outset. Also thanks are due to Kirsty Schaper (Editorial Assistant) and Alexandra Webster (Publisher), who have both been involved in the project and who have offered advice and guidance along the way.

This book could not have been written without the data amassed from two DfES-funded projects: Transforming the School Workforce Pathfinder Project and ICT Test Bed Project. We are grateful to all those involved in these projects at the University of Birmingham for the hard work they put into making them so successful. Both projects were co-led by Hywel Thomas and Helen Gunter, and included: Graham Butt, Antony Fielding, Ann Lance, Rachel Pilkington, Steve Powers, Steve Rayner, Desmond Rutherford, Ian Selwood and Chris Szwed. The ICT Test Bed Project also included Roger Lock and Allan Soares. Celia Brown also co-led the TSW Project at the beginning, but left the University of Birmingham to further her athletic career. Administrative support for both projects was ably provided by Julie Foster and Liz Potts.

Our thanks go to the staff and students of the pilot schools in both projects who welcomed us and accommodated the research into their very busy lives. They demonstrated for us the importance of involving the profession in decisions about educational reform. We would also like to thank the headteachers from the TSW Project pilot schools who have contributed to the book through being interviewed about developments since the Project finished. While they remain anonymous, we would like to give recognition to their generosity in talking about developments in school and their views on how the remodelling processes have unfolded.

Special mention should also be made of Kerry Frew, who translated Chapter 15 from French into English at short notice and for a very modest financial reward.

Thanks to our 'critical reader', Professor Peter Ribbins, whose advice and guidance on a late draft of the book were invaluable, and offered with a characteristic generosity of spirit.

We should also like to thank the School of Education, University of Birmingham for awarding a small Research Development Grant to the editors to ease the production of the book, enabling us to finance aspects of research, travel, translation and meetings.

Last, but not least, the editors would also like to thank the copy editor, Sue Cope, for the time and energy spent in preparing this book for publication.

Graham Butt and Helen Gunter,
October 2006

Glossary of abbreviations

ANC	African National Congress
ASD	Autistic Spectrum Disorders
ATL	Association of Teachers and Lecturers
Becta	British Educational Communications and Technology Agency
BELMAS	British Educational Leadership, Management and Administration Society
BERA	British Educational Research Association
CAD	Computer Assisted Design
CGTV	Cognition and Technology Group at Vanderbilt
CMT	Change Management Team
CPD	Continuing Professional Development
CRT	Classroom Release Time
DEET	Department of Employment, Education and Training
DEETYA	Department of Employment, Education, Training and Youth Affairs
DES	Department of Education and Science
DEST	Department of Education, Science and Training
DFE	Department for Education
DFEE	Department for Education and Employment
DfES	Department for Education and Skills
DPD	Direction de la Programmation et du Développement
EBSD	Emotional, Behavioural and Social Difficulties
EFTO	Elementary Teachers' Federation of Ontario
ELRC	Education Labour Relations Council
ERO	Education Review Office
ESRC	Economic and Social Research Council
FETC	Further Education Training Certificate
GCSE	General Certificate of Secondary Education
GEAR	Growth, Employment and Redistribution strategy
GM	Grant Maintained
GMB	Britain's General Union
GTC	General Teaching Council
HEQC	Higher Education Quality Committee
HLTA	Higher Level Teaching Assistant
HMCIC	Her Majesty's Chief Inspector of Constabulary

HMI	Her Majesty's Inspectorate
ICT	Information and Communications Technology
IFIP	International Federation for Information Processing
ILS	Independent Learning Suite
INSET	In Service Training
IPPR	Institute for Public Policy Research
IR	Industrial Relations
IRU	Implementation Review Unit
IT	Information Technology
ITTE	Information Technology in Teacher Education
IUFM	Instituts Universitaires de Formation des Maîtres
IWB	Interactive Whiteboard
JISC	Joint Information Systems Committee
KS	Key Stage
LA	Local Authority
LEA	Local Education Authority
LSA	Learning Support Assistant
MCEETYA	Ministerial Council for Employment, Education, Training and Youth Affairs
MIS	Management Information System
MLD	Moderate Learning Difficulties
MLE	Managed Learning Environment
NAACE	National Association of Advisors for Computers in Education
NAHT	National Association of Head Teachers
NASUWT	National Association of Schoolmasters and Union of Women Teachers
NCC	National Curriculum Council
NCET	National Council for Educational Technology
NCSL	National College for School Leadership
NEOST	National Employers' Organization for School Teachers
NEPI	National Education Policy Investigation
NFER	National Foundation for Educational Research
NGfL	National Grid for Learning
NHS	National Health Service
NIQTSL	National Institute for Quality Teaching and School Leadership
NOF	New Opportunities Fund
NQT	Newly Qualified Teacher
NRCS	National Revised Curriculum Statement
NRT	National Remodelling Team
NUT	National Union of Teachers
NZCF	New Zealand Curriculum Framework
NZQA	New Zealand Qualifications Authority
OBE	Outcomes Based Education
OCT	Ontario College of Teachers
OECD	Organization for Economic Cooperation and Development

OfSTED	Office for Standards in Education
OISE/UT	Ontario Institute for Studies in Education of the University of Toronto
PAT	Professional Association of Teachers
PDA	Personal Digital Assistant
PFI	Private Finance Initiative
PGCE	Post Graduate Certificate in Education
PIU	Performance and Innovation Unit
PPA	Planning, Preparation and Assessment
PTE	Private Training Establishment
PwC	PricewaterhouseCoopers
QTS	Qualified Teacher Status
RSA	Republic of South Africa
SACE	South African Council for Educators
SAQA	South African Qualifications Authority
SEN	Special Educational Needs
SENCO	Special Educational Needs Co-ordinator
SETA	Sector Education and Training Authority
SGB	School Governing Body
SHA	Secondary Heads Association
SLD	Severe Learning Difficulties
SMT	Senior Management Team
STCA	Secondary Teachers' Collective Agreement
STRB	School Teacher Review Body
SWA	School Workforce Adviser
TA	Teaching Assistant
TDA	Training and Development Agency
TGWU	Transport and General Workers' Union
TLRC	Teaching and Learning Resources Committee
TRB	Teacher Registration Board
TSW	Transforming the School Workforce
TTA	Teacher Training Agency
UNISON	Represents public sector workers
VLE	Virtual Learning Environment
WAMG	Workforce Agreement Monitoring Group

Notes on contributors

Sarie J. Berkhout is Professor in Education Policy Studies at the University of Stellenbosch in South Africa. She teaches Comparative Education, Education Finance and Education Policy Studies to undergraduate and postgraduate students. She has served as a member of several national policy-making bodies related to standard setting and quality assurance in education including moderation of the national school-leaving examination, a national standards body and the standards-generating body for assessment in South Africa. The pervasive interest of her research is a critical reflection on the linkage between equity, education change and its social, economic and political connectedness. Her latest research and articles focus on (de)centralization in education and the implications of different views of power in understanding this. She has also published on the linkage between the qualification structure, assessment and the workplace and rethinking the way education systems are conceptualized.

Kathy Broad is the director of the elementary teacher education programme at Ontario Institute for Studies in Education of the University of Toronto (OISE/UT) and teaches within the initial teacher education programme. Her graduate teaching and research focus upon teacher education, induction and development. Other writing and research interests include literacy education, curriculum, instruction and assessment and transformative leadership for change. A former school principal, she has written literacy texts, resources and assessments for elementary learners.

Graham Butt is Senior Lecturer in Geography Education and Director of Learning and Teaching in the School of Education, University of Birmingham. He has written and researched extensively on issues within geography education, whilst his recent involvement in research projects for the DfES has extended his writing into areas of teacher workload and the use of teaching assistants in schools. His published books include *The Continuum Guide to Geography Education* (2000), *Theory into Practice – Extending Writing Skills* (2001), *Reflective Teaching of Geography 11–18* (2002) and *Lesson Planning* (Second Edition) (2006). One of his previous publications, *Birmingham – Decisions on Development* (1998), was awarded a Silver Medal for Curriculum Materials by the Geographical Association (GA). Graham is currently an editor of the international journal *Educational Review* and is joint commissioning editor of the *Theory into Practice* series of research monographs for the GA. In addition he serves as an external examiner for PGCE, Master's, MPhil and PhD students at a number of British universities and has worked as a consultant for the Qualifications and Curriculum Authority (QCA). Graham is an invited member of the British Sub-Committee of the International Geographical Union (IGU) and has delivered papers at a number of the IGU's international conferences.

Tanya Fitzgerald is Professor of Education at Unitec Institute of Technology, Auckland, and Visiting Research Fellow at the University of Nottingham (2007–2008). Tanya is the Managing Editor of History of Education Review and the New Zealand Journal of Educational Leadership. In conjunction with Professor Helen Gunter, she is co-editor of the Journal of Educational Administration and History from 2008. Her research and publications span two epistemic fields: history of education and educational leadership. Tanya's current research project examines historical and contemporary perspectives on women professors and professional identity.

Helen Gunter is Professor of Educational Policy, Leadership and Management in the School of Education at the University of Manchester, and Adjunct Professor at Unitec, Auckland, New Zealand. Helen was co-director of the Evaluation of the Transforming the School Workforce Pathfinder Project and the ICT Test Bed Pilot Project, and has the led the National Evaluation of the University of the First Age for the past four years. She co-led with Alma Harris and Michael Fielding the Economic and Social Research Council (ESRC) Seminar Series *Challenging the Orthodoxy of School Leadership*. She has written and researched on the modernization of schools, and has a particular interest in knowledge production in the field of educational leadership. Her most recent books include: *Rethinking Education: The Consequences of Jurassic Management* (1997), *Leaders and Leadership in Education* (2001), *Leading Teachers* (2005) and *Living Headship: Voice, Vision and Values* (co-edited with Harry Tomlinson and Pauline Smith 1999). Helen is grant holder for the ESRC project, Knowledge Production in Educational Leadership, and she is researching the origins and development of school leadership in England.

Darius Jackson is Lecturer in History and Citizenship in Education in the School of Education, University of Birmingham. He teaches History and Citizenship on the Secondary PGCE course and the History component of the Primary PGCE course. He also teaches Citizenship at undergraduate level. In his 19 years in teaching, he taught in a variety of secondary schools, ranging from a small rural comprehensive to a large urban girls' school, spending the last 11 years as a head of department. His main areas of research are in the teaching of the Holocaust, how Citizenship teachers are developing a subject-specific pedagogy and how young children develop an understanding of time.

Ann Lance is a Senior Lecturer in the School of Education, University of Birmingham. She coordinates the Professional Studies element of the Primary PGCE course in addition to teaching on undergraduate programmes. A former primary headteacher and editor of *Primary Practice*, she has research interests in school leadership and management, education policy and remodelling of the school workforce. Her publications reflect this range but also include health education issues.

Régis Malet is a Senior Lecturer in Education at Charles de Gaulle University – Lille 3, France, and is President of the French Association of Comparative Education. Prior to that, he was a Research Fellow at the University of Leeds. He is a member of the PROFEOR (Profession – Education – Orientation) research team in Lille. His research is both individual and collaborative and often has an international dimension. His work investigates schools, teaching and training from a cultural and political perspective. His publications include *L'identité en formation. Phénoménologie du devenir enseignant* (1998), 'Anthropologie de l'éducation' (special issue of *Spirale*, 31, 2003), *Modernisation de l'école et contextes culturels* (2005) as well as articles and book chapters in France and abroad.

Rachel Pilkington is Senior Lecturer in ICT in the School of Education, University of Birmingham. Rachel is a Chartered Psychologist, holds a Post-Graduate Certificate in Teaching and Learning in Higher Education and is a member of the Higher Education Academy. Her research has led her to empirically investigate learning with computer-based technology in a wide variety of educational contexts. Her PhD in knowledge-based systems involved her in developing interaction analyses for evaluating and computationally modelling educational dialogue. More recently she has contributed to both DfES-funded TSW Pathfinder and ICT Test Bed Projects. Her current projects include the EU Kaleidoscope 6th Framework Project investigating the conditions for productive networked learning, the Microsoft-funded ECOWiki Project to support students in the collaborative development of web-based educational resources and the evaluation of the JISC-funded Interactive Logbook Project.

Steve Rayner is Director of Research Degree Studies in the School of Education, University of Birmingham. His research interests include the study of individual differences in teaching, learning and special educational management. He has more than 60 publications across this field, including Riding and Rayner (1998), *Cognitive Styles and Learning Strategies*; Rayner and Ribbins (1999), *Headteachers and Leadership in Special Education*; and Riding and Rayner (2001), *International Perspectives on Individual Differences – Cognitive Styles and Learning Strategies*. His interest in style differences in human performance has led to interdisciplinary work researching style in teaching, learning and management, and is reflected in his co-founding and continuing presidency of the European Learning Styles Information Network (ELSIN at www.elsinnet.org.uk/). Additional contributions on cognitive style appear in the *International*

Encyclopaedia of the Social and Behavioural Sciences (Smelser and Baltes 2001) and in *Major Writings in the Psychology of Education* (Smith and Pelligrini 2001). Further recent research work has involved the completion of a number of evaluation studies including the Transforming the School Workforce Pathfinder Project (2002–04), the ICT Test Bed Pathfinder Project (2003), Fostering Inclusion in Dudley LEA (2002–03) and the 'Children as Learning Citizens' – SOCRATES Comenius Project (1999–2003).

Ian Selwood is Senior Lecturer in ICT in Education in the School of Education, University of Birmingham. He has worked in the field of ICT since the early 1970s, initially as head of Computer Studies in a secondary school, followed by six years as advisory teacher for IT. Since 1987 he has worked in the School of Education. His research interests are mainly concerned with the use of ICT to support Educational Administration and Management, and the Management of ICT in Schools. His publications reflect these areas of interest but also include other educational applications of ICT. Recent research projects include contributions to the DfES-funded TSW Evaluation, ICT Test Bed Baseline Study and Impact of Broadband on Schools, and Becta-funded research into the use of tablet PCs. His current research is concerned with ICT and school improvement, and ICT and personalized learning. He is Editor-in-Chief of *Education and Information Technologies* and on the editorial board of two other international academic journals, and Vice-Chair of the International Federation for Information Processing working group on IT in Educational Management.

Elizabeth Smyth is an Associate Professor in the Department of Curriculum Teaching and Learning (CTL) at the Ontario Institute for Studies in Education of the University of Toronto. She was cross-appointed to the Department of Theory and Policy Studies (TPS) in Education from 1999 to 2002, and served as Associate Chair of CTL with responsibilities for professional programmes, including liaison functions with initial teacher education, graduate education and continuing education. At present, she teaches in both the initial teacher education programme (where she teaches courses in the History of Education and in the core School and Society programme) and in the graduate programme (where she teaches courses in Gender and Curriculum, Curriculum Development for Highly Able Learners and in the History of Education). Elizabeth's research interests explore both historical and contemporary elements in teacher education including how teaching as a profession arose in accordance with and in spite of state regulation and how those charged with the task of transmitting knowledge were educated. She is also engaged in a course of research on the impact of women religious on Canadian education. Her recent works include two co-edited collections: Smyth and Bourne (eds) (2006) *Women Teaching, Women Learning*, and Heap, Millar and Smyth (eds) (2005) *Learning to Practice*.

Chris Szwed is Senior Lecturer and Director of Studies for Initial Teacher Education in the School of Education, University of Birmingham. She has held a range of senior management roles within schools and has worked as a Curriculum Adviser within a local education authority (LEA) with responsibility for special educational needs (SEN). Her research interests are in the area of SEN leadership and management within mainstream schools, and primary education. Her doctoral thesis examined the roles and responsibilities of staff working with children with SEN, and subsequent publications, including Jones, Jones and Szwed (2001) *The Senco as Teacher and Manager* have further developed the area.

Lesley Vidovich is an Associate Professor in the Faculty of Education at the University of Western Australia. Lesley's primary research focus is the field of education policy and practices – both in the schooling and higher education sectors – with a special interest in education policy development in a context of globalization and internationalization. She has conducted research in a number of different countries and has published in international journals based in the UK, Europe, North America, Asia and Australia. Lesley has been a secondary science teacher, curriculum developer and tertiary entrance examiner. She has been invited to sit on School Councils, and to conduct consultancy work, in both government and non-government schools. She currently holds an Australian Research Council grant to study higher education policy in Singapore, People's Republic of China and Hong Kong (Special Administrative Region of China).

Chapter 1

Introduction: the challenges of modernization

Helen Gunter and Graham Butt

Introduction

The aim of this book is to critically investigate the current modernization agenda within education, with a particular focus on the remodelling of the school workforce in England. In achieving this aim we concentrate on New Labour's thrust towards the restructuring and reculturing of public sector workforces, whilst also considering the modernization process in education in other countries.

Modernization is a hollow word that can be inscribed with whatever meaning the government and its gurus of the day locate within it. Consequently modernization has become a condensate concept that abridges a range of things to be done: new roles, new work, new power relationships, new values and new employment. The term is also underpinned by narratives regarding the change imperative, which recognize a need to challenge and abandon practices that no longer meet expectations about the future. New Labour is reworking its dictionary and so modernization is becoming an incremental process of upgrading, while transformation is being used to label a reconceptualization. Remodelling can fit neatly under either label because it is about both improving what is there combined with questioning whether what is there should remain. A range of remodelling strategies are currently unfolding as official policies, and the examples we investigate indicate how the *type* of work undertaken, *who* does that work and *how* they do it is being changed. In education it is at the interface between teachers and teaching assistants, as well as through the role of ICT, that modernization is being worked through as a strategy affecting day-to-day practice. We intend exploring such developments, asking questions about what this means for learners and learning.

We aim to explore four important questions about modernization, and the new hybrid of transformation, in the context of state schooling: First, what are the antecendents of the current waves of modernization and what directions is it taking in England and internationally? Second, does workforce modernization, in whatever form, offer meaningful ways forward for the teaching profession in England and in other countries? Third, how is the leadership of change to take place with respect to educational modernization in England and elsewhere? Fourth, what alternative approaches to remodelling might be developed with regard to the workforce labour market in England and in other national contexts?

We do not intend to use these questions to structure ideas or arguments, as we would contend that such a technical handling of complex processes would hide rather than reveal important issues. We have asked our co-authors to use them to do some serious thinking, and so the questions are designed to stimulate rather than control the text. We return to the questions in the final chapter and provide an analysis of where we think things are going, but we are clear that while we can conclude the book we cannot draw definitive conclusions.

We site the analysis stimulated by our questions in two main ways: First, we will draw on data and the experiences of practitioners gathered primarily from the evaluation of government-sponsored projects such as the *Transforming the School Workforce Pathfinder Project* (Thomas *et al.* 2004; see Appendix 1), and the *ICT Test Bed Project* (Thomas *et al.* 2003a; see Appendix 2). Second, we will provide discursive analysis of the processes that are indicative of such projects, particularly by including papers from internationally renowned researchers concerning the reforms in England and how they can be read in comparison with events in their own countries.

Overall, we aim to provide perspectives on the ways in which reforms such as workforce remodelling are located within the process of modernization, with particular reference to how this is used as a conduit for introducing government policy into schools. We aim to both narrate and analyse waves of modernization within context, combining this with a critical evaluation of how remodelling of the school workforce is delivering and anticipating change.

Modernization

Education in England is located within a permanent revolution in the provision of public services. Wave after wave of reform to the structure and culture of the public sector has been taking place since the Second World War with two main trends. The first has sought to extend the public funding of education, and to encourage inclusion and equity; the second has sought to extend private provision of education, enabling differentiation and competition. The first was pre-eminent in the immediate post-Second World War period when gains were made in the extension of secondary and post-compulsory provision to a wider range of people (e.g. secondary education for all from 1944; raising of the school-leaving age to 16 in 1972; and comprehensive schools from the 1960s), curriculum innovation, and the professionalization of teachers; the second trend re-emerged in the 1970s and remains dominant through gains made in the privatization of public provision from the 1980s, the introduction of private sector roles, practices and personnel, and the incentivization of the private sector to offer educational services and products.

These trends are located in very different positions with respect to the role of the state and the purposes of education in an emergent democratic system. On the one hand, education is a public good and schools are institutions through which society's aims for citizenship are realized. This is best expressed by

Marquand (2004) who argues for the public domain that '. . .has its own distinctive culture and decision rules. In it citizenship rights trump both market power and the bonds of clan or kinship'. He goes on to show that the public domain is now in crisis through modernization, and that it is 'both priceless and precarious – a gift of history, which is always at risk' (pp. 1–2). By contrast, Tooley (1995) argues that the problem lies with state provision because it always ensures poor-quality services. He makes the case for markets in education, such that the consumer can both demonstrate voice and exit – whereas in public sector provision the dissatisfied customer can only complain or suffer in silence. Hence education is conceptualized as a private good that should be accessed through purchaser–provider market trading.

New Labour has developed a 'Third Way', through which it has sought to transcend the state market binary and reject 'big government', whilst at the same time recognizing the need for active management. In attempting to avoid the social disintegration caused by deregulated markets New Labour also recognizes the need for social cohesion based on responsibility and inclusion. For education, the shift is away from credentialism towards capability:

> Orthodox schools and other educational institutions are likely to be surrounded, and to some extent subverted, by a diversity of other learning frameworks. Internet technology, for instance, might bring educational opportunities to mass audiences. In the old economic order, the basic competencies needed for jobs remained relatively constant. Learning (and forgetting – being able to discard old habits) are integral to work in the knowledge economy. A worker creating a novel multi-media application can't succeed by using long-standing skills – the tasks in question didn't even exist a short while ago. (Giddens 2000, p. 74)

The lexicon used to describe and popularize this approach is one of 'new', 'modern' and 'modernization'. Fairclough (2000, p. 18) has identified that in the 53 speeches given by Tony Blair in 2 years (1997–9) 'new' occurs 609 times, 'modern' 89 times, 'modernize/modernization' 87 times and 'reform' 143 times.

Analysing modernization shows that it is both a state of being (how the individual and the group thinks about the world), as well as an action (doing what needs to be done to deliver change). Introducing the White Paper on *Modernising Government*, Tony Blair (1999a) argued that 'we should reward success, and not tolerate mediocrity' and 'the "way we have always done it" may not be the best way to do it in the future'. Consequently, modernization is empty until it is filled with an approach to the future through breaking with the past, instilling a 'can do' orientation to secure that future. The challenge to purposes (values), structures (roles) and cultures (habits) is presented as a rationale in itself where all is up for grabs – the commitment to do this is conceived as being energizing, creating a self-generating momentum.

Policy strategies which are designed to both deliver and be a product of modernization have a number of features concerned with standards and accountability: devolution and delegation; flexibility and incentives; and expanding choice (see DfES 2002a). Such strategies are achieved through two main thrusts – the regulation of processes and outcomes, and the deregulation of responsibility and accountability. This can create tensions and contradictions such as the enhancement of the role of parents in exercising choice locally about schools, combined with legal controls over school attendance (and prison for parents of persistent truants), or with respect to guidelines over the content of packed lunches. While the education profession is in tune with the principles underpinning *Every Child Matters* (DfES 2004a) with regard to services focusing on the child, there are concerns that education will be integrated with a range of other public services (e.g. health, welfare, police) in ways that will abolish schools as we know them or integrate these wider services into schools in such a way that a chief executive will be appointed to oversee provision. Hence while an argument can be made that at least someone on the senior team will need to have expertise in education, they may not be a headteacher or even a qualified teacher. The territory on which such policy proposals are taking place is teeming with politics and positioning: from claims that public education and schooling as an agreed principle is not settled and is in the process of being dismantled, to arguments about the 'nanny state' interfering in the private domain, to Bobbitt's (2002) advocated opportunities that the 'market state' is generating for 'turning over education to parents' (p. 242).

The regulative thrust is known as 'new public management'. This combines audits, targets and league tables with longer-term planning, collaboration, social inclusion and 'joined-up government' (Newman 2000). The deregulative thrust is achieved through a differentiated workforce – where the approach is to strengthen hierarchy through the separation of a cadre of trained and licensed elite as organizational leaders (PIU 2001), combined with the deregulation of the workforce by outsourcing, remodelling and civilianization. An example of each of these changes to the workforce can suffice here: first, outsourcing through the tendering of contracts for the delivery of public services by private sector companies in education, health and local government; second, clinical decision-making being remodelled, with doctors expected to link their decisions to resource implications and to transfer some clinical decision-making to nurses and paramedics; third, the work of the police being civilianized through the increase in numbers and change of role of the community support officers, with HMCIC (2004) reporting that 'non-sworn police staff now account for around a third of all police personnel' (p. 34). These are changes that are also evident in compulsory education, where the provision of school services is undergoing rapid shifts in both process and outcome.

Modernizing schools

New Labour's claim about the modernization of schools makes reform both non-negotiable and urgent. As a government insider, Barber (2001) states that 'the vision is a world class education service: one which matches the best anywhere on the planet' (p. 17). A decade of reform has targeted: interventions in the curriculum (e.g. literacy and numeracy strategies); support for social inclusion (e.g. excellence in cities); diversity of provision through structural change and targeting of resources (e.g. specialist schools, beacon schools and academies); and the remodelling of the school workforce (e.g. performance management and pay, leadership training and licensing, removing bureaucratic burdens). Recently the principles underpinning the next phase of the reform agenda have been outlined as:

- **Greater personalization and choice**, with the wishes and needs of children, parents and learners located centre stage.
- **Opening up services** to new and different providers and ways of delivering services.
- **Freedom and independence** for frontline headteachers, governors and managers with clear, simple accountabilities, and more secure streamlined funding arrangements.
- **A major commitment to staff development** with high quality support and training to improve assessment, care and teaching.
- **Partnerships** with parents, employers, volunteers and voluntary organizations to maximize the life chances of children, young people and adults.

(DfES 2004b, p. 4)

Barber (2005), in a speech designed both to celebrate the government's achievements and sustain the reform imperative, argues that there will be continued 'innovation' and 'choice' in order to deliver on standards:

improving children's performance in schools is a question of how well teachers teach in their classroom. The task of everyone else in a school system – school principals, local administrators, teacher trainers, government and other stakeholders – is to align everything they do to ensure that each teacher walks into each lesson with the skills, knowledge, equipment and motivation to teach a great lesson – and find in their classroom pupils who are ready to learn. (pp. 1–2)

This is premised on changing tasks and roles, on how practice is conceived and discussed and on how power relationships are experienced. In essence, it is a reculturing of school staff (DfES 2005a).

The early days of New Labour show a full recognition of the immediate needs to handle workload, not least because the supply of teachers was not meeting existing or predicted demand. Faced with the need to invest in public education and also to secure public accountability for that investment, New Labour had to break the dominance of teachers as providers of education. At the same time they needed to construct claims for the creation of fewer but higher-status teachers. While the achievements of teachers were given some recognition, the emphasis

in reform texts focused on teachers as *the* problem in education. Rapid reform of
the profession was proposed in *teachers: meeting the challenge of change* (DfEE 1998),
where a 'new professionalism' is outlined. This runs through other texts, such as
Estelle Morris' *Professionalism and Trust* speech (Morris 2001) and the remodelling document *Time for Standards* (DfES 2002a). The consistent message is that
teachers have been conservative and self-serving:

> The time has gone when isolated, unaccountable professionals made cur-
> riculum and pedagogical decisions alone, without reference to the outside
> world.   (DfEE 1998, p. 14)

> We need to challenge the cynics who argue that reform is impossible, that
> nothing can ever change; that the challenges are too great. These arguments
> have dogged the public sector for too long. No matter how well intentioned
> some opposition to reform may have been, it has sometimes ended up dam-
> aging the cause it was intended to serve.   (Morris 2001, p. 9)

> None of this was evident 50 years ago. There was little measurement, no feed-
> back, no debate and no teacher held accountable for performance. Individual
> teachers may have taught well but teachers as a whole were, in the professional
> sense, 'uninformed'. There was little scope for identifying and disseminating
> good practice or for creating strategies to improve standards for all.
>   (DfES 2002a, p. 10)

Based on this storying of teachers and their work, New Labour has constructed
a *new* professionalism founded on learning being supported by 'trained
adults', where 'pupils will benefit in the classroom through the help of teachers, teaching assistants and ICT technicians. And learning mentors will also
help ensure they achieve their potential' (Morris 2001, p. 15). In this scenario
the status of teachers and teaching is to be improved through focusing more
on work outside the classroom than inside it (i.e. accessing learning materials
for other adults to deliver, managing other adults, analysing data). What is on
offer to teachers is a shift from the early days of New Labour, where 'informed
prescription' dominated, towards 'informed professional judgement' (DfES
2002a, p. 11). Within the context of the National Curriculum and strategies
(e.g. literacy, numeracy and KS3) and performance management (e.g. league
tables, inspection and payment by results) teachers have been directed
towards 'a greater use of pedagogic strategies. . . greater use of student feedback. . . a commitment to sharing best practice. . . more effective team
working. . . more imaginative use of the growing potential of ICT to support
learning. . . [and] . . . increasingly innovative and flexible timetables and class
structures' (DfES 2002a, p. 12).
    Underpinning this new professionalism is a tension between structures,
delivery and measurable impact. New Labour has sidestepped the established
selection of children by ability (grammar schools), faith (Catholic, Church of

England, Jewish, Muslim schools), sex (single-sex schools) and parental income (fee-paying private schools). Nevertheless, it has sought to enable secondary schools to distinguish themselves further through spreading 'good practice' as Beacon schools, having a particular focus on the curriculum through Specialist School Status and/or enabling consortia of private and public partnerships to receive public funding as Academies. Changes to the composition and deployment of the school workforce cannot be understood without recognition of these 'bigger picture' developments.

Challenges to the boundaries between the private (wealth, faith) and the public (community, equity) mean that the professional ethos, care and commitment of teachers have to be marginalized in favour of delivery and data. Central to this has been the reworking of the headteacher role as 'leading professional' (who teaches and leads on curriculum innovation), towards that of 'chief executive' (who must deliver organizational efficiencies and be accountable for the implementation of external reforms) (Grace 1995). There has been a huge investment in the training of heads as the delivery arm of the DfES through the National College for School Leadership and the mandatory licensing of headteachers from 2009. Furthermore, headteachers and teachers have been pushed and enticed away from public sector governance and expertise (local authority advisors; trade unions; postgraduate study, professional development and research in the universities) towards the private sector (individual and corporate consultants). Consequently, as Ball (2006) has shown, workforce reform is not only taking on private sector practices and language (such as 'workforce', 'leaders'), but is being achieved through and by private sector collaborations. The school is a business located within exchange networks and so change can happen without reference to political dialogue or public accountability (see Woods *et al.* 2007).

The rapidity of change, the complexity of emergent relations, the busyness of those who are most affected – combined with the sheer lack of obviousness about it – means that research which aims to describe and understand what is happening is finding it difficult to keep up. Obtaining access, or even having a voice to speak with those who are experiencing change, is often difficult. There are important debates to be had and issues to be raised about who the workforce are, what they are doing and why. However, it remains hard to develop a critical analysis without facing the same provider capture criticisms made of teachers. The value of educational research is constantly under fire as irrelevant because it is positioned as not solving existing problems that are identified as being urgent. It seems that this book could be characterized as useless, because in the modern world it is the 'spreading [of] good practice' (Morris 2006, p. 4) that matters more than understanding that practice, asking who determines it or why they wish to propose it. Indeed the shift in language from modernization to transformation means that the title is dated, but the ideas are not. Just as the downgrading of management as technical implementation and the upgrading of leadership as strategy has been challenged through research, then we will continue to expose the relationship between what we do, what we call it and who controls this (Gunter 2004a). Central to our aim is an engagement in a discursive analysis of the current changes. The way we achieve this may irritate, because we want to draw on a range of resources that will help us not only to report what is going on, but also to think about what it all means. In particular, we need to consider how policy is encoded, presented and engaged with. We therefore investigate who is transmitting and implementing the reforms, and why. Analysing a range of narratives is not automatically oppositional, but is central to how practice is experienced and taken into account.

Uncovering the realities of what it means to be 'reformed' requires an analysis of research about real lives. Such research shows that teachers become stressed (Bartlett 2004) and may become seriously damaged – both as people and professionals – as a result of being made the objects of a reform agenda which may itself be incoherent and contradictory (Dean 2001; Whitty 2000). It seems, using Ball's (1997, p. 241) analysis, that 'the teacher is increasingly an absent presence' in reform. The combined effect of this exclusion from decision-making, but inclusion through the impact of those decisions, means that performativity triumphs in 'the struggle over the teacher's soul' (Ball 2003, p. 217). Furthermore, questions are being asked about whether teaching will remain a graduate and trained profession, or whether remodelling is a part of a process of deregulation. If ICT software can enable children to learn on their own, and if lessons can be accessed via the Internet and delivered by teaching assistants, then is it necessary for teachers to have a degree and to undergo teacher training? As student debt increases then the prospect of a fourth year after a first degree without earning a salary could affect recruitment. Yet, as Wilkinson (2005) has argued, the relationship between knowledge, practice and role is central to professionalism. It can be argued that teaching assistants are trained 'on the job' to supervise children in order to solve the recruitment and retention crisis; this achieves greater economic efficiency through lower pay and lower status (Gunter 2005a and b). How long can this subordinate position continue if teaching does not have a distinctive set of knowledge claims for a right to practise (Wilkinson 2005)?

Studies of governance show that the policy–practice relationship is complex and that it may be less about the centre directing change and the locality implementing it, but more about how change is interpreted and negotiated within context (Cochrane 2004). Certainly, work that compares reform in England and Scotland (Alexiadou and Ozga 2002; Menter *et al.* 2004; Ozga 2002) shows that 'embedded' policy within 'local spaces' means that 'travelling' policies 'come up against existing priorities and practices'. Thus, 'while policy choices may be narrowing, national and local assumptions and practices remain significant and mediate or translate global policy in distinctive ways' (Ozga 2005, pp. 208–9). Research shows evidence of respect for teacher professionalism in the reform process, not least that 'classroom assistants' do not teach or work independently of teachers (Ozga 2005). The realities of reform show that the intention of reducing the working week to 35 hours in Scotland is itself a time-consuming process, and it is taking time to work through issues of what are essential and non-essential tasks (Menter *et al.* 2006).

Examining teachers at work shows that there is a need to focus on how the individual actively engages with reform through the mediation of core purposes and values regarding pedagogy and a sense of self (see Lingard *et al.* 2003; Stronach *et al.* 2002). Indeed, it has been argued that teachers have contributed to their own situation by making reforms work, even if they did not agree with them. As such they need to develop a form of professional practice which seeks to determine the nature and legitimacy of their work, rather than accept the role of technical implementer (Bottery and Wright 2000; Whitty 2000). Consequently, it is the issue of teachers, their work and the wider workforce that we intend to focus on in this book as we examine what it means to experience current reform strategies.

Remodelling the school workforce

Remodelling of the school workforce was introduced by New Labour into schools in England from September 2003, providing an important site for examining how the modernization project is being worked through. Remodelling is an immediate response to a current and projected shortage in the labour market, but it is equally ambitious in seeking to transform the culture in which change is understood and responded to. The New Labour agenda on improving standards is, in government terms, being jeopardized by reports of low morale – specifically, the media are reporting that one in three teachers expects to leave the profession within five years (Woodward 2003), and around 300,000 qualified teachers are not practising (Horne 2001, p. 15). Workload is regarded as a key issue in England (DfES 2000a, MORI 2002, PwC 2001, Smithers and Robinson 2003), (and in other countries; see, for example, Dibbon 2004, Gardner and Williamson 2005) and remodelling has been developed as the means to solve this.

Reform is more than the employment and deployment of public sector workers. It involves dispositional change, as illustrated by Prime Minister Blair (1999b) in speaking to new headteachers when he stated: '. . . we also must take on what I sometimes call the culture of excuses which affects some part of the teaching profession. A culture that tolerates low ambition, rejects excellence, treats poverty as an excuse for failure'. An upbeat, can-do, energetic profession can, it is argued, deliver globally excellent learning through the speeding up of work using ICT. Hardware and software being used as tools of calculation and communication, particularly through accessing lesson plans and evidence of good practice, means that a teacher with a laptop can work more efficiently and effectively at a time of their choosing. Differentiated and personalized teaching can be a reality through ready-made, online, learning packages. What to teach, how to teach and when to assess are therefore solved in ways that can enable the maintenance of a healthy work–life balance.

In January 2003 a 'historic' National Agreement (DfES 2003a) between the government, employers and unions (except the National Union of Teachers) was signed. Overtly the Agreement sought to solve the poor recruitment and retention of teachers, burgeoning bureaucracy and rising teacher workload. A plan was proposed (DfES 2002a, pp. 6–7) to deliver the reform:

- **contractual change:** to define the work that teachers should not do, including cover; and to guarantee time in the school day for planning, preparation and assessment, and leadership time for headteachers;
- **workload change:** to remove routine administrative work from teachers known as the 25 tasks (DfES 2002a), with an Implementation Review Unit (see IRU 2003) to oversee this;
- **time:** teachers' hours of work which various studies had put at over 50 per week in term time would be reduced (see PwC 2001);
- **support staff:** teachers would have personal assistants and there would be more class support from trained personnel;
- **school support staff:** organizational effectiveness would be enhanced by 'new managers and others with experience from outside education';
- **change management:** headteachers would be trained and supported by a pro-gramme 'to help achieve in their schools the necessary reforms of the teaching profession and restructuring of the school workforce'.

This planned reform has a number of features regarding the change process and a differentiated workforce. Schools were encouraged to establish a change management team to include non-teaching staff in the planning and delivery of reform. The team would take the school through a staged process of: Mobilise, Discover, Deepen, Develop and Deliver, in order to identify where and how change should happen (Collarbone 2005a). Central to these changes was a realignment of the workforce – for example, where schools did not have a bursar either one was appointed or a member of the administrative team was upgraded and trained to manage the budget. Schools also examined their use of technical support, with an emphasis on ICT technicians to enable both a network to be installed and the better use of hardware and software in curriculum delivery and assessment.

The main emphasis has been on increasing the number of adults within the classroom where traditionally only children with special needs and/or those for whom English is not their first language have had additional support. Within primary schools there has been the tradition of employing classroom assistants who have helped the teacher in a variety of ways: through working with individual pupils or groups of pupils; supporting practical activities; supporting pupils using ICT; and/or hearing pupils read. The current shift is to upgrade this work, with the label of teaching assistant (TA) being used as the generic title preferred by the government for those in paid employment in support of teachers, including those with general roles, or those with specific responsibilities for a child, subject area or age group. In essence TAs can provide support for the pupil, the teacher, the curriculum and the school. Higher-level teaching assistants (HLTAs) have greater autonomy and make a significant contribution to teaching and learning activities. They may contribute to the preparation and planning of lessons; monitor pupil progress and participation; provide feedback to teachers; support pupils as they learn; and/or work with whole classes, small groups or individual pupils where the assigned teacher is not present. Training and assessment of TAs, leading to certification as HLTAs against national standards, are designed to formalize and extend their contribution to supporting children, teachers and parents. HLTA status has partly been developed to support smooth progression to qualified teacher status (QTS) for those individuals with the potential and interest to qualify as teachers.

The growth in number, role and function of this varied support staff is located in the phased introduction of remodelling. From September 2003, teachers no longer had to 'routinely' undertake particular tasks, including: collecting money, chasing absences, bulk photocopying, copy typing, producing standard letters, class lists, record-keeping and filing, classroom display, analysing attendance figures, processing exam results, collating student reports, administering work experience, administering and invigilating examinations, administering teacher cover, ICT troubleshooting, commissioning new ICT equipment, ordering supplies and equipment, stocktaking, cataloguing, preparing, issuing and maintaining equipment and materials, minuting meetings, coordinating and submitting bids, seeking and giving personnel advice, managing and inputting pupil data (DfES 2002a). The emphasis was on ensuring a 'reasonable work–life balance', and so time was to be provided for those with management responsibilities to do their work during the day.

In Phase 2, from September 2004, a limit was put on the amount of cover provided for absent teachers, 'with the objective of reaching the point where teachers at school rarely cover at all', and a year later Phase 3 was introduced to ensure guaranteed time for planning, preparation and assessment (PPA) within school time. While invigilation had been listed in the tasks that teachers should not normally do, the new arrangements for removing teachers from this work are located in this stage of the reform roll out. Finally headteachers were to have 'dedicated headship time' in the school day (NRT 2003, p. 3). Underpinning this has been an expansion in the numbers and training of higher-level teaching assistants (41,000 to be trained by the Training and Development Agency (TDA) by 2007), who could do cover in order to release teachers for PPA, with the intention of using this as a route into qualified teacher status (Tabberer 2004).

These reforms are being implemented through a series of agencies:

- The Workforce Agreement Monitoring Group (WAMG) made up of representatives from the Association of Teachers and Lecturers (ATL), the Department for Education and Skills (DfES), the GMB, the National Association for Head Teachers (NAHT), the National Association of Schoolmasters and Union of Women Teachers (NASUWT), the National

Employers' Organization for School Teachers (NEOST), the Professional Association of Teachers (PAT), the Secondary Heads' Association (SHA), the Transport and General Workers' Union (TGWU), UNISON and the Welsh Assembly Government who are all signatories to the Agreement, and have formed a 'social partnership' with the government. The National Union of Teachers (NUT) is not a member. The WAMG provides a strategic overview of the implementation of the National Agreement.

- The Implementation Review Unit (IRU) was launched in April 2003 and is composed of '12 front line practitioners from across England – serving heads, senior teachers and a school bursar' (IRU 2003, p. 2) with the remit to report to ministers on reducing bureaucracy in schools and to 'scrutinise new policy and ensure that it reflects the way schools work' (ibid.).
- The National Remodelling Team (NRT) was formed from the London Leadership Centre team led by Dame Pat Collarbone which piloted remodelling in 32 schools, and developed the change management model (Collarbone 2005a). The remit of the NRT is to deliver remodelling. It was originally located in the National College for School Leadership, but since 2005 it has been relocated to the Training and Development Agency (formerly the Teacher Training Agency).

Ball's (2006) analysis of how the private sector is now undertaking public work is particularly interesting, especially with respect to the NRT whose work has been celebrated by Collarbone (2005a) as follows:

> The NRT is an example of a public–private partnership with the majority of the central team being consultants from the private sector, with little prior experience of education. The idea for such a team arose from the Transforming the School Workforce Pathfinder Project, a precursor to remodelling. The advantages are numerous: this team is not blocked by existing 'assumptions', is able to introduce practices and tools often untried in the education sector, is experienced in working in large organizations and dealing with change, brings a wide range of new skills and experience to the task and is designed to meet the demands of the task. Members of the team are used to working in teams and, perhaps of most value, radiate a 'can do' attitude, no matter how major the task.   (p. 77)

Consequently private sector knowing has cultural capital (Bourdieu 2000), and is seen as essential to securing change. Research evidence is thin on the ground, and the Transforming the School Workforce (TSW) Project evaluation (Thomas *et al.* 2004) has been marginalized, with remodelling being rolled out in advance of the evidence on which it was meant to be based. Official evaluations of the implementation process have been undertaken by the Office for Standards in Education (OfSTED) (2004a) and the National Foundation for Educational Research (NFER) (Easton *et al.* 2005, Wilson *et al.* 2005), although, as yet, there is no major national research project to investigate the experiences of the workforce, or the impact of the changes on teaching and learning.

Remodelling remains a highly political reform and needs to be seen in relation to other changes taking place in the conditions and salaries of teachers – not least the external restructuring of schools through the introduction of Teaching and Learning Responsibility Payments. It is contested by the NUT and UNISON who are particularly concerned about the impact remodelling is having on the principle of teaching being undertaken by a qualified teacher. Both unions note that teaching assistants still lack the necessary training, status and pay structure to undertake the work currently being transferred to them. Indeed, remodelling is regarded as 'un-modern' in its conceptualization, with references being made to Victorian traditions of unqualified teachers and large classes.

Within the context of official evaluations and political arguments, there are 'little voices' (Griffiths 2003) represented in the press where headteachers talk about the benefits of the changes to the work of teachers and the purposes of teaching, and those who identify the lack of funding for the reform and the problems of delivering the planning, preparation and assessment time in primary schools (Gunter *et al.* 2005). In a recent paper about how schools in one local authority engaged with remodelling it was found that there were variations between and within schools about the changes to practice. Hammersley-Fletcher and Lowe (2005) found that some schools were using remodelling to ask questions about practice, while other schools simply saw it as another reform that they had to implement. A wider survey of secondary schools undertaken by MacBeath and Galton (2004, pp. 5–6) for the NUT reports that teachers are still working between 45 and 70 hours per week and that 'so far the work agreement has had little impact on these workloads'. More recently the Office for Manpower Economics (2006) has published the School Teachers' Review Board study on workloads and shows that while secondary-school classroom teachers have dipped under the 50 hours per week barrier, others in secondary and primary schools remain above this. For some the hours have increased, with reports of secondary deputy heads going over 60 hours per week.

Perspectives on modernization

While current published research remains patchy and the stories of practitioners depend on editorial policy in order to be in the public domain, there is a body of research that can be used to understand and examine workforce reform. The chapters in Parts One to Three of this book draw on *The Evaluation of the Transforming the School Workforce (TSW) Pathfinder Project* (Thomas *et al.* 2004), and there is some reference in Part Three to the *Baseline Evaluation of the ICT Test Bed Project* (Thomas *et al.* 2003a and b) (see Appendices 1 and 2 for details). Both projects were commissioned by the DfES from the School of Education, University of Birmingham.

We have divided the book into four parts, the first three directly about reform in England, each of these having a particular theme around work and the workforce, leadership and change and learning. The fourth part provides perspectives on reform in England through the eyes and policy analysis of those working and living in other countries. These chapters stand alone as they examine an issue and make a case, but they are also part of the whole and provide a body of evidence and ideas about what is happening and what it might mean. We have adopted a style through which we want to embrace the reader – as practitioner, as student, as researcher, as policy-maker, as consultant, as taxpayer – into the issues. We have in mind an informed readership, which is located in the midst of the changes and wants to gain some wider understanding of what is happening and what it might mean; a readership that is interested in such events because they work with those who work in schools.

The first set of chapters are written by those who led and participated in the TSW Pathfinder and ICT Test Bed Projects (see Appendices 1 and 2). We wanted to examine the nature of remodelling through looking at roles and time – in particular focusing on aspects of change and its relationship to learning. Our co-authors are our friends and colleagues with whom we have worked on the two Projects and in other research and teaching activities. They have been able to combine their research experience from within these two Projects with their wider knowledge and understanding of particular aspects of research such as leadership (Jackson, Rayner), the workforce (Lance, Szwed) and ICT (Pilkington and Selwood). In several of the chapters we have not only drawn on published research evidence (Thomas *et al.* 2003a and b; 2004) about schools but we have also interviewed a small sample of headteachers from the TSW Project about their recent experiences. We invited these headteachers to participate because the TSW Project data showed that they are leading schools where there are innovative and risky experiments taking place in remodelling. Indeed, remodelling had begun in these schools before the word was 'constructed' and used as a policy initiative. We knew these headteachers would have interesting things to say about extraordinary changes that they and their schools had been involved in for longer than the official remodelling process.

The opening chapter of Part One, by Gunter and Butt, looks at the experiences of schools and draws on post-TSW Project interviews with headteachers. This is followed by chapters by Butt and Gunter who examine issues of workload, and by Lance, Rayner and Szwed who examine changes in the roles and work of support staff. Part Two focuses on organization, and begins with a chapter by Butt and Gunter and uses post-TSW Project interviews with headteachers to examine the leadership issues surrounding remodelling. This is followed by two chapters with thematic links – one by Rayner and Gunter who examine conceptualizations of leadership, and the second by Butt and Jackson who engage with systemic leadership by focusing on networks. Part Three begins with a chapter by Butt and Gunter which uses post-TSW Project data from headteachers on the issues regarding learning and ICT. This is followed by two chapters which examine particular perspectives on ICT – one by Pilkington which looks at the ways in which technology has been used in attempts to create the 'future school' and the barriers this has faced, and one by Selwood which looks at the issues that influence ICT-related change in school with particular emphasis on the management of that change.

A second set of chapters, which have been written by international colleagues who are actively researching the modernization of education and its workforce, are located in Part Four. These co-authors received an invitation from us to participate because they are people who are undertaking important work on the modernization process that we have enjoyed reading and we respect. These researchers are interested in the reform agenda in England, with a particular concern for the changes to both the workforce and work in schools. They are in a unique position to do something that the writing team in Parts One, Two and Three cannot do, that is, to stand outside the English context and generate ideas, where their scholarship allows them to make valid and challenging analysis about what it means.

We have chosen internationally respected researchers from Australia, Canada, France, New Zealand and South Africa, countries where modernization is also unfolding in the national education systems. We have asked the authors to examine what is happening in England from the perspective of their own countries, concentrating on what modernization in general and remodelling in particular mean for their particular settings. This has enabled a very rich and varied set of chapters to be produced where our co-authors have given their own particular emphasis on important issues such as democratic renewal (Berkhout), travelling policies (Fitzgerald), professional preparation (Smyth and Broad), globalization (Vidovich) and comparing national systems and traditions (Malet).

Through these chapters there is an opportunity to see policy borrowing and the globalization of solutions to recruitment and retention as an area for debate about the type of democracy and institutions we want to sustain. The chapters also provide a helpful 'interruption' to the flow of analysis of the English experience of modernization and remodelling by introducing a chance to pause and reflect; to interrupt our thoughts on policy regimes and the almost ceaseless introduction of initiatives and to see things differently. Here we have an 'interruption' of ideas, perspectives, theories and research evidence from other nations; as well as an inevitable 'interruption' of thinking and writing styles. We believe that this is important – the structure and flow of evidence and ideas in the first three parts of the book are 'unpacked' by our international authors, followed by a concluding chapter which draws these arguments together.

We do not follow Collarbone (2005a) in providing 'information' that policymakers in other countries might find 'useful' (p. 75), but instead we engage in critical policy analysis. Hence in the final chapter we return to our sensitizing questions and raise some sensitive issues about current trends. We give recognition to the hard work and gains of those who are making modernization reforms work at local level, but we also reveal the wider trends in which this is located. We conclude that we can generate and reveal alternative stories and practices, and that it is central to professional practice to do so. We do not see knowledge and knowing as a commodity to be traded or imposed as a modern form of colonization. Our job as policy researchers is to do intellectual work as a research practice where we problem pose more than problem solve. To do otherwise would be to act as a ventriloquist and speak reform into existence. The emphasis is on how a major policy development in England can be read, engaged with and interpreted by researchers, analysts and practitioners in other countries. This will generate perspectives, rather than prescriptions, on how change can or should take place in other settings.

Part One: Modernizing the Workforce

This first section contains three chapters where we examine the issue of the composition of the workforce, with a particular emphasis on changes in the role and status of the teaching profession. Uniquely we are able to present data and analysis on what it means for teachers to be required to have a 'work–life' balance. Evidence from the TSW Project is used (Appendix 1) and we have been fortunate to involve headteachers in our presentation of new data on how schools are handling changes to the workforce.

We open the section by presenting a descriptive analysis of what some schools have been doing locally to understand and implement remodelling of the school workforce. Gunter and Butt examine what TSW Project schools were able to do during the short pilot project, and then go on to provide stories of what these schools have continued to work on. What is central to this work is the radical way schools have approached the structures and cultures of workforce employment and deployment, and what this means for organizational efficiency. The next two chapters take this forward by examining the underlying issue of workload, where Butt and Gunter use TSW Project data to investigate how hours of work can be reduced through remodelling, and what it means for teachers and their work. The third chapter in this section digs deep into the development of teaching assistants, and again uses TSW Project data to look at what work is being done, and to what effect.

Chapter 2

A changing workforce

Helen Gunter and Graham Butt

Introduction

Remodelling of the school workforce requires schools to examine their labour needs and costs in order to employ and deploy staff effectively. In this chapter we examine how particular schools have managed this process, drawing on a number of case studies for illustration. These schools were originally part of the Transforming the School Workforce Pathfinder Project – they therefore have not only piloted the workforce changes that are now being rolled out in England as remodelling, but have also implemented such changes for at least four years. Information from the TSW Evaluation Report (Thomas *et al.* 2004) has been combined with more recent data from telephone interviews with headteachers designed to draw out key themes and patterns of practice since the end of the Project in 2003.

The recent reappraisal of the roles and responsibilities of workers in the public sector has led to a shift in the expectations of the types of work employees undertake. As Butt and Lance (2005a) state, 'within the fields of health and education this is leading to a weakening of the traditional job boundaries which have previously defined the work of support staff' (p. 139) and in some respects this underpins the modernization and remodelling of the teaching profession. The expectations of teachers and support staff – in terms of their day-to-day working lives – are indeed changing. This process of change is affecting all those involved in state education, from teachers through to support staff (including bursars, technicians, teaching assistants, clerical assistants, secretaries and even grounds' maintenance staff). In part remodelling can be seen as a response to perennial problems of teacher recruitment and retention, broadly reflecting attempts by central government to shift the current bureaucratic burdens on the teaching workforce, whilst also trying to address issues of work–life balance and job satisfaction.

The National Agreement on Raising Standards and Tackling Workload (DfES 2003a) has particular implications for how all work in school is now managed, organized and resourced. As a consequence of the drive to remodel working practices, employees now at the 'sharp end' of the modernization process have begun to realize the implications of change. This has stimulated calls from certain sections of support staff for greater professional recognition, training, altered pay structures and career development commensurate with a change in roles – as such 'modernization must involve the enhancement of status and work/life balance for all those who work in schools, not just teachers' (Butt and Lance 2005a, p. 140).

Experiencing remodelling

In the TSW Project, the Evaluation Team undertook case-study work in particular schools (see Thomas *et al.* 2004). In many Project schools, remodelling – essentially the reduction of bureaucratic burdens on teachers such that they could be allowed a greater focus on teaching and learning – was achieved through the appointment of additional support staff. However, perhaps more significant in terms of the current situation nationally are accounts from those schools in which the roles and status of many *existing* support staff were altered. It is apparent that in a number of project schools support staff have now become a more visible and important part of the school community as a result of the restructuring of working practices. Such schools have, unwittingly or otherwise, bought into the notion of 'transformational change' introduced in *Time for Standards* (DfES 2002a) which outlined that teachers should not complete a number of 'non-teaching' tasks (then calculated as taking up to 20 per cent of teachers' time). These 25 tasks now come under the purview of support staff.

A brief review of the actions of four project schools, and one 'cluster' of primary schools, gives a flavour of the nature of change both within the workforce and the working practices as a result of the TSW Project:

- **Rural School (11–16):** in this school the whole workforce worked together on remodelling in six change teams. By focusing on issues surrounding the culture and practice of learners and learning the whole staff could engage in challenging current practices and effecting meaningful change. This meant that the definition and enactment of roles could be surfaced and worked through.
- **Lakeside School (11–18):** changes included the appointment of a Display Co-ordinator, which improved the learning environment and impacted on attitudes to the school and learning by the students, and the establishment of an Inclusive Behaviour Unit with the employment of a Unit Officer. The latter had begun to impact positively on behaviour by the end of the Project.
- **Metropolitan School (5–11):** the emphasis was on remodelling learning based on an increase in the number and type of support staff, and changes to their role and status. A Resource Manager was appointed to support the preparation of learning resources; the role of the Senior Administrative Officer was developed in regard to the provision of information and monitoring of the budget, and this was further supported by the employment of more clerical staff to undertake routine work. Teaching assistants were employed to support learning in the classroom, take registers, and some were used to cover lessons to release teachers for planning and meetings.

- **Leafy Suburb School (special school):** a full-time bursar was appointed, which improved management and access to financial data and created a more effective line management system for administrative staff. The involvement and role of Special Needs Assistants improved and interviews showed that there was greater continuity of support for teachers and students. These assistants took on more responsibility for supporting learning and were more confident in their work, while the prime role of teachers in planning teaching and learning was acknowledged.
- **Border Schools' Cluster (four small 5–11 schools):** there is strong evidence that the role of teaching assistants developed in ways that enabled teaching headteachers to have more time to lead and manage the school. Teaching assistants are under the direction of teachers but are taking on work that previously teachers did – such as taking the register, display, marking routine work and working with students in small groups. There is evidence that teaching assistants are more focused and confident in their work. The schools examined the boundaries between teachers and teaching assistants and, while there is variation between the small schools, there is evidence that teachers see their role as being to plan and direct learning, with teaching assistants enabling and supporting this. (Thomas *et al.* 2004)

The TSW Project therefore showed that individual schools in different contexts could raise questions about the type and role of their workforce, making radical changes to the division of labour in schools. This normally took routine 'non-teaching' work away from teachers and helped create time in the school day for teacher planning, preparation and assessment.

Interviews with headteachers helped to access their views on changes to their schools during the life of the Project. For example, the head of Metropolitan School confirmed that the use of teaching assistants to cover classes had overcome initial concerns from both teachers and support staff, but the change meant that some assistants had subsequently improved their range of classroom-based skills. Most notably, one teaching assistant was trained to cover teacher absence by leading learning activities. Similarly, the head of Rural School described the benefits of developing a healthy and inclusive approach to change amongst the staff, detailing how the redefinition of roles had enabled teachers to focus on the core purpose of teaching and learning. New thinking had also led to administrative staff being involved in mentoring children in the school. When an assistant principal left the school, their teaching was replaced separately from their curriculum responsibilities for cover and examinations, which were given to a non-teaching appointment known as a 'curriculum administrator'. Gains such as these have led to more radical thinking around the need not only to remodel work, but also to reconsider the organizational structure of the school. Questions were also subsequently raised about existing classroom and departmental arrangements.

Two schools showed that it was possible to redefine remodelling through focusing on the organization of learning. There are examples of such schools restructuring the week, or reshaping a particular day, in order to remodel the working norms. In Metropolitan School the day was changed, with formal lessons from 8.30am to 2.30pm followed by clubs until 5.30pm. This restructuring supported the remodelling of learning, with a range of stakeholders noting subsequent differences in students' attitudes to learning. Interestingly, in Leafy Suburb School, learning was remodelled through changes to the timetable, so that on Wednesday afternoons 'extension and enrichment' opportunities for students were provided by experts in arts, drama, sport and life skills. This allowed teachers time to meet and plan during the working day – a substantial stimulus to developing the curriculum and changing teachers' working practices.

Remodelling perspectives

Thomas *et al.* (2004) found that the TSW Project led to changes in role boundaries and made the work of support staff more prominent and effective in many schools, although teachers in secondary schools tended to be more resistant to such changes. Headteachers from project schools offered a range of views on the success of the piloting of remodelling and delivery of the Project's objectives. Here we look at particular recurrent themes that relate to remodelling, and offer a variety of thoughts from headteachers. The first section of comments were made by headteachers at, or near, the culmination of the project in 2003; the second section contains arguably more reflective comments gathered through telephone interviews in the academic year 2005/06, some three years after the Project ended.

In 2003 the headteachers interviewed were broadly positive about remodelling. While change management teams had generally been a productive innovation, headteachers did recognize the challenges raised by the composition of the workforce combined with questioning role boundaries. Levels of ambition about what the change could achieve varied within and between schools. For example, the headteacher of Rural School noted that 'the problem was that some of the ideas the change teams were persistent about would never work!' but also stated that 'some staff have difficulty in thinking outside the box – they can be very conservative about change'. This led him to identify the importance of process:

> The ethos of change existed within the school previously, but it can be a risk putting diverse groups of staff together to solve problems. Usefully the staff soon realise that ideas for change need discussion, mean difficulties and call for hard talk!   (Headteacher, Rural School, *Thomas et al.* 2004, p. 47)

Changing the role of support staff was a particular expectation, but also a concern, for many headteachers:

> Support staff are on the telephone booking visits, organising, writing letters. They have moved from washing paint pots to real hard work. However, the

salary structure does need to change . . . . The office has become more efficient and the Senior Administrative Officer undertakes important work regarding the provision of information for the budget and the monitoring of the budget that has relieved the senior managers so that they can focus on decision-making. Resources manager is a new appointment and is seen as a great boost to teaching and learning. The resources manager does save time and is effective.

(Headteacher, Metropolitan School, Thomas *et al.* 2004, p. 56)

While I did assembly she sorted out next week's spellings. I influence this task by directing it and she makes it happen. It's having the courage to let go and having confidence in your teaching assistant. The quality of my life outside of the job has improved. I can do things in the week that I used to have to put off to the holidays.

(Headteacher, Border Schools' Cluster, Thomas *et al.* 2004, p. 69)

Numerous comments were forthcoming about emergent changes in teachers' work:

We've impacted on teachers: they don't do display, only one playground duty, they don't tidy up, do photocopying or produce letters. They have gained a lot out of it. On the INSET day we looked at the list of 25 things that teachers should not normally do and asked the question: 'what do we do anyway?' There is a minimum of two hours non-contact, there is a laptop, we finish early. We use report writers for reports. If teachers have a workload problem then they create it for themselves.

(Headteacher, Metropolitan School, Thomas *et al.* 2004, p. 57)

As a teaching head the job is potentially unmanageable, now it is manageable. This is a massive change. OfSTED is coming and we now have the staffing to handle this.

(Headteacher, Border Schools' Cluster, Thomas *et al.* 2004, p. 73)

Overall there were broadly positive reactions to the Project, although some headteachers noted the complexity in delivery:

Of all the projects we have been involved in, this one worked. It's the only one, really. The reason for this was that it was process led, not product driven. There is a long term advantage in establishing the process because it accelerates the change that the school wants.

(Headteacher, Rural School, Thomas *et al.* 2004, p. 48)

The Project has sharpened our thinking. . . . Irrespective of the funding, the project brought opportunities into reality. As long as we deliver the national curriculum, then it is up to us how we do it. We can do things differently without it all falling about our ears. We now have an early start to the day and it all didn't come crashing down.

(Headteacher, Metropolitan School, Thomas *et al.* 2004, p. 59)

A major issue raised amongst headteachers was the potential sustainability of change after the culmination of this well-funded, short-term project, as the Headteacher of Rural School states: 'There are sustainability issues beyond the life of the project. The teaching staff will soon get used to the level of support they have been given' (Headteacher, Rural School, Thomas *et al.* 2004, p. 47). By 2005/06, headteachers had ample opportunity to reflect upon the sustained impacts of the TSW Project on their schools. Our analysis has shown that individual schools can grasp the opportunities afforded by a large-scale, generously funded, national project and make it work locally (Thomas *et al.* 2004). We provide a further two examples of TSW Project Schools with regard to demonstrating a range of experiences of remodelling. The first one, Country School, was not an original case-study school in the Project, but through the experience of preparing the final report for the school it was clear there was an interesting story to tell in regard to the changes taking place. The second school, Town School, was one of the Border Schools' Cluster of primary schools that formed a case study. The school had a productive experience from the TSW Project, but when contacted again to find out how things had gone the headteacher talked about how they had tried an aspect of remodelling, had learned from it, but had restored the teachers prime role in assessment.

Country School

This school is an 11–16 high school in an urban area in the north of England. Major changes were undertaken in this school during the TSW Project. In particular, two Faculty Support Assistants were appointed to take away the administrative and cover burden from staff, and two Year Managers were appointed to trial the shift of pastoral support from a teacher as a head of year to a trained pastoral manager. The success of this pilot has led the School to make major remodelling changes: first, the two Faculty Support Assistants completed their two-year contracts funded by the TSW Project, and the School then appointed eight Learning Managers who now cover teacher absence. The Learning Managers have been appointed and trained by the school to supervise lessons, and if there is no cover needed then they are allocated to a Faculty to undertake routine administrative work. Second, the two Year Managers have been expanded to five, and so no teacher is a Head of Year. The Year Managers have been trained by the School to undertake the administrative and counselling role necessary for the pastoral support of children.

In the post-TSW Project period the school has expanded its support staff through the redeployment of work around the support team and more significantly the appointment of non-teachers to the following roles:

- **Head of Resources and General Manager:** this person oversees the work and welfare of all support staff and this has freed the bursar to focus on the budget and resource management. He/she is also responsible for cover by the Learning Managers, and for Examination administration and invigilation, and this has taken administration away from an Assistant Headteacher so that senior teaching staff can focus on learning.
- **Buildings and Events Manager:** this person is the site manager, and organizes all events within school such as open evenings and parents' evenings.
- **Network Manager:** this person oversees the ICT hardware and software in school.
- **Webpage Designer:** this person works with teachers to develop online teaching resources.

The status of these support staff is developing through the inclusion of key personnel such as the Human Resources and General Manager on the Leadership Team. The school now has increased the number of staff to 160 with 90 teaching staff.

The changes are directly a product of the way of thinking encouraged by the TSW Project, where issues of cost-effectiveness were engaged with by the school. For example, the funding of the eight Learning Managers costs less than supply cover from qualified teachers. The appointment of the five Year Managers has been based on changing the role of the person who had been the Head of Year, and so either a Head of Year became a full-time class teacher and so taught a full timetable of 26 out of 30 lessons instead of 17 out of 30 lessons, or they left the school and were replaced by a newly qualified teacher who taught a full timetable.

Town School

The school is a 5–11 primary school in the west of England. During the TSW Project the school increased the use of teaching assistant support, appointed additional administrative support and increased the role of the bursar in taking on work that teachers and the headteacher previously did. In particular, the bursar took the register both morning and afternoon, and this enabled the teachers to focus on teaching and learning. This is a small school (head plus 2 members of staff, 38 students) and the use of teaching assistants and support staff in the school is regarded as an overall success. However, the headteacher did note the difficulties of keeping good support staff when financial resources meant that contracts only covered term-time employment, and pay rates needed to be improved.

The school had piloted a change in role for teaching assistants during the TSW Project, and had worked on the boundary between assisting and teaching. One aspect that they trialled and that did not work was the role of teaching assistants in marking children's work. The climate in school was very supportive of this change; in the questionnaire responses at the end of the Project teaching staff agreed that teaching assistants do reduce teacher workload, and disagreed that teaching assistants in their school were underused. Three out of four support staff agreed that they 'would be happy to mark the pupils' class and homework using a clear set of answers', and three out of four said that they disagreed that teaching assistants were underused. Four out of five support staff agreed that they 'would be happy, with additional training, to take over as sole supervisor of the class in the teacher's absence'. They would like to have more planning time, and both teachers and teaching assistants felt there was a need for more training. It is interesting to note that one of the teachers felt that working with teaching assistants freed them up to spend more time teaching, and one did not.

During the life of the Project the support staff at this school had become more positive about marking, but in discussing experiences 18 months later the headteacher explained that this development had not worked in the way they had wanted it to. This was because the teaching assistant was frequently absent from the classroom when the work to be assessed was set, and they did not see the children complete it. Hence they came to the marking process 'cold' outside the classroom. Therefore many took a long time to complete the assessment, and did it poorly. The policy has now changed such that more marking is done within the class, with some of it done by teaching assistants helping the teacher.

What is interesting about these two illustrative examples of how a large secondary and small primary school have continued the remodelling process begun under the TSW Project is the relationship between practice and culture. On the one hand, practice and culture are integrated – as practice is symbolic of 'what is to be done' and culture shapes 'what is usual'. On the other hand, practice can *challenge* culture and generate new practices, or culture can challenge practice, generating new perspectives and attitudes. For example, the headteacher of Country School notes important changes as a result of the TSW Project, and how the school has built on the remodelling approach. He argues that 'the school has more of a "can do" culture. People expect change because it is a way of life'. He goes on to describe how remodelling has been built into the strategic approach to human resource management:

> the people who have been appointed are confident and share our ethos, this has been the right solution for the right time. The Learning Managers have brought continuity and experience. Permanent contracts have been used for the right calibre people. (Headteacher, Country School)

Underpinning this is an approach to change where there are no boundaries to questions that can be asked about purposes and practices: 'we had the message to think the unthinkable and if it benefits the children then we do it. There is no ideological resistance, all is open for change'. And so

> change has become a way of life, and it is about buying into the ethos. It is about the guiding principles about freeing teachers to teach, and to improve learning opportunities. This is our moral purpose and should not be diverted off course with the upset we had, it is about working through this. The message is to stop moaning and do something about it. (ibid.)

The issues generated by these two cases can be developed through our discussions with headteachers from other schools about post-Project developments. The question of whether the workload of teachers could realistically be reduced, or at the very least 'shifted', in an equitable and cost-effective way still concerned the headteachers:

> The school still faces issues of workload. Pathfinder did not really succeed in reducing teachers' workload, but it changed the ways in which they worked. The school operates a performance management review for staff which highlights workload issues and checks that staff are properly qualified for the roles they are now expected to undertake. Stress is still a major issue and so a stress audit is included in the process. Many staff have now changed their job descriptions through remodelling and so this is a focus. The main thing about performance management is ensuring that adults are in the right roles. Workload has not reduced but people feel better about the work they do – however, they are not working less hours! PPA has been guaranteed for three years. (Headteacher, Town School)

> The workload of staff has not really declined since TSW. We have reassigned the 24 tasks, and employed teacher administrative staff, but the workload is still high and seasonal. The start of the Autumn Term still means lots of data gathering for staff, target setting, lesson observations, performance management interviews, etc. (from September to November). The focus then shifts, with the Spring Term being the 'lightest', but the pressure builds again to the end of the Summer Term. Workload problems have not been eradicated to a great extent, but they are now more 'managed'. Teachers no longer photocopy or do stock orders, but do more focused 'higher level' duties'.
>
> (Headteacher, Metropolitan School)

Central to the remodelling of working practices had been the employment, or redeployment, of support staff. Here we consider comments from the headteachers of our case study schools, as well as those of three headteachers from other project schools which we refer to as Avenue, Village and Rural School:

> The restrictions placed on individual schools mean that changing the conditions for support staff is difficult for individual Heads. It is also very difficult for Heads to retain good support staff if they can only be employed/paid in term time. Teaching assistants and other support staff work very well in the school, but it is a difficult situation to maintain. Pay is a significant issue for some support staff . . . . Teaching hours have actually increased slightly, but this has partly been a result of ensuring PPA time. The school has aimed to keep its number of support staff and maintain their hours.
>
> (Headteacher, Town School)

TSW provided funds for more TAs to 'cover' classes. At the start there were some union issues, but this did not come to much. A positive outcome has been that some TAs have been trained to improve their skills – now a Year 6 teacher has a TA who can cover effectively and can lead activities, even when the teacher is away.   (Headteacher, Metropolitan School)

The head of KS4 left and was not replaced directly – funding was used to support other roles and an assistant teacher (HLTA) has taken on their work.
(Headteacher, Avenue School)

Administrative staff are working alongside teachers doing mentoring . . . . The curriculum administrator does cover and exams. This post was created when the school did not replace an assistant principal role. We used resources to replace the teaching and to appoint a curriculum administrator. . . . For teachers and support staff, there has been a redefinition of roles, with refocus on core purposes for teachers as leaders of learning. We need to think about how we remodel the classroom and the department, and how this works.
(Headteacher, Rural School)

The headteachers are very clear that they have used the opportunity of the TSW Project and subsequent remodelling to do different things and to do things differently within their schools. Within context there is evidence of a range of radical changes, where the number and role of support staff has changed and this is regarded as opening up opportunities for teachers to think and practise differently. However, there is clearly a varied approach to what can be achieved within context (not least resources) and how radical a change is envisioned and enacted. For some, they are making changes at the leading edge, while others share their concerns. For example, one headteacher spoke critically of the process: 'Nationally, I'm concerned that remodelling has lost its way. There is a tension between remodelling with teaching and learning . . . . I'm sceptical about the national agenda and whether it will deliver on the radical promise' (Headteacher, Rural School). This does challenge whether change is fundamental or a surface remaking of schools. The emphasis on adult concerns regarding organizational efficiencies seems to be in tension with learning. Hence any discussion about the boundary between teacher and assistant is not just concerned with protection of territory but is about identity and how teaching is a skilled job.

Teachers were questioned, both through questionnaire surveys and individual interviews, about their views on the deployment of teaching assistants in an effort to monitor any change in their attitudes between 2002 and 2003 (Thomas *et al.* 2004). The research findings on whether teachers had accepted the changing roles of support staff in general, and of teaching assistants in particular, point to the readiness of many teaching staff to embrace changes in working practices. There is evidence of a clear acceptance of the enhanced role of such staff, particularly amongst teachers in primary and special schools, and a belief that assistants can reduce teachers' workload. Secondary teachers were more guarded in their responses, seeing fewer direct benefits from the remodelling of the working practices of support staff.

Whilst it was clear from the data that many teachers saw teaching assistants as being key in helping them to carry out their professional duties, it is also obvious that this in itself will not drive change unless teachers can identify *how* to make use of their support to maximize its potential. One key issue which emerges is the importance of listening to what teaching assistants themselves have to say, particularly in relation to their role (Clark 2002; Quicke 2003; Tilley 2003). A second and related issue was the opportunity for teaching assistants to discuss practice with colleagues outside their own immediate working environment. Some teaching assistants were able to converse with their counterparts across the case-study schools, and this opportunity to reflect upon practice may be a key area for consideration in putting remodelling programmes into action. A third issue related to confidence: confidence on the part of the teaching assistants to undertake new roles, and confidence on the part of the teachers to delegate elements of their work. Building confidence is not a short-term enterprise and needs careful consideration before role structures are altered and new ways of working implemented. Finally, the issue of workload for teaching assistants needs careful consideration, for there is little point in shifting teacher overload into another direction, only to find the same problems with the recruitment and retention of teaching assistants a few years down the line (Dixon 2003). Our interviews highlighted a variety in practice here. On the one hand, there were people whose new roles were encouraging them to be 'Jills of all trades' (Moyles and Suschitzky 1997), while, on the other, there were examples of teaching assistants working in a much more focused manner within a single classroom context, for example. While these four issues emerge from the examination of limited data, they provide lessons to take account of within a much broader national context.

The students' views, primarily gleaned from a number of focus groups in case-study schools, are more fragmented and less reliable in assessing the impact of remodelling. Whilst many welcomed the influx of new technology, appreciated capital build programmes or favoured the restructuring of the school day, others tended to hold rather conservative views on the use of teaching assistants in the roles traditionally taken by teachers. Adverse comments were received from some secondary school students concerning the use of assistants to cover, teach or assess learning, with the 'regular teacher' being viewed as the only person who could possibly fulfil these roles.

Conclusion

Despite the government's imperative that remodelling is a 'must do', the processes involved are complex and the focus for change differs from school to school. Some schools have opted to shift the status, roles and function of their support staff; some have reorganized their school day; whilst others have addressed the reorganization of teaching – often through the increased use of technology. Most schools are still very much engaged in implementing changes in traditional working practices and expectations.

A key focus for expenditure during the Project was the provision of more support for teachers, often through employing (or redeploying) teaching and classroom assistants. Where this has occurred successfully, teachers have generally welcomed the outcomes of remodelling. The national 'cross-section' of views of education staff afforded by the Evaluation has suggested that there exists a degree of mutual acceptance and respect between teachers and teaching/classroom assistants, as well as a willingness to experiment (to some extent) in the shifting of role boundaries. This is particularly noted where there have been tangible reductions in teachers' hours worked, improvements in work–life balance and a diminution of overall workload. Nevertheless, we should still be aware that Thomas *et al.* (2004) found that most teachers continue to work an average of 50 plus hours each week.

What is less clear is how such 'gains' can be driven forward at the national scale. Harnessing the positive aspects of a short-term, well-funded, government-supported project across all England's schools is obviously problematic. The 'sustainability issue' was raised by a number of headteachers, as well as other members of the school workforce. It could also be argued that a significant proportion of Project schools (who, we must remember, were all invited to take part in the pilot) had *already* made some headway on the issues surrounding remodelling before they participated in the pilot. Therefore certain strategic and structural questions may have already been addressed in Project schools, within which the benefits of additional project resources to further the schools' goals were quickly recognized by senior staff.

Of potentially greater significance in terms of the success of the remodelling of the school workforce is the need for cultural shifts amongst staff before change can occur. Staff in the pilot schools often had to be persuaded to 'buy into' the TSW Project by senior colleagues. Many remained reluctant or resistant. The goals of the Project had to be seen as a priority by all staff – who were then expected to make large investments of time, effort, intellect and emotion into ensuring that the Project's aims were realized. Incentives were offered, such as the 'quick win' of laptops and the longer-term expectation of reduced workload, but not all staff saw their investment in the Project as worthwhile. After all, not everyone chooses to have their working lives remodelled and restructured, particularly if the personal and professional gains seem less than tangible. Many teachers have questioned whether such changes have any prospect of achieving what they see as the most important goal – raising the level of achievement of the learner in the classroom.

This chapter has provided perspectives on the realities of workforce reform. It has shown what schools within context can do, and has generated important issues regarding the pace and nature of change on the ground, combined with how people feel about that change. We have documented how schools within the TSW Project used the opportunity to increase the number, role and scope of the workforce, and what this has meant for culture and practice. The testimony of the headteachers has generated two vital issues that need more investigation: first, how remodelling is actually impacting on the type and nature of work, workload and work–life balance, an issue we intend to examine in Chapter 3; and, second, how remodelling is actually impacting on the work of teaching assistants and their contribution to purpose and practice, which we intend to examine in Chapter 4.

Chapter 3

Workforce, workload and work–life balance: the initial impacts of modernization in English schools

Graham Butt and Helen Gunter

Introduction

The official aim of remodelling the school workforce is to reduce bureaucracy and to free teachers to focus on teaching and learning. Where successful, reforms have usually involved both a shift of 'non-teaching' work from teachers to support staff (such as teaching assistants, clerical assistants, technicians and bursars) and a change in the culture of schools – in the process traditional working practices have been challenged and altered. This remodelling of the workforce mirrors a series of reforms visited on other public sector employees in England. However, within education, modernization is 'edged' by considerations of recurrent problems of staff recruitment and retention – as well as long-standing issues of performance, standards, job satisfaction, work–life balance and pay. As such

> the urgency of finding practical solutions to excessive workload problems has been increased by perennial concerns about poor teacher recruitment, loss of a high percentage of new teachers from the profession in their first years of teaching and an increasingly ageing population of teachers nationally.
> (Butt and Lance 2005b, p. 402)

With almost 60 per cent of teachers who choose to leave the profession before retirement age stating that 'workload' was a significant factor in their decision (Hastings 2002), the mere recruitment of more teachers is not the simple answer to deep-seated issues of work–life balance.[1]

The principles on which the modernization agenda is founded have a logic of practice: as the overall quality of the national workforce increases and role boundaries blur then the possibility of reconsidering working practices presents itself. Thus employees might be expected by their employers to take on responsibilities that they had not previously been considered capable of – in essence a process of redefining 'who does what' (Butt and Lance 2005a). Gunter *et al.* (2007) make clear that underlying such reforms are attempts to change the cultural norms that sustain traditional ways of working, often through the introduction of a change process which gathers representatives from the whole workforce into change management teams.

The New Labour government believes that support staff in general, and teaching assistants (TAs)[2] in particular, can help to drive up standards and reduce teacher workload in schools. Its investment, since 2000, of around £350-million to recruit teaching assistants, to provide for their training and to create greater clarity of their roles and qualifications pathways reflects the government's belief that support staff can enhance modernization. However, the process of change has been disjointed – only being supported by the publication of exemplars of different schools' use of TAs (e.g. DfES 2000b), rather than through the provision of clear national strategies, policies and guidelines. A certain nervousness has also traditionally existed about the extent to which TAs might 'take over' the roles and responsibilities of qualified teachers. This is reflected in the words of Estelle Morris, a previous Secretary of State for Education, when she asserted that 'the greater involvement of trained teaching assistants in the learning process in no way detracts from teachers' own unique professional skills and distinct responsibilities. In fact, it reinforces the teacher's role' (DfES 2000b, p. 1)

Changing hours, changing roles

Thomas *et al.* (2004, p. 7) found that in 2002 teachers were working over 50 hours per week. Other surveys in England (e.g. MacBeath *et al.* 2004, PwC 2001, STRB 2004) and internationally (e.g. Dibbon 2004, Gardner and Williamson 2005) confirm the endurance and consequences of such long hours. New Labour responded to evidence by commissioning PricewaterhouseCoopers (PwC 2001) to undertake a study into workload and to identify options. They confirmed the intensive nature of term-time work, the lack of control and ownership of work and concerns about the pace and manner of change. Teachers argued that their workloads were not being well managed either nationally or locally. This is something that the then Secretary of State, David Blunkett, had identified as a key issue: 'yes, teachers do work hard – but it is clear from inspection and other evidence that some schools manage teachers' time better than others' (Blunkett 2001, p. 6). PricewaterhouseCoopers (PwC 2001) provided options for how schools could tackle workload issues regarding the use of support staff and ICT. The DfES decided to launch a 'pathfinder' initiative to trial these strategies and so see how schools could engage with workload reduction. The Evaluation of the TSW Project provides 'a unique opportunity to witness intensive change in a sample of schools, and to begin to understand what it means to embrace and experience what became known as remodelling' (Gunter 2004b, p. 2). The 32 Pilot Schools produced Change Management Plans regarding interventions they intended to make to reduce teacher workload and to improve work–life balance (see Part Two for more detail on the change processes). A central aim of the Evaluation was to measure the impact

Table 3.1 Reported weekly hours by teachers

Occupation	N 2002	Mean hrs 2002	N 2003	Mean hrs 2003	N 2002 & 2003	Change in hours
Primary						
Headteachers	13	57.2	11	55.1	10	−4.3
Deputy heads	19	56.4	15	50.8	13	−7.2
Class teachers	136	52.7	133	50.1	124	−3.7
Secondary						
Headteachers	12	58.4	10	56.8	7	−3.1
Deputy heads	54	55.4	56	53.4	49	−1.8
Heads of faculty	92	52.1	80	50.5	61	−0.01
Class teachers	477	49.9	421	49.1	311	−1.2
Special						
Class teachers	53	52.8	49	49.0	47	−3.5

Source: Thomas *et al.* 2004, p. 7

of these interventions on the nature of work, hours of work and attitudes to work (see Appendix 1 for details about the methodology). One of the key findings of the Evaluation was that the Project 'made an impact in reducing the working hours of teachers, led to change in role boundaries between teachers and other members of the school workforce, and made support staff more prominent and effective in schools' (Thomas *et al.* 2004, p. ii). As a result of remodelling, class-room teachers across all types of schools involved in the Project reported a reduction in hours worked: ranging from 3.7 hours per week in primary schools, to 3.5 hours in special schools and 1.2 hours in secondary schools (see Table 3.1). However, a caveat must be added concerning these figures. The actual hours worked by teachers in different schools varied considerably – a fact which is masked by the use of means; we therefore cannot assume that *all* teachers benefited equally from a reduction in 'hours worked'. Indeed, interviews with a cross-section of staff in schools revealed that for significant numbers of them weekly hours worked actually increased during the life of the Project.

Interestingly data from 'comparator' secondary schools – schools included as 'controls' from which questionnaire data were collected but in which no project-based remodelling interventions were made – show similar trends in the reduction of teachers' hours. Here teachers experienced a reduction of 1.9 hours work each week, a slightly larger decrease in hours than that achieved in the Project secondary schools (1.2 hours).[3]

The Evaluation of the Project also included an investigation of the time teachers spent on work outside the school day, during evenings, at weekends and in holiday time (see Tables 3.2 and 3.3). Teachers were asked 'to indicate the time you normally work during the school week' against three categories – evening, Saturday and Sunday – with options ranging from zero to more than three hours worked. Their replies for 2003 are shown in Table 3.2, together with the percentage change in working hours for 2002 and 2003.

Table 3.2 Teachers' evening and weekend work (hours and percentage change)

Time in hours		N 2003	2002 mean	2003 mean	02–03 change
Special	Eve	70	1.9	1.7	−0.34
schools	Sat	70	1.2	1.3	−0.27
	Sun	70	2.5	2.1	−0.67
Primary	Eve	184	1.8	1.7	−0.22
schools	Sat	184	1.2	0.9	−0.33
	Sun	184	2.4	2.1	−0.41
Secondary	Eve	641	2.0	1.9	−0.12
schools	Sat	641	1.3	1.2	−0.11
	Sun	641	2.4	2.3	−0.23

Source: Thomas *et al.* 2004, p. 9

Table 3.3 Reported work by teachers outside term time

Occupation[5]	Change in days
Primary	
Headteachers	−1.2
Deputy heads (1)	−5.7
Class teachers (2)	−2.5
Secondary	
Headteachers	−2.6
Deputy heads (1)	−1.7
Heads of Faculty (3)	−0.6
Class teachers (4)	−1.4
Special	
Class teachers (2)	−5.5

Source: Thomas *et al.* 2004, p. 8

When Thomas *et al.* (2004) examined teachers' patterns of work during the evenings and at weekends, 95 per cent of teachers reported doing some work at these times. During a 'typical' evening, teachers in special and primary schools stated that they worked for 1.7 hours, whilst those in secondary schools worked for 1.9 hours. With respect to working on Saturdays, the mean hours in 2003 were 1.3 (special), 0.9 (primary) and 1.2 (secondary); and for Sunday the means were 2.1 (special and primary) and 2.3 (secondary). In terms of the change in hours teachers worked each week between 2002 and 2003, there is therefore a modest, but uniform, fall in hours across all school types – ranging from 0.11 per cent (less than 7 minutes) to 0.67 per cent (about 40 minutes) (Thomas *et al.* 2004).

Again, comparing the data for those teachers who completed questionnaires in *both* years of the Project, there is a fall in reported working time for the period outside the school term (Table 3.3), ranging from an average of 5.7 days for

Table 3.4 Maxima and minima of changes in teachers' weekly hours worked (by school type)

School type	Maximum reduction of teachers' hours	Minimum reduction, or increase in teachers' hours	Range of changes in teachers' hours
Special	8.7	0.6	8.1
Primary	13	(2.5)	15.5
Secondary	5.6	(2.1)	7.7

Source: Based on Thomas *et al.* 2004, p. 28

primary school deputy heads to 0.6 days for heads of faculty in secondary schools.

As such we can conclude that the interventions made during the Project had a small, but beneficial, impact on the hours that teachers worked during evenings, at weekends and outside term time. Importantly, we must also consider how these figures vary on a school-by-school basis rather than as an aggregate for all teachers in an entire sector of schools. These data show a wide variation in the range of weekly hours worked by teachers across the 32 Project schools (see Table 3.4).

There were very considerable differences in the impact that the Project made on hours worked in specific schools. Indeed, within each school there were often significant variations in the hours worked by individual staff members – some teachers may have seen their hours reduce sharply; others experienced an increase in hours worked. This suggests that any 'solutions' to teacher workload which promise reductions in hours worked based on aggregate data must be treated carefully, as local conditions within specific schools may not correlate closely with mean trends.

The nature of teachers' work

In both questionnaire surveys teachers were asked to respond to a set of detailed questions about the time they spent on different activities. Here we report on the outcome of the survey undertaken in 2003, at the end of the Project, using secondary school data (Figure 3.1) for illustrative purposes.

Secondary school teachers in the pilot schools reported that in 2003 some 44 per cent of their time was committed to teaching, and 11 per cent to other forms of pupil contact. The proportions of time given to these activities were essentially the same in special and primary schools, each being within 2 per cent of the corresponding secondary school figures. For teachers in secondary schools, supporting learning absorbed 20 per cent of their time – comparable figures being 15 per cent in special schools and 20 per cent in primary schools. Some 6 per cent of teachers' time in secondary schools was given to school and staff management, compared with 12 per cent in special schools and 9 per cent in

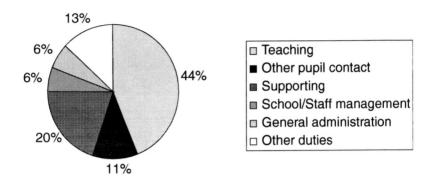

Figure 3.1 Teachers' work in secondary schools

Source: Thomas *et al.* 2004, p. 11

primary schools. Teachers in all schools reported spending 6 per cent of their time on general administration, with 'other activities' accounting for between 12 per cent and 13 per cent of their time. In reviewing the responses from those who replied in both 2002 and 2003, there were only negligible increases in the time allocated to the 'teaching' category in all schools – the most significant shift being a 3 per cent rise in the amount of time primary school teachers spent teaching (Thomas *et al.* 2004).

Reviewing the data across all three sectors, the biggest reported change occurred in the time teachers allocated to making display items (one of the activities contained within the category 'supporting learning'). Here there was a large fall in the time spent by teachers in special and primary schools, and no change in the secondary schools. This suggests that reducing (or removing) time spent on display work was a targeted 'quick win' for many teachers in primary and special schools. Teachers also showed significant changes in the time they allocated to 'clerical items' (general administration) each week – secondary school teachers reported a fall of some 22 minutes spent on such work, although this was lower than the 58 minutes saved among primary school teachers and 45 minutes in special schools. Clerical work also accounted for more of the teachers' time in secondary schools – where teachers spent, on average, 66 minutes per week on such work – than in either special or primary schools (33 minutes each). This indicates activities which, in secondary schools in particular, might more appropriately be done in future by clerical or support staff.

Overall, data produced by Thomas *et al.* (2004) show a reduction in the amount of time teachers spent on tasks that could be done by others – tasks subsequently taken up in a number of schools by support staff and teaching assistants. Unfortunately this change is not yet reflected in schools nationally, as many still struggle to implement the workload agreement (DfES 2003a). Indeed the School Teacher Review Body Report (STRB 2004), published following the implementation of the agreement in 2003, revealed that the workload of primary teachers had actually *increased,* on average, from 51.8 hours to 52.5

Table 3.5 Teachers' job satisfaction – personal (response shown as a percentage)

Please indicate what you think about each statement:	Type	N	Dissatisfied	Satisfied
The actual job itself	Spec	69	7	93
	Prim	180	9	91
	Sec	622	18	82
The degree to which you feel 'motivated' by your job	Spec	68	4	96
	Prim	184	8	92
	Sec	625	18	82
The kind of work you are required to perform	Spec	66	11	89
	Prim	183	17	83
	Sec	630	33	67
The degree to which you feel you can personally develop or grow in your job	Spec	68	15	85
	Prim	183	20	80
	Sec	629	25	75
The degree to which your job taps the range of skills which you feel you possess	Spec	68	16	84
	Prim	184	14	86
	Sec	629	29	71
The degree to which you feel extended by your job	Spec	68	18	82
	Prim	184	14	86
	Sec	631	27	73

Source: Thomas *et al.* 2004, p. 16

hours per week between 2003 and 2004 (ibid.). The reasons for this are believed to relate to lower staff numbers in primary schools, which may limit their ability to be flexible in remodelling workforce arrangements.

Teachers' views on job satisfaction and quality of life

As well as trying to find ways of reducing the hours worked by teachers, the Project was also concerned with increasing their job satisfaction and establishing a more equitable work–life balance. Importantly, job satisfaction is not simply a function of hours worked – therefore it does not necessarily follow that reducing the number of hours that teachers work will automatically lead to improvements in their levels of job satisfaction. In an attempt to identify the factors associated with job satisfaction, Thomas *et al.* (2004, pp. 16–18) examined the responses of all members of the school workforce to two sets of statements: one focused on satisfaction with personal factors related to their own job (Table 3.5), and the other on how organizational issues impact on job satisfaction (Table 3.6).

In their responses to the six 'positively worded' personal statements (see Table 3.5) teachers revealed strong overall levels of job satisfaction. The highest levels reported in 2003 were mainly from teachers in special schools, although these satisfaction levels were almost all very slightly lower than those recorded in 2002.

Table 3.6 Teachers' job satisfaction – organization (response shown as a percentage)

Please indicate what you think about each statement:	Type	N	Dissatisfied	Satisfied
Communication and the way	Spec	68	44	56
information flows around	Prim	182	36	64
your organization	Sec	631	58	42
The style of supervision that	Spec	66	35	65
your superiors use	Prim	180	22	78
	Sec	621	41	59
The way changes are	Spec	68	41	59
implemented	Prim	180	31	69
	Sec	627	55	45
The way in which conflicts	Spec	69	36	63
are resolved in your	Prim	183	32	58
organization	Sec	626	46	54
The psychological 'feel' or	Spec	69	17	83
climate that dominates	Prim	183	23	77
your organization	Sec	627	47	53
The design or shape of your	Spec	68	31	69
organization's structure	Prim	181	18	82
	Sec	629	43	57

Source: Thomas *et al.* 2004, p.17

The responses of primary school teachers showed the next highest satisfaction levels, whilst those of secondary school teachers involved in the Project were the lowest. Nonetheless, all teachers reported levels of overall satisfaction, rather than dissatisfaction, against each of the 'personal' statements.

The responses to the statements on satisfaction with the organization show broadly similar trends to those relating to the teacher's job, with teachers in special schools again producing the highest level of satisfaction and those in secondary schools the lowest. However, the percentages reporting themselves as being 'satisfied' against these statements were all lower than those awarded to the 'personal' statements. For two of these statements – one concerning 'communication' and the other on 'the way changes are implemented' – levels of dissatisfaction are higher than levels of satisfaction for secondary school teachers. Again the changes in satisfaction levels recorded from the start to the finish of the Project were negligible.

Although the Project Evaluation could find no consistent relationship between job satisfaction and hours, there was evidence that, for secondary school teachers, reducing the hours worked impacted on satisfaction levels:

In 2002 and 2003, no significant relationships were established between reported hours and levels of job satisfaction and levels of motivation; this was the case in special, primary and secondary schools. However, when change in hours between 2002 and 2003 was examined, the results for teachers in secondary schools showed a significant correlation between job satisfaction and change in hours worked and it was in the expected direction with job satisfaction increasing as hours fall.   (Thomas *et al.* 2004, p. 17)

In a similar fashion to the enquiry into job satisfaction, staff were asked to respond to two sets of statements – one 'positive' and one 'negative' – about their quality of life (Thomas *et al.* 2004, pp. 18–20). These statements sought responses on the teachers' personal life, their aspirations, work and working environment. Again answers were generally positive, although the most negative response from teachers was to the statement 'I enjoy work now more than I did 12 months ago'. With respect to overall trends of agreement or disagreement with the statements, secondary teachers were the most negative and special school teachers the most positive. The most significant negative shift in teachers' responses from 2002 to 2003 was in relation to statements about whether their work in school was valued, whether it was a good use of time and whether workload issues could be discussed with senior managers.

The statement that teachers from all sectors responded to most strongly revealed that they felt they needed 'the time to do the job as it should be done' (95 per cent agreement). High levels of agreement were also seen in response to the statements 'My job makes me feel exhausted by the end of the workday' (between 85 and 88 per cent of teachers agreeing) and 'I want to reduce the hours I work' (79 per cent to 88 per cent agreement). The pattern of responses showed that secondary school teachers were more dissatisfied with their quality of life than teachers in either primary or special schools.

Teachers' solutions for excessive workload

As part of the questionnaire surveys and interviews held in pilot schools, teachers were invited to express their views on possible solutions to excessive workload. When analysed, these responses highlight a number of strategies which teachers across all sectors believed would reduce their workload problems (see Butt and Lance 2005b). The most frequent observations are briefly outlined below and form an interesting counterpoint to the interventions which the government currently believes will effect change. A small selection of statements made by teachers in the pilot schools is included here for exemplification purposes.

Perhaps not surprisingly, teachers from all schools requested that more *time* be made available for them to do their work. Specifically, this would take the form of provision of some non-contact time for teachers in primary schools, whilst in secondary schools teachers requested that their existing non-contact time be protected. When asked what this 'additional' time would be used for, teachers expressed a wish to carry out further planning, marking and lesson observations:

With non-contact time kept free it is easier to plan and do practical work –
this eases the workload at home.
(Teacher, Metropolitan School, Thomas *et al.* 2004, p. 57)

Across all the schools there was a call for more *teachers*, alongside a clearly stated
belief that the roles and responsibilities of teachers should be further clarified.
In some schools the Project had resulted in teachers wanting to be trusted to
'do their job' and to further exercise their professional judgement on educational matters:

Teachers should be free to devise their own ways, to think differently.
(Middle Manager, City School, Thomas *et al.* 2004, unpublished data)

Most teachers are traditionalists by heart, with a genuine feeling for the children. But these approaches are rightly questioned and challenged. We live in
a changing world. We do want to see reflective practitioners being developed
in school. Boundaries for professionals do need to be defined, but they also
need to be flexed if we are genuinely going to see a relationship between
quality and time in this development.
(Senior Manager, Conurbation School, Thomas *et al.*, 2004,
unpublished data)

A common wish was that *class sizes* could be reduced. Many teachers, across all
sectors, felt that smaller class sizes would cut down on assessment demands and
improve pupil behaviour:

The solution to workload problems is straightforward – less pupils to teach
and smaller class sizes!
(Teacher, Metropolitan School, Thomas *et al.* 2004, unpublished data)

Bureaucracy was mentioned as causing a significant workload issue in many
schools, often in the context of the need to simplify aspects of monitoring, assessment, recording, reporting and accountability. Teachers felt that assessment data
could be generated and managed more effectively in schools, in particular citing
better use of ICT to store, prevent replication of and enable easier access to the
data. There was a common request, particularly amongst teachers in primary and
special schools, for the employment of more *support staff* – although a significant
minority of teachers expressed the view that this would only reduce workload if
such staff were used more effectively than in the past. In particular, teachers identified a need for more clerical and administrative support:

More administrative staff has meant the reduction of demands on teachers
and has raised standards. The introduction of Year Managers has also reduced
the demands on teachers.
(Teacher, Metropolitan School, Thomas *et al.* 2004, p. 58)

The clerical assistant has made an impact through doing letters and answering the phone. They are a godsend. They take the workload away from teachers.
(Middle Manager, Village School, Thomas *et al.* 2004, unpublished data)

The demand for more, better-deployed, better-trained *teaching assistants* was also clear – with a requirement for dedicated planning time for teachers and teaching assistants to work together also being voiced:

I would like to see more teaching assistants, next year will be SATs and I have an extra programme to boost reading. I need a teaching assistant.
(Teacher, Village School, Thomas *et al.* 2004, unpublished data)

I personally think Teaching Assistants can follow a plan set by a teacher and because of their knowledge of the pupils they can manage the situation to support learning.
(Middle Manager, Rural School, Thomas *et al.* 2004, unpublished data)

[The Teaching Assistant] is almost doing the same job as me. I value the Teaching Assistant as a colleague and there is a high degree of trust, although it might be different with another Teaching Assistant.
(Senior Manager, Rural School, Thomas *et al.* 2004, unpublished data)

Finally, the impact of *government initiatives* on teachers' workload had not gone unnoticed by teachers in many pilot schools. A strong view was expressed that the number of national initiatives should be reduced, and that schools should be given more flexibility to develop their own plans.

I feel we need less initiatives and a clearly defined period of consolidation. There is also a desperate need for more trust to be shown in the professional's judgement – an acceptance that the teacher is well placed to know what is appropriate for the needs of pupils – and much less rhetoric and 'spin'.
(Middle Manager, Rural School, Thomas *et al.* 2004, unpublished data)

Whilst most of these suggestions for workload reduction require more resources from government, they do not necessarily all propose major shifts in the working patterns of schools. However, the employment and training of more support staff and teaching assistants certainly require additional resources, or the spending of existing resources differently, and are closely related to changing patterns of work in many schools. The final item, on government initiatives, represents a call for fewer government demands on schools (Butt and Lance 2005b).

Conclusion

Survey data from the TSW Project reveals that teachers in pilot schools reported a clear fall in hours worked between 2002 and 2003, with those in special and primary schools experiencing a larger reduction than their secondary colleagues. There was a consistency to the pattern of reduction in the hours they worked outside term time, and during evenings and weekends (Thomas *et al.* 2004). However, the data from a much smaller number of teachers in 'comparator' secondary schools also showed significant time reductions, often without Project funding to remodel working practices.

Looking at the time teachers gave to different tasks during the Project, there were only small reported reductions (if at all) in the proportion of time spent 'teaching', as might be expected. However, analysis of eight 'non-teaching' items, which could be done by other members of the workforce, showed a marked shift in teachers' allocation of time – albeit greatest among teachers in special and primary schools. Here opportunities had been taken for achieving 'quick wins' in saving teacher time, often by removing certain aspects of their daily work – such as the creation of displays, or the completion of routine administrative tasks. That the data show such changes reinforces the findings of the interviews, where teachers identify (amongst other things) 'clerical' tasks as an area where they could spend less time. Many teachers in Project schools therefore appear to have taken the opportunity to act on their beliefs as to where time could, and should, be saved (ibid.).

The Project was also concerned with measuring any impact of remodelling on job satisfaction and work–life balance. Thomas *et al.* (ibid.) found no systematic relationship between job satisfaction and hours worked, although there was a relationship between a reduction in hours worked and an improvement in satisfaction from the 'job itself' among secondary school teachers. These findings give emphasis to the proposition that job satisfaction is dependent upon a more complex set of factors than simply 'hours worked'. As Butt and Lance (2005b) conclude:

> It is apparent that highly motivated people often gain much satisfaction from their work and choose to work long hours – as such many teachers' sense of satisfaction and motivation seems to be embedded in a larger set of beliefs and attitudes reflecting, say, their commitment to their job, good working relationships with colleagues and children, and positive school ethos. This may partly answer some apparently intractable questions such as: why do some teachers apparently like working long hours, even when there are opportunities to avoid this?; why has there not been more of a welcome for the increased use of classroom-based support?; and why is there little realisation that working mainly during term time may create a heavier workload than working over a larger number of weeks through the year? (p. 420)

In a further study by Lance (2004), primary teachers did not object to working long hours if they had a reasonable control over *when* they carried out their non-teaching duties. With a networked laptop, which easily linked home with work, teachers could more successfully juggle domestic and professional commitments and therefore improve their quality of life.

Hargreaves (1994) recognizes the complexity of many teachers' relationship with time, work and personal life. In seeking to understand what happens when society changes, but the basic structures of teaching and schooling do not, he notes that 'teachers become overloaded, they experience intolerable guilt, their work intensifies and they become remorselessly pressed for time' (p. x). Each of these factors has at least some resonance with the findings of the Project Evaluation (Thomas *et al.* 2004). Referring to a 'Faustian bargain' between the quality and quantity of time teachers have available to them, Hargreaves identifies that for many teachers time is not simply an objective constraint but constitutes a more subjective 'horizon of possibility and limitation' (1994, p. 95). The ever-tightening controls on teachers' time – which are often bureaucratically driven – are at odds with the more personal, flexible ways in which teachers manage their time in an effort to deal with the simultaneous demands their job creates. As such, 'it may be more helpful to give more responsibility and flexibility to teachers in the management and allocation of their time, and to offer them more control over what is to be developed within that time' (Hargreaves 1994, p. 114).

Reducing the time worked by teachers in attempts to redress the imbalance between 'work and life' is not merely a statistical issue – as the government seems to believe – but has a number of more complex facets. For example, only limited consideration has been given, thus far, to the effects on teachers' motivation of intensifying their work whilst simultaneously deprofessionalizing many of their responsibilities. The multilayered nature of teachers' work, how they think and feel about it and the emotions they bring to it – especially feelings of anxiety, frustration and guilt, which Hargreaves (1994) recognized in the mid-1990s – has not yet been adequately considered in workforce remodelling. Teachers' motivations about their work are therefore complex and not easily manipulated. They relate to a work–life culture that is hard to define, and even harder to reshape.

The Project Evaluation found little compelling evidence of the impact of teaching assistants in reducing teachers' work, although teachers in the pilot schools revealed a weak relationship between a fall in hours worked and a more positive view of the potential of teaching assistants to reduce workload. Remodelling has certainly occurred through the deployment of teaching assistants in non-traditional roles in many of the pilot schools, but we are uncertain as to the extent to which this change has become embedded.

The experience of remodelling appears to have been positive in most pilot schools, but the transfer of such gains from a well-funded one-year project to permanent change in working culture and practice at the national scale will not prove to be straightforward. It was clear from the data that some teachers saw teaching assistants as being key in helping them carry out their professional duties, but it is also obvious that this in itself will not drive change unless teachers can identify *how* to make use of their support to maximize its potential. These issues are dealt with in Chapter 4.

Chapter 4

Challenging and changing role boundaries

Ann Lance, Steve Rayner and Chris Szwed

Introduction

This chapter will consider the shifting of role boundaries and job responsibilities within schools and the ways in which such practices are producing a remodelled workforce. It is significant that remodelling has focused on organization and personnel issues, rather than directly on learners and teaching. In the following discussion, therefore, we present three case studies illustrating different approaches which schools have taken to remodel the roles undertaken by support staff. The first case study, of Urban Primary School, is related to supporting pupils with special educational needs, and demonstrates how one school is redefining roles developmentally to enable the special educational needs co-ordinator (SENCO)[1] to act in a strategic role, with teaching assistants acting in an operational capacity (Szwed 2004). The second of the case studies is taken from one of the TSW Project pilot schools, and shows how Central School has restructured its support staff by reviewing and extending some of their roles. The third case study was a special school, Conurbation School, also involved in the TSW Project. It provides an insight into how the remodelling process affected role shift for support workers within school that reinforced emerging notions of a changing professionalism and professionality. The question of challenging and changing role boundaries is finally reconsidered in the light of the TSW Project and the National Remodelling Agreement (DfES 2003a) and continuing reform of schools in England.

Changing roles and functions in education

Modernization is a contemporary political discourse establishing an agenda for change across a range of public services, including health, education, criminal justice, local government and the civil service. This change is construed as largely being driven by new technology (ICT) and as a continuing process of reform driving improvement of the public sector that has not successfully been transformed by marketization (Newman 2000). Although the modernization agenda continues to focus on accountability as a key purpose, reflecting a concern for efficacy, efficiency and performance, it has more recently reflected a broader concern for social inclusion as part of public sector reform. This has led to Newman (ibid., p. 46) stating that reforms such as remodelling are now concerned for 'best value, partnership, public consultation and democratic renewal' which can be seen as going beyond the 'outright assault on public services which took place under Conservative administrations'. Within this notion of modernization is the idea of lifelong learning; a concept of the citizen as an active, engaged and informed community member; of work as task-focused and supported through new technologies providing opportunity for the socially excluded; and of multi-agency approaches involving collaboration and cooperation across different parts of the public sector. Remodelling of the school workforce is therefore part of a wider initiative aimed at a better provision for diversity reflected in recent policy presented in *Every Child Matters* (DfES 2004a).

If we focus on the education sector of public service reform, and consider the four factors identified as critical in the implementation of modernization (DfES 2002a), this chapter is concerned with the 'flexibility and incentives' category. Here the emphasis is on a fundamental shift away from traditional workforce roles and boundaries, encouraging the relinquishing of existing contractual employment arrangements. Thus job redefinition has become a 'cornerstone of the. . . remodelling of the teaching profession' (Butt and Lance 2005a, p. 139). It is not only a review of teachers' roles which is implicit in this process, but also a reappraisal and, in some cases, expansion of the roles of support staff. It is this group of staff which are of particular interest in this chapter, not least because 'schools now employ significant numbers of teaching assistants' (Clark 2002, p. 18). The reform, however, affects both teaching and non-teaching staff as a modern school workforce is recast and a new professionality is produced. Perhaps more critically, this process raises the question of the continuing relationship between the teacher and those para-professionals making up the non-teaching staff in a school. Issues such as status, terms of employment, trust, professionalism and expectation begin to surface, and reflect much of the content in the following discussion.

Changing role boundaries in relation to special educational needs

The signing of the National Agreement (DfES 2003a) introduced important changes to teachers' conditions of service, signalling a continuing movement towards the remodelling of the school workforce in England. The increased number of teaching assistants in schools and changes in the expectations of their role have had significant implications for teaching assistant management within schools, especially for SENCOs, as many teaching assistants are mostly engaged in supporting children with special educational needs. The National Agreement also acknowledged the pressures that schools were under to tackle unacceptable levels of workload. This is particularly pertinent in the area of special needs coordination. Therefore there is clearly scope and reason to reconsider and challenge traditional boundaries within the area of special educational needs coordination.

The New Labour Government both within the revised Code of Practice (DfES 2001a) and within its national standards sought to define the role of the SENCO, and all mainstream schools are expected to have such a designated teacher. The SENCO is required not only to possess skills in teaching children with special needs but also to develop management techniques in order to communicate with and influence professional partners in action for special educational needs. Central to this partnership is the role of special educational needs teaching assistants or LSAs (Learning Support Assistants). However, Gerschel (2005) reports that the management of teaching assistants in schools, especially primary schools, is often complex and ill-defined although the revised *Code of Practice* (DfES 2001a) added the area of line management of teaching assistants to its description of the SENCO role. Gerschel (2005) recommends that the SENCO, to be effective in managing the change process and the teaching assistant team, must have an established role and a strong voice in senior management and decision-making.

Consideration of the SENCO workload is timely given the recent UK Government initiatives relating to reforming the workforce (DfES 2002a). The proposed changes express an aim to 'restructure the teaching profession and to reform the workforce' and include 'a concerted attack on any bureaucracy that gets in the way of what matters most – teaching and learning and raising the standards of pupil achievement' (ibid., p. 3). More recently the IRU Annual Report (DfES 2005b) reported on progress towards reducing the bureaucracy associated with SEN and found that in spite of DfES efforts to support schools in this area they had had little impact in practice. Kelly (2006) drawing advice from the Implementation Review Unit (DfES 2005b) asks schools and local authorities (LAs) to 'identify administrative tasks concerned with special educational needs that could be carried out by staff other than qualified teachers'(p. 1). A concern here is for the implications of transfer of work upon the role and status of the SENCO and school provision for pupils with SEN.

Case Study 1: Urban Primary School[2]

Urban Primary School is a 4–11 primary school with 400 pupils, situated in a metropolitan area serving a well-established district of mixed housing. It has an excellent record for supporting children with SEN, as recognized by OfSTED in its last inspection where SEN was seen as a strength of provision. The SENCO role is undertaken by the Assistant Head who is a member of the Senior Management Team (SMT), although over half her weekly timetable is allocated to SEN. The school has nine teaching assistants who support SEN work.

The SENCO is responsible for managing their work. The SENCO reports few difficulties in fulfilling the SENCO role. The three factors which help her fulfil the role are a very supportive headteacher and governing body, SEN viewed as a high priority in the School Improvement Plan and 'an excellent SEN team who are well trained and committed to their roles'. These points are endorsed in the school's last OfSTED report which said that the SENCO and staff are hard-working and support the headteacher in promoting teamwork and productive relationships.

The role of the SENCO within this school is clearly a strategic one. The main emphasis within the work is on a consultative and advisory role. The SENCO is clearly an experienced and valued member of staff.

What is clear is that the whole school share a commitment to SEN and its high priority within the school. Working relationships amongst staff are strong and the school has invested heavily in resourcing SEN. LSAs are given a clear role with a job description, performance management review and programme of professional development. Within this programme, negotiated and supported by the SENCO, training is undertaken in a particular area of SEN and then the LSA becomes the lead person in this activity supporting other staff members, both teachers and other LSAs. The SENCO is allocated time for the role and has the autonomy within the role to utilize the resources in the most appropriate way. The Head and Governing Body of the school are very supportive and it is evident that the Head and SENCO have a shared vision for SEN.

The main SEN resource identified by management is clearly the school workforce, and the SENCO has built up a large team for which she has direct line management responsibility. Although class teachers are given autonomy in setting up programmes for children with SEN in this school, there is a large team of nine teaching assistants. The SENCO as a senior manager is involved in their appointment, deployment, monitoring and professional development. This is an extensive management role and one which she acknowledges is quite time-consuming. Weekly SEN team meetings and individual LSA performance meetings are scheduled 'to ensure smooth operation of policies'. The SENCO has full responsibility for the SEN budget including staffing, buying services and resources.

The SENCO within this case study is an established, experienced teacher who has built up the role since the introduction of the original 1994 SEN Code of Practice. She talks of the importance of SEN within the school, the supportive whole-school ethos and the importance of inclusion. It is clear that the role of SENCO is seen as pivotal in the development of the school. A comment from the Head indicates this:

> Our school prides itself on supporting children's special needs and its inclusivity. It is crucial, however, that the area is well led. The SENCO provides a wonderful lead. She is a sensitive and experienced member of staff who others can look to for advice and support and I can rely on to provide the vision and direction in the area.

In a discussion of how the role has developed she is keen to point out that her appointment as SENCO was carefully deliberated by the school management.

> When the Code of Practice was established the Head felt that this role was very important. He felt that as Head it would be difficult to fit in with all the other

responsibilities but that it should be a senior manager, someone with good knowledge of the school, so that was a choice of myself or the Deputy Head.

In discussing the school's policy on inclusion it is clear that whole-school commitment and support is key to the policy. As SENCO, a lead part of the role is 'keeping staff informed of inclusion matters, assessing children and ensuring the right provision, then working closely with teachers and support staff to achieve that provision'. A response to the question 'Do you see yourself as champion of inclusion?' was particularly insightful:

> I always raise the status of children with SEN on the SMT. I am lucky here because the Head and governors are very supportive of SEN. I do need, however, to take a proactive approach to inclusion. We are including more children with SEN all the time. We could not do this without the support of the staff, and my role is clearly to lead the way forward in helping them to achieve success.

This last statement clearly emphasizes a leadership role. The way in which this is carried out varies, but there is a great commitment to leading by example in relation to interpersonal skills, i.e. being ready and available to support staff and parents. Teaching assistants are viewed as part of the whole-school team; they even have their own performance management systems linking closely to targets stated in the school development plan. What is evident within this case study is how the roles and responsibilities of teachers, SENCO and teaching assistants have been formulated and trialled, and are constantly under review.

Given the importance of the role in relation to whole-school developments, the designation of the SENCO role is clearly an issue for schools. A significant finding alongside that of sufficient time allocation for the role is the benefits of membership in the SMT. Decisions on resourcing and policy in SEN are often taken by the SMT leaving out the SENCO. Effective SENCOs, as acknowledged in the literature (Cowne 2003; Shuttleworth 2000) and as witnessed in the case study, need good managerial and interpersonal skills, an ability to understand whole-school issues and developments and the credibility and respect of colleagues in order to take these developments forward. A more innovative approach, however, is to consider the development of teaching assistants in enhancing their skills to be able to take over some of the bureaucratic tasks of the SENCO. This development is clearly in line with *Reforming the School Workforce* proposals (DfES 2002a, p. 1) to create 'new support staff roles filling roles at every level in the school, so that teachers can focus on teaching'.

What is meant here is, however, open for debate. Such a development could be interpreted as implying that the role of the SENCO no longer needs to be undertaken by a qualified teacher. Indeed Warnock (2006) told the SEN Inquiry that she believed the role of the SENCO as teacher was under threat as schools in different parts of the country were employing teaching assistants to do the job. She suggests that this casts a shadow on the concept of a new professionalism and calls for a reconsideration of the status and training of SENCOs. Wilkinson (2005, p. 243) in a separate consideration of the impact of workforce reform on teachers as professionals argues that remodelling as it is currently being developed threatens teachers' professional jurisdiction. He argues that there is no explicit analysis of knowledge base or description of a teachers' expertise, in current government policy, which explains or justifies teachers' retention of any area of responsibility in school. He continues this argument by asserting that without '. . . an explicit articulation of teacher knowledge, stipulations about the proper roles of teaching and support staff are unreasonable and arbitrary'.

However, there is a more positive note within the IRU Report (DfES 2005b) which recognizes the need to strengthen the role of the SENCO, realizing the benefits of using SENCOs in a strategic role across the school rather than spending time on bureaucracy. This is in line with several recent commentaries (Cheminais 2005; Gerschel 2005; Layton 2005). Central to our discussion here is a concern for an evolving rather than transforming role of the SENCO, and the importance of context, that is a management and leadership role specific to the context of SEN and inclusion. This will involve SENCOs in managing both teaching and non-teaching colleagues and enabling others to work more effectively as a manager/member of multidisciplinary teams.

In a final analysis, do we actually need a teacher to fulfil the SENCO role? Or is the appropriate question to ask should we transform or reform role definition for the SENCO? What is evident is that dealing with special educational needs is a challenge for every teacher every day and it is essential that we should not absolve teachers of this responsibility in any way. As we have noted, the role of the SENCO is more in line with being able to empower others in developing innovative practice to further support special educational needs within their classroom. Gerschel (2005) reports that teaching assistants expect to be better informed, prepared, trained and supported and have better pay and career prospects. The SENCO is central in managing this change process, but to be effective must have a strong voice in senior management and decision-making in order to take a whole-school perspective as this case study has illustrated.

Changing role boundaries by restructuring support staff

Workforce remodelling is a major element of government policy, not just within education, but also in other arenas such as the medical world and other public services. It is a major plank of the government modernization programme – the role of para-professionals is extended to allow the professionals to concentrate on their major function. While some schools have been reluctantly drawn into this endeavour, suspecting that this is merely a means of saving costs on education spending, remodelling is a major development within Central School. As a pilot participant in the TSW Project, the school has fully embraced government policy in the remodelling of its workforce. While some primary schools have either reluctantly reviewed the roles of support staff, or made adjustments to meet the demands of the remodelling agenda, the school has taken a national lead in a wholehearted approach to this work.

Case Study 2: Central School

For Central School (a large urban primary school with 800 pupils) a major aspect of remodelling has been the restructuring of the role of teaching assistants:

> What a lot of schools have done is not do it properly, which is they've assimilated them [teaching assistants] across onto a new pay scale. But they haven't restructured. But there's a big opportunity to restructure support staff.
>
> (Senior Manager)

The restructuring of teaching assistants has been organized to mirror the teaching management structure. In a four-phase system with a teacher acting as phase coordinator, a HLTA has now been appointed to each phase (Scale 4). Two of these HLTAs act as team leaders who manage and support the whole group of teaching assistants throughout the school. Two other levels of teaching assistant fall into the categories of being qualified (Scale 3) and unqualified (Scale 2). Within the qualified group, there are two further levels of teaching assistant (Scale 3 plus 1 and Scale 3 plus 2.) On Level 3 a teaching assistant is expected to work with groups of no more than 8 children, so those working in Foundation Stage with groups of 15 children are graded at Level 3 plus 1. Those on Scale 3 plus 2 take on an extra defined responsibility which could be, for example, pupil mentoring or management of support staff students.

An important outcome for the school in this restructuring programme is that hours of work for some teaching assistants have now been extended so that they can participate in a range of activities which take place beyond the school day, such as planning meetings, pupil assessment and out-of-school activities. Moyles and Suschitzky (1997) highlight the importance of the involvement of teaching assistants in the cycle of planning. They see this as critical for effective learning to take place, and this is similarly identified by Goddard and Ryall (2002, p. 31). These writers emphasize the need for 'teachers and teaching assistants to plan and discuss activities in order to ensure understanding and so maximise benefit and efficiency'. It is, for example, argued that time is given for teaching assistants to report on pupil progress when they have been supporting groups of children within a class. It is not appropriate to assume that the presence of extra adult support within the classroom is necessarily beneficial to pupils' learning. It is important that communication between teams of adults working with classes of pupils is given careful attention. It is clear that teachers acknowledge that having such support necessitates their spending time beyond the immediate contact hours to support planning and preparation (HMI/OfSTED 2002). This expansion of the roles of teaching assistants has facilitated opportunities for this vital communication to take place outside class time. A subsequent issue for all schools is how to avoid the simple idea of teacher release for PPA by non-teaching staff that results in the latter making no contribution to the process of planning and assessment.

At Central School the role of the HLTAs involves them in working in teacher-led teams for planning. HLTAs receive regular training and carry out their role with confidence and commitment. More controversially, HLTAs undertake whole-class teaching, with the support of another assistant, in specific circumstances. They are based in a particular phase, within which they undertake cover teaching, and are also members of the planning team. This is welcomed by staff:

> By having people in the school who they [the children] already know and hopefully have respect for, it's a smoother transition if somebody's away. And whoever is away they know that the teaching is at the right level – they know that what's being taught is what they want being taught.   (Support Staff 1)

There is awareness on the part of the senior management team that this issue is one which requires careful monitoring and a balanced approach:

> One of the problems we have with it, of course, is that this then takes them away from what they should be doing, and they're doing very valuable work. So it's just getting that balance.   (Senior Manager)

The work of teaching assistants is highly valued within school, and their flexibility and enthusiasm has thus far enabled this remodelling to work well.

This acknowledgement of worth and contribution is evident in speaking with teaching assistants and in listening to their discussion on the school website. They talk about being part of a team whose knowledge and experience is valued. They appreciate having regular weekly meetings to which they contribute agenda items, and from which they receive management feedback. They appreciate having clearly defined responsibilities. They also are appreciative of the carefully monitored programme of training which is provided for them, both in-house and outside the school. Moyles and Suschitzky (1997) underline the need for 'individual strengths' (p. 104) to be taken into consideration in the organization of training for support staff. Such needs are best identified by giving attention to the views of teaching assistants as well as those of teachers. Goddard and Ryall (2002) emphasize the need for there to be 'regular open communication channels' (p. 31), in order to ensure that this type of dialogue takes place. This seems to be in operation at Central School.

The smooth transition into this remodelling at Central School may be attributable to a number of issues. Firstly, the size of the school and its flexibility of budget have allowed the school to invest heavily in this initiative. In addition to the funding which was being committed to the basic support of this restructuring, the school has also undertaken a commitment to training for support staff in order to support their career progression. Secondly, there has clearly been careful thought given to the management of change, where members of staff are encouraged to pilot change before it is built into practice. The concerns of teaching assistants are also taken into account. There is a need for sensitivity of approach towards teaching assistants on the part of teachers, not least because of the more powerful and highly remunerated positions of the latter. As Mills and Mills (1995) highlight in their discussion about the relationship between teachers and teaching assistants, there is a need for 'each partner . . . to respect the integrity of the other' (p. 125). This is particularly important in the context of the management of change, especially when the restructuring of roles is concerned. Hayes (2003) similarly underlines the importance for teachers in training to be respectful of the roles which other significant adults play, and urges that the high levels of commitment shown by teaching assistants should not be taken for granted by their teacher colleagues. Tilley (2003) reinforces this from a teaching assistant's perspective, speaking of her determination to make her role work through 'much good will' (p. 36). This atmosphere of mutual respect is one which has to be carefully nurtured.

At Central School there is a sense that all staff are working towards achieving the best they can for the pupils, thus reflecting a child-centred approach. This remodelling initiative, which embraces government policy, may have fallen on more fertile ground here than in other primary schools, because reflection on current practice and piloting change is embedded within the staff culture:

> I think it's the management team. Because they're very committed to the school, they want to get what they can for the benefit of the children. And I think that just flows through, trickles down, and everybody is just, 'Well, we'll try this because it might benefit the children'.   (Support Staff 1)

> I think we're all working as a team. We've all got the same goal, we all want to meet the same objective with the children. So you're taking the children's needs into consideration more than anything else.   (Teacher)

The success of this restructuring programme is related to much more complex issues than the single process of implementing a new structure which affects role boundaries. It has been introduced into a situation where a positive whole-school culture of collaboration has been embedded over a long period of time, and where there has been a long-term 'investment in people'. It raises questions about its replicability in other schools where attention is less focused on the people within those institutions.

Challenging role boundaries in the special school

The contemporary context for the English special school is typically one of adopting a strategic lead and managing change that embraces both workforce remodelling as well as the broader UK Government agenda for social inclusion and equity in the educational system. The special school is a unique form of provision, and its place in modernizing and transforming the educational system is potentially key to the notion of an integrated children's service (see Burnett 2005). Yet in a policy mix which continues pressing for a new professionalism reflecting stated concerns for both standards of excellence and social justice (see Newman 2000), the special school is particularly vulnerable to closure. It is arguably caught in a nexus of political reform and an ideology of educational inclusion (Rayner *et al.* 2005). In remodelling terms, this uncertainty presents a challenge that requires a process of making sense of issues linked to professionalism, professionality and boundary change for both the special school workforce and the special school (see Hoyle 2001; Burnett 2005; Wilkinson 2005). The special school has a short-term future if it does not succeed in both remodelling its workforce but also reforming its educational function – the alternative is to face being closed down.

Case study 3: Conurbation School

Conurbation School participated in the TSW Project. At the time of the Project the school had 225 children with complex learning difficulties across the full secondary school age range (11–19). The school catered for children with a range of special educational needs (SEN) including children with severe learning difficulties (SLD), moderate learning difficulties (MLD), emotional, behavioural and social difficulties (EBSD) and autistic spectrum disorders (ASD). The school workforce during the TSW Project comprised 28 teaching staff and 45 support staff (1, 2 and 3). The support staff included: 27 teaching assistants working with children, 4 technical support staff providing assistance with ICT and other equipment, 6 medical staff and 8 school site-based and office staff.

The aim of the school in participating in the TSW Project, expressed by the Headteacher and many of the staff, was to improve how the school managed its time and workforce. The effect of the Project on school development appears to have mostly impacted upon the question of role definition and conceptions of professionality and professionalism. Interview respondents explained that:

> Most teachers are traditionalists by heart, with a genuine feeling for the children. But these approaches are rightly questioned and challenged. We live in a changing world. We do want to see reflective practitioners being developed in school. Boundaries for professionals do need to be defined but they also need to be flexed, if we are genuinely going to see a relationship between quality and time in this development.   (Senior Manager)

> Special Needs Assistants seem to have more responsibility, especially on Wednesday afternoon. They combine with speakers from outside agencies and

manage the afternoon. Different kinds of specialists are bought in. SNAs have more responsibilities on Wednesday. Through Pathfinder some Teaching Assistants have more responsibilities as a result of differentiated roles being offered and applied for. (Support Staff 2)

The impact of the remodelling project on its teaching staff was mostly felt in the area of role responsibility and a reduction for the teaching staff of some administration and extra-curricular activity. This was linked to the restructuring development of the non-teaching staff. Several staff in interviews at the end of the Project commented upon this effect:

The workload as a teacher has reduced, now that we have a Reprographics Technician and don't have to use LTAs to do such work. This has impact on the quality of lessons. (Teacher)

Special Needs Assistant reorganization has led to my being involved in class more. Since the start of the Project I've been more involved with the children. All of the Learning and Teaching Assistants and other non-teaching staff have been working in different ways. (Support Staff 1)

The issue of role definition and job specification was perceived as part of a bigger picture describing developments in collaborative practice and working partnership that was compared to that of doctor and nurse in the health services context. It should also be noted that this kind of teamwork had been a feature of this school for a long time. As one member of staff explained:

As a grandparent of a child in a mainstream school I would feel strongly if I thought my grandchildren were being taught by a classroom assistant. If you thought they weren't being taught by a fully qualified person you'd be very unhappy. Within this school it is very different. I don't think it's a bad thing here. (Support Staff 3)

A second aspect of the TSW Project, in terms of school development, was the drive towards improving systems. This involved role expansion for non-teaching staff and particularly the effort to transfer record-keeping and paperwork from teaching to other staff. This aim was clearly established in the school's change plan, and the evaluation data showed that respondents generally perceived an intention to extend and enhance clerical support for the teaching staff. One member of staff commented that:

The Project has allowed the creation of a full-time post of Central School bursar. This has helped to make financial management more accessible and transparent. There is also a greater access to resource management for all of the staff. Secondly, there have been new lines of management introduced for the office staff. Out-of-school working for administration, previously paid for

by goodwill, has been introduced. Overall, there have been definite improvements in the structures for support work.   (Support Staff 3)

A central aim of the TSW Project and the National Agreement was workload
reduction for the teaching staff. As explained by a member of the support staff,
the Project was therefore perceived to be primarily centred on the task of
improving teaching and learning as part of an effort to release time for teachers.

Pathfinder has emphasized the extra work teachers do – we try to relieve them
of workload. I now work with a senior teacher on Wednesday afternoons.
People work all hours, struggle on, it's only through Pathfinder that we've
given it some consideration. So, it is these issues that have been highlighted
by Pathfinder.   (Support Staff 1)

Overall, the effect of participating in the TSW Project as described by the school
workforce was a sense of impact and change and, while this was perceived positively, it was tempered by uneasiness over the issues of sustainability and wider
applicability. There was a sense of a renewed emphasis being placed upon the
importance of dedicated staff teams and partnerships interacting throughout
the school week. The reshaping of professional identity and working practices
for both the teaching and non-teaching staff was less clearly stated but also
strongly felt by many members of staff.

Conclusion

Several themes emerge from the three case studies presented here and more
recently in evaluation studies of the National Remodelling Team in England
responsible for supporting the National Agreement (Wilson *et al.* 2005; Easton
et al. 2005). The first report (Wilson *et al.* 2005) noted that outcomes of the
remodelling process included support staff consistently gaining a greater
degree of responsibility and an improved career structure. Key factors facilitating these outcomes were identified as a willingness from school staff to work differently and change their current practices, the availability of funding and a
commitment from support staff to take part in professional development activities. Similar findings, reflecting remodelling and non-teaching role developments, were also reported by HMI for Education and Training in Wales (2005).
These early findings were subsequently reaffirmed in a second evaluation in
which the researchers found more evidence of professional development
opportunities for support staff (Easton *et al.* 2005). The report also stated that
respondents believed systems and support networks established through the
remodelling programme should be used to roll out new policy such as the *Every
Child Matters* programme.

   Our own appraisal of the current remodelling is perhaps less positive than the
NFER evaluation and reveals additional issues reflecting change management

and restructuring of role boundaries in the school workforce. This includes good management of the following aspects of the remodelling process:

1. balancing between a consideration of role redistribution and resource capacity;
2. ensuring good pace and sustainability in planned change;
3. enabling transitions and distribution of networking within and between groups in the workforce;
4. working with intended and unintended outcomes in change management;
5. agreeing conceptions of educational professionalism and professionality.

The most immediate concern emerging from this appraisal is for the continuing direction of remodelling and government policy – and what this means for the role and job of being a teacher or member of the support staff. While *meltdown* and *crisis* have been words more usually associated with teacher recruitment and retention when used in connection with education reform, these words might perhaps now be as easily used to predict changes to professionality that might well occur in a remodelled school workforce.

For example, Ball (2003, p. 226) writes persuasively that educational policy in England since the 1988 Education Reform Act has seen an intensifying attrition of the soul of the teaching profession. An emphasis in policy upon an internal market ideology, the so called 'terrors of performativity' and a transformational leadership linked to managerialism are all identified as having resulted in a steadily corrosive effect upon what it means to be a teacher. Ball explains that

> The policy technologies of market, management and performativity leave no space of an autonomous or collective ethical self. These technologies have potentially profound consequences for the nature of teaching and learning and for the inner-life of the teacher.   (p. 226)

Allied to this longer-term effect of recent policy is a worry that conceptions of teaching and schooling underpinning the reform exercise actually reflect a model of learning that is entirely grounded on the idea of knowledge transmission. Education perhaps is simply construed, firstly, in terms of its utility to produce a skilled workforce and economic capital; secondly, as schooling in terms of a model of cultural and social training; and thirdly, with formal learning as a delivery system for knowledge. 'Chalk and talk' is replaced in the transforming education model by a computer screen with image and text. While none of this is in itself a bad thing, what is worrying, given our original acceptance of the claim that remodelling will facilitate improved social justice and equity in education (Newman 2000), is a disregard for the learner, learning and teaching process. Further, this approach also reflects a similar disregard for the primacy of a human relationship between the learner and teacher.

The point here is that this idea of education strips away the interpersonal dimension in learning and teaching. There is an emphasis upon particular knowledge and skills, with little or no concern for personal, emotional and social development. The human and ethical dimension in learning is either relegated or separated from the core task of teaching. In this way, it is not surprising, for example, to anticipate further restructuring of role boundaries, with teaching assistants becoming Heads of Year, or a SENCO, and the worth of a pastoral curriculum duly consigned to para-professional activity. In this respect, it is tempting to assert that, while Ball may be correct to suggest we face a continuing battle for the teaching profession's soul, there is more immediately an urgent need to protect its heart.

The exercise in remodelling the school workforce creates a time to rethink deeper concerns about professionalism and an integrated school workforce. Role responsibility and working boundaries are by definition increasingly complex in a less certain and changing context. Reinforced by the press of new technologies and political accountability, there is clearly an agenda of imposed instrumental reform impacting upon the educational sector. This change is affecting professional boundaries and identity. Working well in a team, across a network or as a member of a project, however, requires a secure sense of professional self, status and identity. Flexibility and innovation flourish in a context which offers the practitioner some certainty and trust, as well as an opportunity to learn. Growth of this kind is perhaps not simply transformational, nor is it technical remodelling, but rather an educative process that ideally comprises a cycle of innovation and learning, adaptation and development.

Part Two: Modernizing the Organization

We present three chapters in this section of the book. Here we explore the ways in which schools in England have approached organizational and cultural change. We focus on the realities of leadership, and we not only present data from the TSW Project (see Appendix 1) about headteachers and their work, but we also link the schools to wider networks contracted to deliver change.

We begin this section with a chapter by Gunter and Butt which highlights the accounts of particular headteachers who led the change process in schools that were originally involved in the TSW Project. Original project data are supplemented by new data gathered from interviews with headteachers some two years after the TSW Project ended. The next chapter extends the key themes introduced by the headteachers by examining the role played by leadership in bringing about change, questioning whether there is anything new in the forms of leadership expected in modernization. The issues of change management and distributed leadership are considered, leading to a theorizing of the 'new' leadership process. The concluding chapter in this section looks at the role played by 'change agents' in school modernization. In particular the work of external consultants and School Workforce Advisers (SWAs) is explored, such that the tension between 'private' and 'public' agents of change is brought to the fore.

Chapter 5

Leading a modernized school

Helen Gunter and Graham Butt

Introduction

All headteachers are accountable for the delivery of a remodelled school work-force in their schools. In this chapter we examine headteachers' experiences of leading this change in particular schools who were part of the Transforming the School Workforce Pathfinder Project. These headteachers not only led the sub-stance of the change in the type and role of members of the workforce but also the change process that is now being used in schools across England. Here we draw on data from the Evaluation Report (Thomas *et al.* 2004), combined with new data from interviews with some headteachers two years after the Project ended. We tell the stories and then draw out the key themes and patterns of practice that these cases generate.

Experiencing leading and remodelling

Each TSW Project school had to go through a formal change process of: first, attending regular London Leadership Centre 'global' events where the change model of Mobilize, Discover, Deepen, Develop and Deliver was intro-duced, and the headteacher/school was supplied with a copy of Michael Fullan's (2001) book *Leading in a Culture of Change*; second, participating in strategic monitoring where each school had to complete forms staged at various intervals based on the change model in order to record progress and outline the next steps; and third, establishing a change management team sup-ported by an external school workforce adviser who facilitated strategy and implementation.

The TSW Project was not the only contracted Project that many of the schools were involved in, with some having received funds from Excellence in Cities, Educational Action Zones, Beacon Status and/or Specialist School Status. Successful implementation is associated with schools having created almost seam-less links between these and the TSW Project. Indeed, securing change in schools might seem to be more likely if new initiatives are introduced into a school in a way that demonstrates their linkage and integration with existing activities.

We can illustrate this by drawing on evidence from the case studies under-taken by Thomas *et al.* (2004):

- **Rural School:** the approach has been to develop distributed leadership through an inclusive approach to participation in and responsibility for change. All staff were members of one of six change teams and each team worked on a particular change goal, e.g. homework, ICT and the curriculum. The school was already very successful in regard to learning outcomes and had begun to work on remodelling prior to the Project. The Project gave additional resources to enable innovations around developing the classroom of the future, supported by new ways of designing the curriculum and a new school day. Staff were encouraged to engage in 'blue skies thinking' and to have open debates which generate strategies for improvement.
- **Lakeside School:** the driving force behind the Project was the change management team made up from staff at all levels. The majority of staff interviewed reported that they felt positive about the way in which this team had operated, though the pace of change and some operational difficulties were commented on.
- **Metropolitan School:** the Project had accelerated change that the school had already embarked on and provided new opportunities for development. A key strategy has been to increase staff involvement in the change management team and to begin to shift towards a culture of distributed leadership within the workforce. The change team was composed of team leaders from all parts of the school and it was challenging for teachers and support staff to be involved in a collective approach to development. The evaluation found that this was regarded as having been successful, and staff state that they have grown in confidence through their contribution.
- **Border School's Cluster:** the management of change within the cluster has mainly been positive, with change management teams working on strategy in all four schools. Positive comments have been made about the collaboration, with the anticipation of developing stronger links in the future.

The TSW Project case studies show members of the workforce identifying positive gains to their working lives and being supportive of the processes they have experienced. It is also the case that there have been negative experiences, either through the paradox of the high pace of change within the short life of the Project or frustration that changes did not happen quickly enough. The students at the case-study schools were generally supportive of the initiatives in their schools, and were able to articulate the positive impact these had on their learning.

The case studies also highlight the concerns that members of the school workforce had about the future. There were many comments about sustainability and whether the additional resources, often seen as crucial to enabling the changes, would be sustained. Set against these concerns was the recognition in some of the schools that the Project had given them confidence to begin to manage resources more creatively, creating a new-found sense of freedom. In order to gain an understanding of what longer-term change involved we approached some of the pilot and case-study headteachers two years after the

TSW Project had finished to obtain their views on the change process. We present five stories of ongoing change from headteachers:

Town School (small primary school within the Border Schools' Cluster)

The TSW Project has had a positive influence on the school and continues to do so. The most lasting impacts are the capital-spend and staffing changes, although not all of these developments have been funded through the TSW Project. Some of these changes have kept going, but this has only been possible through an increase in base funding. Teaching hours have actually increased slightly, but this has partly been a result of ensuring PPA time. The school has aimed to keep its number of support staff and maintain their hours. Most changes brought about by Pathfinder have been permanent, but it was apparent from early on in the Project that the DfES expected certain outcomes and had certain beliefs about what would change teachers' workload.

A further major change that continues, which Pathfinder introduced, is the role of consultation, and in essence Pathfinder was about introducing cultural changes to schools. Consultation has become central to how the school works, and therefore the Development Plan is created as a result of consultation with all the school's staff. Although the change management team no longer exists in the school in name, its role has continued. The change management team way of managing is all about getting all staff to put forward their views in a professional way. We have whole-staff meetings once a month, which also includes parents, governors and children. These meetings have been central to the creation of priorities within the next Development Plan. I am currently seconded by the LEA for 1 or 2 days per week to work as a remodelling adviser for primary schools, and schools are generally very receptive to the introduction of change management teams and I would say that about 50 per cent of primary schools have introduced them.

I believe I have become a better head as a result of Pathfinder. It has changed the nature of my job and the way I work. I am no longer the one source of information and support when issues arise. Much of the administrative work I carried out is now done by the Staff Manager, and the financial work by the School Bursar. Aspects of health and safety management and premises management have also been shifted away from me.

The school still faces issues of workload. Pathfinder did not really succeed in reducing teachers' workload, but it changed the ways in which they worked. The school operates a performance management review for staff which highlights workload issues and checks that staff are properly qualified for the roles they are now expected to undertake. Stress is still a major issue and so a stress audit is included in the process. Many staff have changed their job descriptions through remodelling and so this is a focus. The main thing about performance management is ensuring that adults are in the right roles. Workload has not reduced but people feel better about the work they do – however, they are not working less hours! PPA has been guaranteed for three years.

The conditions that most support staff work under in most schools are archaic. The restrictions placed on individual schools mean that changing the conditions for support staff is difficult for individual heads. It is also very difficult for heads to retain good support staff if they can only be employed and paid for in term time. Teaching assistants and other support staff work very well in the school, but it is a difficult situation to maintain. Pay is a significant issue for some support staff.

The size of this school is a major factor to consider in any change process. This school is very small (38 students) – this makes some things very easy to change and others not! Pathfinder came just at the right time for this school as it was about to enter a period of change. However, not everything Pathfinder introduced worked. For example, the idea that teaching assistants might become more involved in marking and assessment was not successful – as they were often not in the classroom when the work to be assessed was set, and did not see the children complete it. They came to the marking process 'cold' outside the classroom. Many therefore took a long time to assess work, and did it poorly. The policy has now changed such that more marking is done in the classroom, some of it by TAs.

It seems to me that Pathfinder's approach of grouping various types of schools (large, small, primary, secondary, etc.) worked brilliantly for the cross-fertilization of ideas and practices. It gave an insight into how other schools were approaching modernization and remodelling within very different contexts. However, the least successful changes in schools are imposed from above. The best solutions are those that schools generate themselves. This creates a tension between national and local agendas for change. When I eventually leave the school, the change will be permanent and embedded. The wider school staff now have the skills and qualities to work in and run a modernized school. For example, the ICT changes have become embedded within the school. This is both in the context of teaching and learning and in the school office.

My experience of working with other heads and staff is that they feel that the National Agreement has been under-funded. My main criticism of Pathfinder is that it actually introduced too much money into the remodelling and modernization programme for schools, a situation which was not sustainable. This has had a negative impact on many schools who have had to change back their systems because they no longer have the budgets to sustain them. Pathfinder needed very careful financial management by schools – indeed I tended to use expensive solutions to problems precisely because I knew that a lot of money was available during the life of the Project. This does tempt heads to work in this way – again an unsustainable situation. There was therefore a tendency to find easy (but costly) solutions rather than working hard to find sensible solutions that did not involve larger costs.

(Headteacher, Town School)

Metropolitan School (5–11 urban primary school)

During the TSW Project the school introduced a restructured school day, starting 30 minutes earlier at 8.30am and finishing 15 minutes earlier. Fifteen minutes was also taken from lunch. Staff have been very positive about these changes, which have been maintained, and there has been no major negative impact (such as increased lateness to school by pupils). Psychologically staff see the 8.30 start as positive as it allows them an opportunity to 'avoid' the rush hour. As part of the restructuring of the day, the school provides after-school clubs. This has been a struggle, particularly with respect to staffing the clubs. This is an increased workload issue, and staff no longer volunteer for the clubs and there are no funds to support this work. The school site now closes at 6pm which means additional staffing up to that time. The fact that more children stay on for the extended day facility has meant an increase in staffing costs.

All classes now have interactive whiteboards and the school has an intranet. The TSW Project provided the impetus for increased IT use, and laptops have helped immensely, but these [and all IT equipment] are prone to breaking down and need replacement. IT support staff are hard to find and costly, and since TSW the school has employed an IT graduate, but funding this in the longer term will be problematic. There are financial implications for who manages the IT systems.

The change management team in school wasn't continued because it was seen as being 'of the moment'. We have stayed with our original leadership team and team leaders. Change management teams were only beneficial at the time of development.

The school has made a reasonable financial transition since the Project, but this has been as a result of constant savings and budgeting. I am always aware that to retain levels of resources I need to closely monitor savings. The school is only allowed to retain 5 per cent of its budget for each year – this means budgeting longer-term for staffing changes is difficult. We cannot look for support staff funding more than one year ahead.

The workload of staff has not really declined since the TSW Project finished. We have reassigned the 24 tasks, and employed teacher administrative staff, but the workload is still high and seasonal. The start of the Autumn Term still means lots of data-gathering for staff, target-setting, lesson observations, performance management interviews, etc. This happens from September to November. The focus then shifts, with the Spring Term being the 'lightest', but the pressure builds again to the end of the Summer Term. Workload problems have not been eradicated to a great extent, but they are now more managed. Teachers no longer photocopy or do stock orders, but do more focused higher-level duties.

Remodelling and modernization does not come cheap! Also there is some initiative fatigue and there aren't the opportunities to sit back and reflect on current practice and procedures. League tables are a concern, as is the constant focus on a narrow curriculum. The TSW Project was about being creative. With the pressures of targets/standards/league tables you can't be creative. (Headteacher, Metropolitan School)

Avenue School (special school)

I didn't want the TSW Project to be a one hit wonder and so we used it as a catalyst for what we wanted to do anyway. I wanted the gains to be sustained and so would not take some of the risks that other TSW schools did. One thing we have done is to continue to extend the Associate Teacher (i.e. Teaching Assistant) role developed during the Project into the Higher Level Teaching Assistant. When the head of KS4 left, this role was not replaced directly, but the funding was used to support other roles, and an assistant teacher has taken on the work.

We have reviewed administration work and we continue to audit this. We check to make sure we have not slipped back to where we were before the Project. We ask the administrative staff to make sure that teachers are not doing administrative work, and we use the Project questionnaire to check up on work and workload. Capital expenditure has been used to build a new entrance and this continues to benefit the school. The developments in ICT were seed-funded through the Project and the school has continued to invest in this.

My role was remodelled in the Project and this meant some of my work was taken away, which meant I could do more strategic work, and at the moment I am the head of two schools in a local federation. We have extended ICT across the two schools so that policies are in common and there is video conferencing. Laptops have been extended to Higher Level Teaching Assistants (HLTAs), and members of the leadership teams all have personal digital assistants (PDAs), and mobile phones to aid contact.

The school did not have a change team because we did not need a new group formed. Consultation for the Project was through the groups that already existed, and there is a high degree of participation in the school. The change process was good to follow, but it seemed to be more about reporting and filling in forms, though this process gave it rigour, I have to say that the external support was very good.

Overall, the TSW Project allowed the school to extend and build on what we aimed to do, it gave authority to the changes, provided seedcorn funding. It enabled the school to do what we wanted to do. The process is kept under review and it has enabled the school to be extended into a federation with another school. There is the perception that the TSW schools could only make the changes because of the money, and so the gains made are not replicable. Hence TSW Project schools have been sidelined. No one has bothered to find out what we actually did and so other schools have not benefited from the learning in the schools. Remodelling has ignored us and we have not been involved in the training.

(Headteacher, Avenue School)

Rural School (11–18 comprehensive school)

Since the TSW Project I have changed schools. At Rural School I was at a time in my career where I wanted to rethink headship, and I was working hard at the school – around 80–85 hours per week. I really needed to rethink my working week for myself, but I also realized that I was modelling long hours that others took a lead from. The TSW Project made me think about my job, the core purpose of my role, how I make decisions and how I work.

The experience of the TSW Project has helped me to develop priorities for both schools, the structures for learning, and thinking about work–life balance for staff. In the new school we have a five-term year with two-week breaks in-between. We have a work–life balance week at this school and it is midway in a term where there are no meetings or trips. I have appointed three cover supervisors in the first term, and use others to help with invigilation. The ideas that I worked on at Rural School are being implemented at my new school.

The gains for teachers and support staff have been a redefinition of roles, with a refocus on core purposes for teachers as leaders of learning. I think we need to think about how we remodel the classroom and the department, and how this works. For the students, they are now working with a wider variety of adults with a range of skills. The gap between teachers and support staff has improved, and in this school there are 14–15 support staff who are now form tutors, and so there are 2 adults for every tutor group.

Administrative staff are working alongside teachers doing mentoring. We have a curriculum administrator who does cover and exams. We created this role when the school did not replace an Assistant Principal role. In addition to this we restructured the leadership and middle leadership group. I don't know if this is directly due to the TSW Project, but what is clear for me is that the experience of TSW has made me think differently.

The big issue is sustainability. There are a lot of issues that we looked at when I was head of Rural School but they have not been implemented. There is a new head with a new direction, and if there is this type of change then it does take the school in a different direction. Also we have to remember that the TSW schools had money and so it is a difficult argument to win with other heads. Some schools have made changes over time and beyond what the TSW schools did, and so they didn't really need the money. However, I do wonder if I would have had the same sense of purpose if I had not been the Head of a TSW school. Some of the TSW schools did change things, but many only paid lip service to the Project.

The TSW Project made me a more effective head, and has been incredibly valuable. Deep change takes time and will take time to get embedded into schools. I do think that nationally Remodelling has lost its way. There is a tension between remodelling with teaching and learning. The National Remodelling Team have refocused on Extended Schools, and it seems Remodelling has lost its way. There is a tendency to focus on the contract and not on teaching and learning. So overall, I would say that it has been positive for heads and for schools, but I am sceptical about the national agenda and whether it will deliver on the radical promise.

(Headteacher, Rural School)

Country School (11–16 urban high school)

The school has more of a can-do culture because of the Project, and people now expect change because it has become a way of life. And the new staffing review has not been a headache because of the remodelling we have done. We have had a policy that wherever a teacher leaves we always look to see if some of the duties that he or she performed need to be done by a qualified teacher; in fact this is a process we are engaged in all the time whether a teacher leaves or not.

During the Pathfinder Project we appointed two Faculty Support Assistants, two Year Managers, we bought 90 laptops so that all teachers had one, and we installed a wireless and administration network. Since the Project finished we have appointed eight Learning Managers who cover lessons when a teacher is absent, and this was because of the success of having the two Faculty Support Assistants during the Project. We have now increased the number of Year Managers to five and we no longer have Heads of Year. We have appointed a Head of Resources and General Manager who is a member of the Senior Leadership and Management Team and oversees all support staff, does cover and exams. We have appointed a Buildings and Events Manager who takes care of the buildings, anticipates problems, organizes open evenings, organizes parents' evenings and organizes family learning day. There are now about 110–120 laptops in school so that all teachers and the bursar, Learning Managers and Year Managers have one. There is a Network Manager and the ICT facilities have developed well. We have a web-page designer who worked with the English Department to develop teaching resources and is now working with Design and Technology.

A big gain from the Project is that a new way of thinking developed, for example, the appointment of the Learning Managers costs less than the cost of supply cover used to. Getting rid of the Heads of Year and appointing the Year Managers also costs less because a Head of Year taught 17 out of 30 periods, whereas a main grade teacher teaches 26 out of 30, and so the school gets more teaching from a teacher, and the pastoral work is covered by a cheaper Year Manager. The Heads of Year either took on a fuller timetable or left and were replaced by a newly qualified teacher. The people who have been appointed are confident and share our ethos; this has been the right solution at the right time. The Learning Managers have brought continuity and experience. Permanent contracts have been used for the right calibre people.

The support staff have developed well. For example the Human Resources and General Manager joined the leadership team after a year and this has added a dimension to the strategic development of the school. There are now 160 staff and 90 of these are teaching staff. Teamwork has developed really well, and there is a good interaction between staff. People are more accepting of teamwork. The wireless network has been liberating because you can work where you want to, and you can see staff working on laptops around the building. The ICT capability of staff has developed, but if the system goes down then people clearly have become more dependent on it. There is an events log-on wireless network and this cuts the paperwork. There are some pluses and minuses with students logging in, but it is being used more and more.

We have replaced all laptops since the original TSW Project ones. We needed an initial investment into hardware, software and people. Then we trained the staff and things have moved in stages and people have grown in confidence. At the OfSTED inspection in May it was reported how well ICT was being used to deliver lessons. ICT is now an integral part of assessment and recording. Registers are taken on the laptops, with photo ID on this as well. ICT also generates reports. It is used for target-setting and monitoring, with a traffic light system of Green 'on target', Amber 'borderline' and Red for 'difficulties', on the basis of which interventions can be made.

I do wonder whether things were done too quickly under the TSW Project, particularly the change plan, and we did need more time to do this. But maybe the urgency made us go in a creative direction. One gain is that there has been cultural change, and we are trying to spread our practice by setting up conferences for other schools. We have also made our job descriptions available to schools locally.

We didn't want the Change Management Team (CMT) to be a talking shop but to do things – we didn't want it to be too big. We had a twilight session for all staff and informed them that we were forming a change management team, and that we wanted it to be a conduit for staff views and ideas, and to deliver on workable solutions. It has 9–10 people: Head, Deputy Head, and representatives from all staff, including teachers who had promotions, teachers on the standard scale, governors, support staff, and a representative from the NUT. The change management team has stayed and while the composition has changed it is still representative of all. There are meetings of staff to evaluate the changes – what works well and what we need to do – and this is then fed to the CMT. It's been a good experience to see how ideas can be put forward and see if they work. The staff and the CMT were given the message to 'think the unthinkable' and if it benefits the children then we would do it. We decided that there would be no ideological resistance and everything is open for change.

We could have done without the upset to the staff and the propaganda from some media coverage of the NUT action over the changes, but this was a major change and you go through pain and then come out the other side. Our experience of this means that if someone comes up with something, an idea, it does not really look to be so radical. But change does not happen overnight – it takes two to three years – and quick fixes based on people is a problem because if the person goes then the change goes. What schools need to work on is longer-term cultural change and this means that you can sustain things even if people go. Change has become a way of life, and it is about buying into the ethos. It is about the guiding principles about freeing teachers to teach, and to improve learning opportunities. I liked the Fullan idea of this being our moral purpose, and I am of the view that we should not be diverted off course with the upset we had, it is about working through this. If something is tough then the message we give out is to stop moaning and do something about it.

(Headteacher, Country School)

Conclusion

What these stories show is that working to reduce workload is hard work. Huge amounts of time, energy and credibility have been invested in developing these schools. There have been highs and lows in these experiences, with concomitant gains and frustrations. From these stories and our analysis of the whole change process, the Evaluation Team have identified that there are four main meanings that can be developed from the TSW Project (see Gunter *et al.* 2007).

The first interpretation is that change in schools is linear. This can be illustrated with the change model and how each school has had to produce and monitor a change plan. In this way change has a beginning, a middle and an end. The rationality of the change is evident in the formal beginning with the production of an evaluation report for each school based on the baseline data; and the formal completion through the evaluation report for each school based on the end-of-Project data collection and measurement of change (see Appendix 1 for details of the methodology). Such linearity, combined with external direction and surveillance of the process, illustrates the twin features of New Labour modernization: investment and accountability. Each of the schools secured additional resources to trial remodelling and had to go through a rational process in order to demonstrate how those resources had been used and to what effect (Thomas *et al.* 2004).

A second and connected interpretation of change is that there can be planned intentional change processes where the aim is to challenge and possibly overturn long-established structures and cultures. So a change in practice means that which is different can be identified, and the stories are full of examples of proactive strategizing where questions about who does what, why they do it, how they do it and whether they should continue to do it come up for discussion and intervention. Illustrative of this is how County School trialled innovations in the covering of lessons and new ways of handling pastoral care during the TSW Project, and then built on this in the two years following, with Learning Managers and Year Managers appointed to what had traditionally been teachers' roles. What this indicates is the interplay of cultural change, or 'what is done around here', with the practice of what needs to and should be done.

We have argued elsewhere (see Gunter and Rayner 2007; Gunter *et al.* 2007) that while the two forms of change illustrated above have been central to reform strategies, there are other change approaches that are evident in the data. Therefore the third interpretation of change is one where the experience of change, with all its messiness and incoherence, is given attention. What story-telling does is to enable the person to emplot their life and to give it a sense of meaning, but within this the actual experiences of what it has been like to live through the change can be made visible. In this way, experiential change processes are located within the working practices of those who have witnessed and lived remodelling, and so change is relative to what can be perceived and felt. We are mindful that headteachers have dominated the data, but they have made aspects of the process transparent. For example, while the headteachers, and hence their staffs, were told to think differently in change management teams, this cannot be legislated but has to be developed over time. It may or may not happen to all, it may or may not be understood by all, and it may or may not be sufficiently visible to be recognized or measured. For example, Metropolitan School did not begin with a linear change in regard to the organizational matters of remodelling but with the learning needs of students. From this a new timing of the day emerged and the school worked on securing this as a means of developing innovative learning experiences. The school has done what the Project required in relation to reviewing roles and staffing, but they have done this from the perspective of learners and learning. The experience of taking back control over educational purposes means that there has been learning about what the school can do without fearing the performance regime shaming them in public or putting their livelihoods in danger.

A fourth and connected area of interpreting change is through recognizing the political processes through which people reveal their histories, their personal views and their values. There is a game to be played; some play it well, some do not. Consequently, change is a matter of what is possible through negotiation and deal-making. Local circumstances visible through a cocktail of personalities, events and position-taking therefore are a part of the change process, and so matters of credibility, influence and legitimacy play their part. For example, matters of sustainability of the gains from the TSW Project are not just about the sufficiency of resources to employ and deploy the workforce or to have a rolling programme to upgrade the ICT system, but are a result of how choices are framed and made. What works may only work locally, and it may only work through a trial-and-error process as illustrated by Town School's experiments with TAs and marking. Reviewing the 25 tasks that teachers should not now normally do (see Chapter 1) is not simply a matter of having a rational plan but is about how professional identities have been formed and developed. It is about how members of the workforce have undertaken work in good faith because if they had not done certain things (including photocopying by teachers) then students would not have had the learning materials they needed. Hence asking teachers to change their practice is not simply concerned with their giving up work they agree needs to be done (see Thomas *et al.* 2004), but is about how secure they are that the work will happen in ways that will enable them to focus on teaching. Connected to this are matters such as the low status and pay of teaching assistants, and how teachers can only delegate to TAs if time is provided for such leadership work to take place.

A final point is that the politics of change are such that, as Hoyle (1999) has argued, micropolitics are evident in schools in two ways: first, the way external policy is engaged with internally; and second, the way internal relationships operate through the mix of people and their histories. The TSW Project is an interesting way to examine how these two interplay: on the one hand it is an external policy thrust that the schools had to make work within their particular setting; and on the other hand the Heads are clear that they had built on the opportunities of the 1988 Education Reform Act and site-based management. Therefore the Project was more 'bottom up', as they participated in it and used it to accelerate changes in place or in their plans. Hence while change is officially rational and linear, with the aim to achieve an equilibrium between the central and school-based policymaking, there is another perspective that sees change as a political process of gains and claims. We examine these matters further in the next two chapters, where in Chapter 6 Rayner and Gunter challenge the dominant discourse of heroic leadership, while in Chapter 7 Butt and Jackson examine how private sector networks have developed in order to sustain the official model of leadership.

Chapter 6

Remodelling leadership
Steve Rayner and Helen Gunter

Introduction

This chapter explores remodelling through a focus on leadership, and considers whether there is a new form of leadership, or merely a restatement of previous approaches. Southworth stated, when considering the launch of the National College for School Leadership (NCSL) in England, that:

> School leadership is often taken to mean headship. Such an outlook limits leadership to one person and implies lone leadership. The long standing belief in the power of one is being challenged. Today there is much more talk about shared leadership, leadership teams and distributed leadership than ever before. (Southworth 2002, p. 3)

The way in which a distributed form of leadership has been central in much of the remodelling agenda is considered in our discussion, focusing in particular on a model of change management in the remodelling process. In addressing the core principles of remodelling leadership from both a theoretical and practical stance, we move toward a greater understanding of what remodelling leadership may really mean within the context of education. More specifically, the chapter will present an analysis of the following:

- models of official leadership promoted by government to enable modernization;
- distributed leadership and its role for describing and understanding the practice of the transforming change management model;
- theorizing about educational leadership generated from the TSW Project and subsequent data gathered in evaluations of the National Workforce Agreement.

Leadership in education, finally, is re-presented in a number of variations but always as a purpose, function and activity that is continuing to evolve. It reflects both a changing world and our understanding of what it is to lead – as a process and as an event which takes place. We argue that the form of leadership being presented within remodelling is about organizational efficiency and effectiveness, rather than about learners and learning or what we would recognize as educational leadership (Gunter 2005a and b). Educational leadership draws from researching and theorizing in education, is practised within education and is intrinsically educational. Following Gronn (2000), we argue that leadership is a relational interaction, and educational leadership is only realized in a complex interaction of structure and agency, generating leadership that is a social and socializing practice.

Modernizing the education workforce through leadership

There is a position taken in the literature that the field of educational leadership has recently witnessed a fundamental reappraisal of definition and function (see, e.g., Bush *et al.* 1999). Some writers claim this as an overdue exercise, citing a failure of researchers and research in providing a more clearly mapped terrain of the field (e.g. Bush *et al.* 1999; Gronn 2002; Gunter and Ribbins 2003). Others (e.g. Barber 2001; Caldwell 2004; Hallinger and Snodvings 2005; Istance 2005), justifying and indeed contributing to an 'establishment' leadership model associated with notions of commerce, service reform and business management, criticize the field for irrelevance. Such writers claim that the profession requires a particular kind of leadership associated with reform that will both meet the needs of the modern world and facilitate school improvement and educational effectiveness (see Caldwell and Spinks 1998; Dalin 1998; Reynolds 1992).

This latter *government-approved approach* to school leadership unsurprisingly influenced the Transforming the School Workforce Pathfinder Project (see Collarbone 2005a). This approach might be described as a blended cocktail of transformational leadership, managerialism and performativity (as defined in Ball 1997, 2003; Gunter 1997) and previously critiqued in the writings of Gleeson and colleagues (Gleeson and Husbands 2001). While this model is advocated in policy documents for England as a working model fit for purpose in a world shaped by the ideology of an educational marketplace (see DfEE 1997a, 1998; DfES 2001b, 2002a, 2003a, 2004b, 2005a), it should be remembered that it is a particular approach to leadership. There are in this approach a specific set of beliefs about the nature and value of public service, the utility and commodification of education and the primacy of a managerially driven accountability.

School workforce modernization has been for some time a *big idea* for government. It has been located at the heart of policy in England since the Education Reform Act (DES 1988), and has been directly tackled by New Labour since 1997 (e.g. DfEE 1998). Indeed, it sits in the vanguard of an attempt to modernize the entire public services sector. The reform drive is reinforced, in turn, by a notion of transformation linked to meeting the challenges of a new world. Bentley and Miller (2003) argue that the successful transformation of schools calls for a 'new professionalism' in which teachers' work is increasingly research-based, outcomes-oriented, data-driven and team-focused. At the same time, it is described as simultaneously globalized, localized and individualized, with *lifelong professional learning* the norm for the evidence-informed specialist. The parallel is drawn with the specialist in medicine. This idea of evidence-based practice and data-driven development as a predominant *modus operandi* for supporting an 'account-able professionalism' has seen a similar modernizing rationale applied to educational research reinforcing a particular emphasis upon performance and result (see Cordingley 2004; Sebba 2004).

Draper (2005) offers support for the urgency in implementing this kind of leadership policy, in an interesting analysis of demographic and social forces impacting across the UK workplace. Reform is justified in a real-world rationale presented as particularly relevant for remodelling the school workforce in England. Demographic and economic data are used to demonstrate that the shape and nature of the school workforce must change in order to ensure efficacy. Draper (ibid., p. 49) writes plausibly that the issues of professionalism and teacher recruitment or retention are a key to modernizing education. He suggests that the existing profile for the school workforce in England is one reflecting a division between two groups: the first group are traditionalists who resist change and the second, modernists, who welcome a new professionalism. In an analysis reminiscent of recent political history in England, the resistance to reform and modernization is cast as a recalcitrant and foolish denial of a changing world and the need to reshape within this real world. Draper captures much of the current debate surrounding remodelling leadership and workforce modernization, but this is more extensively and critically presented in Gronn's (2000) analysis of shifting changes in the structure of global labour, with its implications for education leadership and a redefinition involving a phenomenon called 'distributed leadership'.

A powerfully privileged response to this need for reform and change, it seems. is one of two distinctive forms of remodelling leadership (see Table 6.1). The first is in the guise of an established approach described by Collarbone (2005a) in an account of the TSW Project and is transformational leadership. This model of leadership is described by Leithwood (1994) as leadership associated with a concern for the following key orientations:

- building school vision;
- establishing school goals;
- providing intellectual stimulation;
- offering individualized support;
- modelling best practices and important organizational values;
- demonstrating high performance expectations;
- creating a productive school culture;
- developing structures to foster participation in school decisions.

Murphy and Hallinger (1992, p. 86) also attribute the adoption of transformational leadership to 'changes in the policy context of schools' but argue that this is a normative change in which school leaders are being asked to 'undergo a metamorphosis, to change from transactional to transformational leaders'

Table 6.1 Two types of leadership in modernizing schools

Type A – Traditional	Type B – Emergent
Leadership resides in individuals	Leadership is a property of social systems
Leadership is hierarchically based and linked to office	Leadership can occur anywhere as a social practice
Leadership occurs when leaders do things to followers	Leadership is a complex process of mutual influence
Leadership is different from and more important than management	The leadership/management distinction is unhelpful
Leaders are powerful agents	Leadership is powerful synergy
Leaders make a crucial difference to organizational performance	Leadership is one of many factors that may influence organizational performance
Leadership is data-based and target-led	Leadership is knowledge-based and learning-centred
Leadership is technical and instrumental	Leadership is social and political
Effective leadership is generalizable	The context of leadership is crucial
Leadership is transformational – it delivers impact	Leadership is transformative – it empowers and grows

Source: after Simkins 2005

(p. 81). Following Simkins (2005, p. 12), we would argue that this debate has captured the surfacing of a traditional and an emergent definition of educational leadership. These are described in terms of key features in Table 6.1. The traditional type of leadership reflects transactional and transformational models of leadership. The emergent type of leadership reflects a distributed and critical model of leadership.

Bush and Glover (2003) agree that the transformational model is comprehensive in that it provides a 'normative approach' to school leadership which focuses primarily on the process by which leaders seek to influence school outcomes rather than on the nature or direction of those outcomes. This model when applied to a managerial approach to performance is characterized by an emphasis upon the technical aspects of professional service, reflected in language associated with business, commerce, marketing or accountancy; examples include terms such as audit, delivery, product and impact, and are reinforced by a curious mix of quasi-religious terms such as transformation (instant change), mission, vision and charisma; the school context in which this is applied involves local management of finance, site-based management, winners and losers, profit and loss and a belief in an implicit benefit from open competition that in itself is presented as a guarantee for service equity (provision that will ensure a good fit for diversity, creativity, selectivity, choice and opportunity). Transformational leadership, to sum up, describes a particular type of leader-centric process based on increasing the commitment of followers to organizational goals. Leaders seek to engage the support of teachers and galvanize a vision for the school so as to enhance capacities for goal achievement (Gunter and Rayner 2005).

A second form of remodelling leadership seems to be grounded on the idea that a changing world is a reality and requires a new form of educational leadership, just as it requires a modernized or new educational professional. Hartle (2005) offers a typical summary of this position in a description of the structural forces determining this direction,

> It is evident that the functions and form of secondary schools is changing and that school leadership pathways will become more complex as a result of a more diverse work environment. Internally, there is a drive towards shared leadership, which in theory will create more opportunities for leadership development. (p. 18)

The kind of leadership expected in a post-modern world characterized by rapid and accelerating change, a knowledge economy that is fluid and uncertain and a workplace characterized by a technology-driven accountability of performance is critiqued by Gronn (2002), who argues that

> the property of distribution [represents] the hallmark of a different kind of phenomenon, but one which has emerged only in conditions peculiar to the fast capitalism of late modernity. That is, distributed systems are 'a leitmotif of late twentieth century life' and arise only because of an 'exponential growth in variety, variability and diversity of all sorts in all areas. (p. 428)

A conclusion reached is that such 'realities' exist and are impacting upon the workplace across the globe and this does indeed have implications for school leadership.

> With the possibility of distributed leadership first raised more than four decades ago, a revised unit of analysis is long overdue. Although recent workplace restructuring has been the trigger for a reawakened interest in distributed practice, a number of studies in the taxonomy predate these developments, either in their subject matter or in their publication date. A key question, therefore, is whether distributed leadership is new or whether commentators are beginning to recognize a phenomenon which has always existed? (ibid.)

The distribution of leadership, in Gronn's mind, seems to be an inherent part of leadership *per se* but to have been re-emphasized in the global trends impacting upon contemporary society. To cope with the unprecedented rate of change in education as it is being experienced by practitioners – and it should be noted that in many ways an inherent presumption of constant change was subjected to a hot-housing effect in the TSW Project – there is sense and purpose in locating leadership in a distributed way across the workforce.

There is continuing debate and disagreement about the meaning of 'distributed leadership'. It is identified by Leithwood *et al.* (2004) as a 'promising development' in the school response to national reform initiatives in education (see also Bennett *et al.* 2003; MacBeath 2005). The nature of change as a process demanded by reform policy appears to point to an emerging practice that is inclined towards redistribution. It is based on what we would argue is an unhelpful distinction between strategic leadership (including all of the features of this approach to leadership usually associated with the transformational model) and operational management (including an approach usually associated with securing efficient and effective use of resource and good levels of institutional performance). Put more simply, the distinction between 'doing the right things' as strategy, and 'doing things right' as operational activity, reflecting separate and distinct actions of a practitioner exercising leadership, is misleading if not simply wrong. Similarly, the notion that distributed leadership is a tool for the technical exercise of re-engineering the educational professional, or implementing new reform, is equally misplaced (Gunter 2005b). Educational practitioners are perhaps doing what they have continued to do through a long and constant programme of change initiatives impacting schools over more than three decades in England (see Farrell and Morris 2004) for an example of workforce response to change initiatives and government policy; Wilkinson (2005) for an analysis of threats to teacher jurisdiction in the remodelling exercise). Practitioners are clearly translating policy in a process that is about combining personal and professional values in a continuing exercise of educational practice. This involves leading and leadership of teachers at every level of the school structure, from classroom to assembly hall, from support staff to members of the governing body (Gunter 2005a).

Teachers may be seen as exercising a form of *reluctant compliance* while attempting to hold true to a set of values and beliefs underpinning a deep-set professionality (Farrell and Morris 2004). There are perhaps further related reasons for practitioner resistance to the reforming of professionalism identified by Hoyle (2001), including threats to prestige, status and esteem. Similarly, educational leaders are engaged in translating policy while *playing a game* of managing reform that is about continuously re-presenting and confirming values and beliefs about an *educative process*, yet simultaneously ensuring participation in a bid culture and policy arena that offers the payback of social and political capital and resources for their school. Behind this activity often sits *smart thinking, astute positioning* and *strategic compliance* that might be reasonably described as part of an enduring teacher professionalism (see Rayner and Gunter 2005a and b; Rayner *et al.* 2005). Nevertheless, the pressures of educational policy and accountability are very real and dominant, as practitioners experiencing school inspection, change initiative fatigue and, in a worse case scenario, the notice of a *failing school* testify. Leaders and leadership can easily slip into a position of being *lost in translation* as policy is implemented, whilst change management forms an operational management stretched across the organization. Such management is perhaps wrongly described as distributed in a transformational aspiration and a prescriptive dispersal of delegated instruction (see Spillane *et al.* 2001).

A significant piece of research and resulting conceptualization of processes of power within organizational arrangements has been undertaken by Gronn (2002), who is less interested in the normative purity of distribution in ways that remain top down and are aimed at seducing followers to accept reform. Rather, he is concerned about the ways in which the division of labour operates, where distribution is an accepted feature of how people work together. Gronn offers a taxonomy of distributed leadership in an effort to define the phenomenon and argues for four types of related distributed leadership:

1. Co-performance–intuitive working relations;
2. Co-performance–institutionalized practices;
3. Collective performance–intuitive working relations;
4. Collective performance–institutionalized practices.

He argues that the principal change in the operational form of this leadership has been in the application of an increased incidence of conjoint agency, in the form of networked computing. This, in turn, has produced several social and structural shifts in organizational management across the workplace reflecting a phenomenon we can confidently call distributed practice:

- cross-hierarchical synergies entailing negotiation of role boundaries;
- friendship activities facilitating conjoint agency between allied interests;
- trusteeship in the form of an oversight of executive power, to check the *corrupting influence* of power on executives and to prevent harm to *those affected by its use.*

Gronn (2000) draws our attention to how distribution is not just the product of a role incumbent's position, i.e. the headteacher distributes tasks to others, but is a feature of practice. He argues that

> the choice posed by these or other similar approaches which privilege agency ahead of structure, or vice versa, rests on a false ontological dualism. The dualism is false because neither constitutive element of social reality, agency nor structure, reduces to the other; rather, the relationship between the two is always one of interplay through time: each element is analytically distinct from, but is ontologically intertwined with, the other. (p. 138)

This leadership practice is generally one that we think is continuing to mutate in a number of different forms as it reflects a local context yet contributes to a restructured and modernizing education service. All of this is construed as interaction or interplay between agency, structure and location. The trend is also located in a wider policy context – current political pressure for accountability, commodification of provision and service improvement – reflecting different constructions, values and beliefs about how we should define both leaders and leadership in the school system.

Leading interplay in TSW Project schools – managing change and distributed practice

The action and interaction of leader agency with structure located within a particular context is the 'real stuff of leadership'. The external demand for change is integral to this activity but it is greatly reinforced, or perhaps aggravated, by the demand for continuing improvement and demonstrable results produced in the existing policy of raising standards and school reform. The approach to change and leadership underpinning remodelling in the TSW Project is evidenced (Thomas *et al.* 2004) and described in summary by Collarbone (2005a). Official policy documents argue that remodelling is not an initiative, but is about change. This is claimed to incorporate carefully managed processes and tools designed to enable schools to own and manage their own restructuring agenda. This change management model is presented as reliant on team-working and distributed leadership. It is a transformational model of leadership emphasizing *quick wins*, and a continuing policy drive toward reform. The remit of the National Remodelling Team (NRT) in England is to support this approach. It is a public–private partnership with the majority of the central team being consultants from the private sector (see DfES 2003a, 2004b). The idea for such a team was introduced by the TSW Project London Leadership Centre team, albeit Collarbone claims that it emerged from the experience of the Project. The NRT reflects a commitment to notions of business management thinking, and of encouraging school leaders to think outside of the box as well as nurturing the creative capacity of envisioning and blue skies thinking. The advantages identified in this approach include the team holding no existing assumptions; it offers new practices and tools often untried in the education sector; it is experienced in working with large organizations and dealing with change; and it brings a wide range of new skills and experience to the task.

It is important to consider this process as it was presented in the TSW Project and in our own explanation for remodelling leadership. The change management model advocated by the Project leadership team required that there were three core elements in the change process if it was to be successful. These three elements reflected the characteristics of transformational leadership and are:

- a compelling reason for change;
- a clear vision of the future;
- a coherent plan for getting there.

The change process as presented is a directed agenda used to assertively drive towards identified goals and organizational improvement. A five-step change process formula was given to schools in the Project. It comprised the following actions:

(i) *Mobilize* – recognize the need for change, a school change team and opportunities for delivery of change.
(ii) *Discover* – focus on workload, assess the change readiness and build staff commitment.
(iii) *Deepen* – develop the scale and scope of the change and confirm a change initiative plan.
(iv) *Develop* – develop a vision and strategy for change, the potential solutions, combined with the delivery plan.
(v) *Deliver* – implement the change initiative plan and monitor effectiveness.

School leaders were trained in the operation of this scheme at so-called 'global events' organized as part of the pilot project. The process was structured as a variant of the 'improvement cycle', reflecting the structure of plan, do and review. Collarbone claims that this scheme is self-directed as it places the school in control of planned change and through the devices of a *change management team* and a *change plan* also involves the whole school community. Secondly, she states that the scheme is tried and tested, both in the commercial sector and in education. Thirdly, the process as directed during the Project relied upon a wider network of support in the form of change consultants – a strategy repeated in the work of the NRT.

Collarbone suggests that this approach to remodelling leadership will be a key tool in the reshaping of schools and education in the future developments of policy and provision. It will give school leaders the ability to:

- develop collaborative and inter-agency partnership of a community-led educational provision;
- ensure successful management of change required in the remodelling exercise;
- build trust, redesign jobs, change organizational structures and develop learning cultures;
- nurture the social partnership between government, employers, unions and others in order to
- enable an effective and efficient education service.

What is not considered anywhere in this account is the way in which all of this relates to learning and teaching and, more crucially, the nature of the relationship between learning and teaching and the question of teacher professionalism. The redefinition of what it is we understand education to be is presumed rather than explained. In respect of educational leadership, these values are key to the formulation of practitioner purpose, identity and function (see Stronach *et al.* 2002). A genuine distributed leadership pattern, however, is less about traditional notions of leader–subordinate relations in ways that deliver organizational efficiencies and more about distributed social and socializing practices forming a basis for new types of practitioner leadership and professional partnership. For this to work in the school setting, critical work is needed in the area of professional identity, boundary exchange and problem-posing/problem-solving consensus in the reworking of purpose, function and practice.

The following consideration of this leadership interplay based upon the experiences and an evaluation of the TSW Project will hopefully illustrate the point here: that is, there is a type of remodelling leadership emerging from the work of schools involved in reform which is less about the transformational imperative and more about pragmatic leadership. The latter is intent on growing a strong professionalism that is about protecting the educative process, reflecting sound educational values and a professional integrity. This might be summed up as good teachers wanting the children to learn and holding to a commitment for each child fulfilling their potential. To do this, good teachers want to make a difference. For this to happen, they need to be focused upon the process as well as content of a school curriculum, and the nature of the learning and teaching relationship. All of this in spite of a continuing remodelling drive towards a resource-focused operational excellence and a target-saturated culture of performativity that is threatening the soul of the teaching profession (see Ball 2003).

As identified by Rayner and Gunter (2005a), key features of the remodelling exercise in the TSW Project case studies included the change plan and the change management team. As part of the TSW Project each school was required to produce a change plan, reflecting the clearly stated intention to innovate and reform approaches to professional practice. For example, at one case-study school, the strategy was to develop the use of ICT through the provision of laptops for teachers; to support the development of teaching resources and facilitate networking; and to introduce an electronic communication, attendance and reporting system to give staff more accurate and readily available information about students. New members of the support staff were appointed including the Inclusive Learning Unit Officer heading up the new Inclusive Learning Unit, a Technical Support Assistant, a Creative Assistant and a part-time Bursar Assistant. A second formal and important organizational site, engendering potential distributed practice, was the change management team. All schools were required to set up a change management team to plan and oversee strategic change. Schools were encouraged to include membership from across the workforce and, with the support of an external School Workforce Adviser, also aimed to engage in blue skies thinking about the opportunities afforded by the Project. Our reading of data about planning and the change management team reveals how the disposition to contribute has been witnessed and has revealed a form of *distributed practice* reflecting how people made sense of the relationship between professional practice and the work involved in the Project. For example, members of the school workforce reported positive experiences of the CMT that included the following testimony:

The change teams have been fantastic! People have been constructive and helpful and it's good to have the ideas from a cross section of staff. It's an interesting model of change, but the Head is seen as being supportive and open minded about the change management process so this has helped. We are an open school that embraces change and staff have been kept well informed and interested in being involved.

(Rural School, Middle Manager, Thomas *et al.* 2004, p. 46)

The management of the school has changed in a positive way, the change management team has more positive ideas. Management has changed for the better, it is a more positive school.

(Metropolitan School, Support Staff 2, Thomas *et al.* 2004, p. 55)

The success of the Project for me is that it's been about the team approach to problem solving and decision-making. It's not just for the Senior Management Team to make the decisions it's about all the staff being involved. (Rural School, Teacher, Thomas *et al.* 2004, p. 47)

The implications for educational leadership of remodelling as experienced in the Project were perhaps more far-reaching than realized, or probably fully understood, by many involved. The evaluation data show problems with change management teams that required problematizing leadership role identities before any worthwhile boundary shift or restructuring might be sustained as part of the remodelling exercise:

Often teachers wanted instant change – which is unrealistic.

(Rural School, Middle Manager, Thomas *et al.* 2004, p. 46)

I had no real contact with my change team. I was part of the team initially but it was teacher centred. I went to one of three meetings but did not feel that administrative staff had a real role to play.

(Rural School, Support Staff 3, Thomas *et al.* 2004, p. 46)

It was a shock to have the change plan proposal to re-structure the school year accepted in July and then rejected. This gap between the instruction to think 'blue sky', then face a 'grey mass of rain' was very disappointing. To some extent, this was made worse by the DfES pushing for regular reports, making it seem as if we were being asked to 'dig up the seed every week to check for growth'. There was an obvious need for trust and a little show of belief in the school. Above all, the pace and time frame of the Project meant we were often pushing against the grain.

(Leafy Suburb School, Senior Manager, Thomas *et al.* 2004, p. 61)

These three illuminative examples show that distributive leadership cannot be imposed on professional practice: first, changing boundaries takes time and has to grow from within practice rather than being used to direct practice; and second, fabricated distribution can be seen through very quickly, as there is little credibility of the school developing a forum for different members of the workforce to come together to make decisions if, in reality, decisions are actually made by the DfES.

What seemed to be missing from much of the discourse was how teams, working together as adults, would make a difference to learners and their learning. This is certainly the case in how remodelling leadership has been understood during the roll-out across the country. In 2003, the DfES (2003a) published the National Agreement. In it, the claim was made that this initiative:

- relies on the involvement and participation of the entire school community;
- revolves around a change process that is a tried-and-tested way of managing change in schools;
- is underpinned by a wide network of support involving LEAs, the National Remodelling Team (NRT) and the signatory organizations.   (p. 2)

More recent evaluations of the National Agreement conducted by OfSTED (2004a), HMI for Education and Training in Wales (2005) and the NFER (Easton *et al.* 2005, Wilson *et al.* 2005) provide further data on how the Project inspired means of managing change and distributing leadership in schools tackling the policy of school remodelling.

In the NFER study (Easton *et al.* 2005, p. 45), the CMT was found to be widely used (although not always), forming a key vehicle for introducing changes in workforce structure. In a case study, communication is identified as a key success factor. One respondent commented,

> We discuss everything in staff groups. Everyone is clear that the focus of the school is on standards and all our work has to improve standards. A quarter of respondents also reported that extensive communication and the involvement of all stakeholders were needed to establish and maintain remodelling.
> (ibid., pp. 59–60)

The main elements of the change management team role as described by respondents to a survey questionnaire were identified as:

- communicating with and informing other members of staff (81%);
- leading remodelling within the school (79%);
- disseminating information about remodelling (72%);
- attending internal and external remodelling meetings (69%);
- representing staff interests as part of their role (51%);
- communicating and informing students (20%).   (ibid., p. 65)

The 'official' formula for remodelling, reflecting the TSW Pilot, was found to be widely applied; for example, the first stage involving 'mobilization' – in which headteachers advise the school's intention to participate and appoint a change management team which is briefed on the rationale for remodelling – engaged the remodelling process and the roles of team members. A change plan for completing the remodelling process, or a 'Remodelling Initiation Document', is then discussed and created by the change management team (Wilson *et al.* 2005, p. 47). This instrumental use of the change management team and a transformational model of leadership is emphasized here, and interestingly, the use or linkage of the team to student-related matters is negligible. Remodelling, as a technical operation, has little to do with students, teaching students or learning.

A report on workforce remodelling by HMI in Wales reported little use of the CMT. Their evaluation also described the most serious concerns for workforce remodelling to date, that is, a lack of impact upon standards of learning and teaching, and the poorly developed use of PPA allocation as part of the restructuring of teacher workload. This narrow focus on the main aims of the exercise ignores leadership aspects of the initiative, yet reveals a flaw in the work to date reflecting a gap between the effort to re-engineer teaching and learning and the very self same activity of learning and teaching.

This example of accounting as evaluation is mirrored in the earlier report in England by OfSTED (2004a). Their evaluation also found that schools were not taking into account the raising standards aspects of the National Agreement, nor was there evidence of linkage between the remodelling drive and the school improvement plan. Reinforcing this approach to restructuring the operation of school and workforce was a general emphasis upon resource management. This took the form of a managerialist perspective – in which the appraisal of the efficiency and effectiveness of human, physical and material resources being deployed to raise standards and value for money was held to scrutiny and audit.

At this point, it is timely to return to the precise purpose of remodelling leadership as reflected in government policy. The DfES (2005a) in perhaps its most explicit fashion to date has recently stated that:

> The new teacher professionalism agenda will build on and embed the achievements from the National Agreement to deliver further improvements in teaching and learning and in teachers' motivation and morale. The Five Year Strategy for Children and Learners proposes that 'career progression and financial rewards go to those who are making the biggest contribution to improving pupil attainment, those who are continually developing their own expertise, and those who are helping to develop expertise in others.' Underlying the new teacher professionalism is the aim that professional development is an ongoing part of the everyday activities of a teacher rather than a separate activity which adds to their workload.   (ibid., p. 9)

The question 'what's new in this?' is left hanging. But the answer is 'quite a lot' – for what is being proposed is an engineering of professional development that reflects the construction of competences-based training, and an official mandate for managing the definition of a 'good professional'. How this affects wider aspects of educational leadership and the future of the remodelling exercise is considered in the final part of our attempt to answer the questions raised at the beginning of this chapter. We suggest there is an emerging form of remodelling leadership occurring in schools, but it is far from clear how this will mutate or develop except to say that it will not simply be an officially prescribed transformational model of leadership.

Conclusion

The nature and scope of change within the TSW Project involved schools in examining the division of labour in ways that perhaps reflected a continuum ranging from a flow of delegation and mandate, through to other forms of more democratic or dispersed activity. More interesting still is the revelation of diffuse practices in ways that demonstrated the interplay between the agency of the person and the structures that stifle and encourage that agency (see Rayner and Gunter 2005a; Gunter and Rayner 2007). We believe it is important to understand and engage with these structures so that the social and socializing potential of participation is realized: for example, how does experience of change in the workplace and in people's wider lives impact on dispositions to work and professionality? How do we practise leadership in ways that challenge the structures of change so that we know what the change is, who is promoting it, for what purpose and why?

The educational leadership challenge, it seems, is about ensuring dialogue, coherence and continuity, albeit with much greater flexibility so that it can adapt to more fluid contexts characterized by uncertainty and change. This represents the greatest and most immediate challenge for those who work in educational institutions. We are in full agreement with Simkins' analysis (2005) of an existing dichotomy of educational leadership, in which he argues for the primacy of professionals seeking to make sense of their work as they 'lead leadership', rather than the received wisdom of seeking out what works and is deemed to be 'best practice'. Context is key to the success of educational leadership, as is the actuality of leading which is not solely the property of the official school leader (see Gronn 2002). Certainly, in our appraisal of the remodelling experience in the TSW Project, we found evidence to support our notion of changing patterns of leadership facilitated by an interplay between agency and structure.

This form of leadership is seeking to sustain, develop and make sense of good and successful practice – it does not imply a normative notion of best, or ideal, practice. The pressure exerted by impacting forces upon the school leader and practitioner leader should not in any circumstances be underestimated. These take the form of policy directives from government, popular pressures from differing groups comprising the school's immediate community and less tangible, but equally powerful, forces reflecting social change. Certainly, the postmodern shifts in knowledge construction and social structures characterized by ambiguity and fluidity impacting upon education leadership are making it necessary to develop more flexible and distributed kinds of practice. It is probable that the forms of remodelled leadership presented in this chapter reflect similar roles to those observed amongst native American tribes, as reported by Bryant (2003). What is essential, however, in the growing of such distributed practice is a consistent and coherent set of values that in the previous example of a non-hierarchical and function-related system of leadership was provided by tribal cultures. In our own context, this set of values should ideally reflect an educational professionalism and professionality.

Indeed, Rayner and Gunter (2005a) identified the challenge of 'games professionals play'. In the existing Zeitgeist, it is not surprising that this activity is often mistakenly described as entrepreneurial, but it is perhaps more accurately understood as a series of politically inspired interpretations of policy mandates imposed by central government on the work of a school. As Rayner and Gunter (ibid.) commented when reviewing leadership and the remodelling exercise in the TSW Project, the experience for the practitioner

> is an emotional and intellectual roller coaster ride that looks increasingly like an exercise in control and crisis management but is actually a creative constant: sharing in the process of making sense and securing sensibility for a school community. (ibid., p. 10)

It is this work of a leader in the professional context that will continue to form the developing model of a new leadership required for serving the core professional purposes of education. It will undoubtedly become increasingly more fluid in structure, distributed in nature and affected by the continuing information and technology revolution. It will above all else need to facilitate and nurture groups of practitioners in making sense of the collective and educative endeavour. It will, therefore, in all likelihood, take the form of a leadership that is increasingly concerned with making explicit a set of professional values and beliefs that can inform a renewal of what it is to be a teacher and to teach.

Chapter 7

Networking change – the role of change agents in school modernization

Graham Butt and Darius Jackson

Introduction

This chapter explores the function of various 'change agents' contracted by schools. We refer to the work of those agents who are principally located outside schools, but who may sometimes be utilized by schools to effect internal change. The broad delineation of such agents, as applied here, encompasses both organizations and individuals – although we are mindful that the actions of individuals are often perceived as being contiguous with those of the organization they represent. The work of a diverse collection of organizations involved with creating or promoting change – such as the DfES, local authorities (LAs), WAMG and the National College for School Leadership (NCSL) – is briefly considered. In the case of individual change agents we primarily consider the work of School Workforce Advisers (SWAs), although reference could also be made to change management personnel within LAs[1] and the wider community. This last category is fairly eclectic, being comprised of governors, consultants, parents and 'interested parties' from commerce, industry, charities, trusts and universities.

In our reflection on the work of external change agents in schools – rather grandly conceptualized by a previous Minister of State for School Standards as constituting 'coalitions for reform' (Miliband 2003) – we have sought to understand which factors influence their effectiveness, also focusing on their contribution as private consultants to the configuration and nature of publicly funded education. The main focus of our analysis is the promotion of change with respect to the broad modernization agenda now set for schools in England. This implies an appreciation of the models and concepts these agents implicitly, or explicitly, apply in their attempts to change schools and the ways in which they visualize their role in bringing about modernization. Often the change process involves some degree of wider networking by schools, which is also briefly explored.

Since the signing of the National Agreement on teacher workload in January 2003, and the earlier publication of *Time for Standards* (DfES 2002a), schools have been required to address the remodelling of their workforce. According to David Miliband, the School Standards Minister at the time, the starting point for these changes was 'not complex', but required a simple focus on the fact that every child was special and had a right to fulfil his or her potential. As such, every school was expected to bring out the best in their students through the creation of new 'styles of teaching, organization and support for learning, culture and an ethos of aspiration and respect' (Miliband 2003). Importantly, this would be achieved by the whole school staff – not just the teachers – working in a remodelled, efficient and modernized way. The National Agreement was therefore conceptualized as a 'new start' which offered 'real change in teachers' contracts. Real change in workload. Real change in classroom support, with new training and career development opportunities. Clear evidence that the government is for real, the agreement is real, and the benefits are for real' (ibid.).

This 'reality' is challenging. Since 2003 both the national and education press in England have regularly reported incidents of teacher, headteacher and union resistance to workforce remodelling and modernization – not least the immediate rejection of the Agreement by the largest teaching union, the NUT. Despite government claims that reform would put teaching at the cutting edge of public sector modernization, many schools have been slow to embrace change. Against this backdrop we explore the role of officially endorsed external change agents and attempt to evaluate how useful they currently are in creating change – this implies a focus on school leadership, as the main conduit for change. However, we should not ignore underlying considerations of the importance of what and how we teach, teacher recruitment, workload and work–life balance, continued professional development and performance management. These are all essential elements of a reformed teaching workforce, but must represent secondary considerations in our concise analysis of the ways in which change is instigated.

Collarbone (2005b) reminds us that the government's focus on education has shifted since the turn of the century towards encouraging schools to have a greater ownership of the change process – 'schools increasingly leading reform, indeed, schools at the *heart* of reform'. The emphasis has also shifted towards greater 'personalization of change', with children ostensibly placed at the centre of the change process and schools being expected to draw upon their own skills and expertise to effect change. In itself the concept of personalization as a model of public services provision deserves greater analysis, arising as it does from marketing theory (see Leadbeater 2004). Nonetheless, a major aspect of remodelling, encouraged by the government, has been a greater collaboration between schools and further reliance on external agents to help instigate change – whether these agents come from within schools, LAs or other sources. New collaborative partnerships and networks for change now include 'LEAs, Consultant Leaders, NCSL's regional providers, governors' organizations, the Diocesan Boards and many others. Their role is to challenge and support schools in implementing the [National Workload] Agreement and in identifying forward-looking ways of remodelling the school workforce' (Collarbone 2005b). Not surprisingly the success of such eclectic partnerships and networks varies.

Leadership and external change agents

New Labour governments from 1997 envisioned the modernizing of the education workforce as an issue primarily concerned with workload and working practices, rather than directly with teacher recruitment, retention or pay. The 'problem' is framed not in terms of teachers teaching too much, but rather of their being overburdened by additional bureaucracy, cover and administrative tasks. The main solution advanced has been centred on the remodelling of the whole education workforce, such that greater numbers of support staff are employed to carry out the tasks that teachers should no longer routinely be involved with. This places many teachers in a stronger organizational leadership role. As Miliband (2003) asserted: 'the key is that teachers become leaders of a team dedicated to higher standards of learning of students. They have the support worthy of leaders, and the responsibility of leaders to organize learning to serve children'. In essence this implies the enhancement of teacher effectiveness primarily through their leadership of support staff – some 350,000 of whom work in schools (compared to around 400,000 teachers) – particularly in roles of administration, pastoral, managerial and, more controversially, pedagogical work. The enhanced status of teaching assistants, and the recent creation of higher-level teaching assistants, is significant here.

It has been acknowledged for some time that leadership in schools is not solely a matter for headteachers. However, there is a degree of uncertainty about the extension of leadership to include middle managers in schools (Bennett 1999, p. 289). This is because middle managers have an ambiguous role: are they there to manage the implementation of decisions, or to represent their subject in discussions? How does their subject leadership relate to leadership situated higher up in the management structure? How much autonomy does a subject department have in schools? These issues have made it hard to move the focus of education leadership away from headteachers. Indeed, Gunter (2005c) states that the role of the 'headteacher as leader' has been regularly strengthened by governments over the past 25 years. This is further underlined by comments such as those made by Maurice Smith HMI, whose observations on the key characteristics of high-quality leaders in schools conclude that: 'Above all, leaders provide role models for all with whom they come into contact. People notice the personal qualities of leaders, and these come in a mixture of forms: inner calm, compassion, judgement, and a consistent confirmation of vision and the values which I believe all institutions should construct together' (Smith 2006). Gunter (2005c) similarly notes that through the use of techniques originating from non-educational settings, headteachers have often been reified as transformational leaders who are expected to demonstrate motivational, inspirational and influential attributes. She concludes that the current drive for school workforce remodelling has largely reaffirmed and strengthened the headteachers' legitimacy in these roles – although evidence suggests that such leaders rarely achieve success on their own! Hence the increasing use of models of distributed leadership, networked communities and the increasing use of external agents for change. However, we need to be cautious about our understanding of the term 'distributed leadership'. As Gunter (2005a) argues, distributed leadership does not currently exist in many English schools, as Collarbone (2005b) seems to claim, but *delegation* certainly does. Distributed leadership, unlike delegation, relies less on the existence of hierarchy and more on shared practice. It is therefore hard to achieve true distributed leadership within a system that is inherently hierarchical, where headteachers are regularly trained and 'measured' on their implementation of policy.

Collarbone (2005b) draws parallels between the government's agenda for modernizing public services and the educational scenarios outlined by the Organization for Economic Cooperation and Development (OECD) at the start of the millennium. These include using schools as *core social centres* – where they act as 'the most effective bulwark against fragmentation in society and the family. Schools are strongly defined by collective and community tasks' – and schools operating as *focused learning organizations*, whereby they develop flexible, state-of-the-art facilities and engage in 'high levels of R and D, professional development, group activities, networking and mobility in and out of teaching'. It is important to note that both of these scenarios no longer view teachers as 'gatekeepers of knowledge', but rather as facilitators of learning both in schools and the local community. Needless to say, such changes require a shift in mindset, culture and behaviour – successfully encapsulated, as Collarbone (2005b) reports, in the views of one student at an NCSL 'future sight day' when he stated 'the school of the future will have lots of adults in it helping us to learn – they will be seen as teachers but not just subject teachers. We will be taught by artists and business people and people from the community who have got skills that we want to learn. These people will probably do other jobs as well, they won't just be teachers'.

This implies the replacement of the 'hero leader' – 'one individual promoted to headteacher, a person endowed with superior knowledge and skills, almost single-handedly leading the school forward' (ibid., 2005b) – with a system built around greater delegation of work from above. Again, it is arguable whether this is truly 'distributed leadership', or simply a way of ensuring that staff are trained to undertake (in a reasonably compliant way) tasks that are handed down to them. (See Chapter 6 where Rayner and Gunter argue that distributed practice is a more productive way forward for understanding how people work together.) Without an equitable and accepted way of either distributing or delegating work schools will never become intended centres of learning communities – which are open for the entire year, offering a broader curriculum and being the focus for a range of community services.

Making it work – views on the effective use of external change agents

Hopkins and Jackson (2003) note that all schools currently operate in the context of significant 'outside forces' that shape their actions – forces they represent as 'external opportunities', focusing on their positive potential to contribute to school improvement. Nevertheless, they also appreciate that some agents of change can have a negative impact which may 'destabilise, debilitate and paralyse' schools. This can create a dilemma of choice – which are the external change agents that schools should embrace? Which should they ignore or avoid? Some external change agents are not easily sidestepped (such as OfSTED, DfES, LA), whilst others may be embraced (or avoided) according to the perceived benefits (or costs) to the school. External change agents may ultimately possess the ability to build capacity and confidence in schools or to create positive opportunities for schools to improve their current ways of working. Firestone (1989), Fullan (2000) and Jackson (2000) offer examples of such practice. Hopkins and Jackson (2003) therefore believe that external change agents should ideally be embraced, for they '[strengthen] the linkages within networks or with universities and other partners and [open] the school up to learning from and with others' (p. 92).

Fullan (2001) suggests that a successful leadership model in a culture of change will require, amongst five other key components, a commitment to relationship building. These relationships will often be personal and individual, but will almost certainly also have a community, partnership or networked element. Collarbone (2005b) visualizes that a part of building such relationships in education involves the development of learning cultures. She believes that leadership has to exist across four community domains:

i.   building community within schools;
ii. building community between schools;
iii. building community between schools and local communities – which involves parents, local businesses and local and wider community groups; and
iv. building community in a multi-agency context – the most challenging as it involves the values, beliefs, cultures and accepted norms of a wide cross-section of professionals.

Collarbone (2005b) concludes that:

change teams will be enabled to develop an understanding of the multiple agendas which exist. By deepening that understanding and becoming more widely aware of the issues at stake, it will be possible to develop and deliver appropriate solutions for the context in which the new, extended, school organisation will exist. It becomes possible to tap into the full fund of intellectual, social and organisational capital available.

The establishment of learning communities and social partnerships with schools cannot be achieved overnight, nor are they solely about resolving the immediate issues of modernization and remodelling. Forming communities and partnerships requires major cultural change for many schools, especially for those that have tended to look inwards, or who have traditionally relied on LAs for their external stimulus for change. Future management of change will rely, at least in part, on sustainable local partnerships, networks and collaborations. Even if headteachers do not tend to employ external agents of change, they would be wise to 'maintain their awareness of what is happening beyond their own environment, partly to gather intelligence related to the latest developments in policy and practice. This enables them to be proactive rather than reactive to external change' (Day *et al.* 2000, p. 49).

Partnerships for change – the tensions

Although partnerships between schools and external organizations and individuals are regularly conceptualized in almost wholly positive terms by the government, there are inevitable tensions in establishing and sustaining such arrangements. Bennett *et al.* (2004) recognize that the partnership in educational provision established between central government and schools is often merely rhetorical, choosing to focus on the seemingly more significant role of LAs as a key source of agency. They see the concept of partnership as problematic, questioning the extent to which LAs and schools – constrained as they are by accountability and codes of practice – can ever enter into true partnerships. The history of these partnerships is important. For example, the introduction of legislation which enabled the creation of grant-maintained (GM) schools by the Conservatives in the late 1980s effectively removed the link between certain schools and their LAs. However, despite the abolition of GM schools following the formation of the New Labour Government in 1997, the creation of (broadly similar) foundation schools meant that the ties between many schools and their 'parent' LA have remained problematic. The current situation is one where such partnerships are marked by different levels of school autonomy often determined by the degree to which the type of school (such as community, voluntary aided, trust, specialist, etc.) is 'distanced' from the direct influence of the LA. Additionally, central government has made 'attempts to draw a wider range of agencies into the process of educational improvement . . . [such that] partnerships have replaced formal accountability hierarchies in the rhetoric of government ministers and officials' (Bennett *et al.* 2004, p. 218). It is perhaps significant that the TSW Project was initially launched *without* the direct involvement of any LAs, although some authorities were approached by the DfES to help with the nomination of suitable schools to be involved in the Project. This appears to have been a deliberate act – although ironically the LAs have subsequently played a more central role in remodelling, as the government has been forced to concede that their involvement has been necessary to achieve localized implementation of change.

The concept of 'partnership' therefore presents problems, so much so that Bennett *et al.* claim that 'little is known about what factors contribute to creating successful partnerships between local or national bodies and schools' (ibid.,

p. 220). A variety of definitions of different types of partnership exist (see, for example, Furlong and Whitty 1995; Osborne 2000; Riley 1998), but most agree that trying to identify a one-dimensional concept of schools' partnerships with their LAs is ultimately unsuccessful. Partnerships may be very different according to the particular school, head, professional officer, consultant or governing body under consideration. One is dealing with a complex range of individuals and groups with divergent agendas, functions, motivations and beliefs.

Judging the success of a partnership or network can also be problematic. Bennett *et al.* (2004) feel that such judgements are not straightforward with respect to public services and non-profit-making organizations, the concept of success often revolving around a sense of mutual advantage and dynamism. Added factors, such as expectations and accountabilities (each of which may change over time) complicate this notion further. However, some believe that it is possible to identify core characteristics that underpin effective partnerships. Huxham and Vangon (2000, p. 297), for example, point to notions of 'collaborative advantage', 'trust', 'organisational maturity' and 'two way systems' as the crux of such partnerships. The most important consideration is that both parties have something to gain. Importantly, successful partnerships also need clear purposes, an end point for their work, a definite (often small) number of partners whose roles are clearly differentiated, and the ability to 'give way' on both sides should sticking points be experienced. Bennett *et al.* (2004) define this as collaboration, mutual accountability, voluntary commitment and an equal pursuit of shared goals.

Fergusson (2000) notes the link between modernizing managerialism and partnership, collaboration and networking. Here the benefits of 'co-operation, effectiveness, efficiency and public service' (p. 214) are brought to the fore, perhaps without sufficient realization that there should also be a commonality or purpose, clarity of objectives and a degree of reciprocity for both parties. In essence, 'partnership has the potential to supplant the rampant institutional individualism fostered by market-managerialism. But it does tie its participants largely to the modernizing agenda around which it is constructed' (ibid.). The suggestion is that private finance initiatives (PFIs), for example, enable private corporations to have a controlling hand in public services, often intensifying the modernization process and leading to an intensification of managerialism. There may also be an anticipation of a rise in academic performance, which many private organizations would expect as a consequence of their financial involvement. This may ultimately blur the boundaries between the roles and functions of the private and public sectors.

The role of SWAs in the TSW Project

We now turn to a consideration of the role that individual change agents can play in the process of remodelling school workforces. As part of the data collection phase of the evaluation of the TSW Project (see Appendix 1), 13 SWAs were interviewed by telephone[2] (Thomas *et al.* 2004, p. 5). The SWAs occupied an important position in the change management of schools involved in the Project, being introduced as 'change agents' at the start of the two-year project. Our intention was to ascertain through (approximately) 30-minute-long semi-structured interviews what attracted these people to the position of a SWA, what they saw as the purpose of SWAs, how they were to approach their role and how well they thought they had been prepared. A variety of probe, or extension, questions were also included for use as the researcher thought appropriate.

The semi-structured interviews conducted as part of the evaluation of the TSW Project sought specific responses from headteachers, senior managers, teachers and support staff regarding *their* thoughts on the SWAs who acted as change agents for their schools. This data set was not large and the responses were somewhat inconclusive. One reason for this was that although the Headteacher, the School Change Management Team and certain members of senior management might have met the SWAs on at least two or three occasions, the 'rank and file' of staff often had little or no recollection of who the change agent was. Indeed, rarely did the SWAs involve themselves with whole-school meetings – although in fairness this was not within their brief. Nevertheless, headteachers and SMT members who had significant contact with the SWAs were broadly very positive about what they brought to their schools. In special schools the overwhelming view was that SWAs had been effective, whilst three schools also stated that collaboration with other external agents and the local community had improved. Thomas *et al.* (ibid., p. 34) report that in primary schools 20 teachers and 12 support staff stated that the SWAs had been effective, with 11 schools reporting improved relationships with other external agents. However, in secondary schools only 11 teachers and 3 support staff commented positively on SWAs, with 4 teachers and 2 support staff taking a contrary stance. Interestingly, the lack of involvement of the LAs was perceived negatively by staff, many of whom may have been unaware that the authorities had not been included in the Project. Across all the schools, there were comments about the 'lack of interest' of the LAs and assertions that their role in the TSW Project had been 'limited or non-existent' (ibid., p. 34), almost certainly a misinterpretation of the levels of involvement the LAs had been permitted.

The SWAs represented an extremely varied, professionally accomplished group. They were almost all attracted to the project by a belief in its aims and objectives, with the majority (n = 10 of 13) making statements about 'freeing teachers to teach', 'raising standards', 'reducing teacher workload' and 'remodelling the profession'. Others spoke of the project appearing to be 'professionally challenging', 'exciting', 'interesting' and 'worthwhile'. All respondents had already been involved in some form of work in change management, institutional improvement and workload reduction, although not exclusively within education (in fact four respondents had not previously worked in, or closely with, schools). The motivation to join the Project varied – some SWAs had been approached directly by PricewaterhouseCoopers (who had completed a previous workload study in 2001) and asked to apply, whilst others had gained information through various agencies or were approached to nominate themselves by the London Leadership Centre. In their previous careers the SWAs had variously worked as headteachers, independent consultants (both within and outside education), educational advisers, HMI/OfSTED inspectors, civil servants, employees of leadership centres, change managers in the public sector (Probationary Service, social work, Social Exclusion Unit, Prime Minister's Office) and consultants. One adviser, who had a strong background in education, readily welcomed the involvement of 'lay' members who had little previous experience of schools: 'It's good that the advisers are not all ex-heads – I welcome the input of people who have different experiences and perspectives and who have an alternative view on how problems might be solved' (SWA 1).

When questioned about their purpose within the Project the responses of the SWAs were often similar, although certain individuals stressed particular (often personal) expectations. Most used words such as 'encourage', 'help', 'motivate', 'support', 'advise', 'guide', 'facilitate' to describe their relationship with schools. The following comment is typical of the tone: 'Being an adviser is not about telling schools what to do, but helping them to understand where they want to get to and the means by which they can achieve this' (SWA 2). Others were slightly more directive, stating that their role as SWAs was 'to challenge the approaches schools take to change, especially if they are not radical enough at present. To show them the benefits of other ways of managing' (SWA 3). Nonetheless the general message coming from the SWAs was that they saw their roles as being to 'help and advise, but not to take ownership of change – as a counsellor rather than director' (SWA 4), or as a 'critical friend'. One adviser commented that 'we want to help schools work as teams, but also ensure that they do not develop a dependency culture. Schools must become independent within the timescale of the project, becoming autonomous with respect to their workload management' (SWA 4). The scale of their task was generally perceived to be substantial, with three advisers commenting that their contribution to reducing staff workloads in schools might be 'small, but significant'. The general mood of the advisers at the start of the Project was upbeat, with many talking about being 'excited', 'challenged', 'enthusiastic' and 'inspired' by the importance of the task ahead of them. However, the irony of having to sustain an increase in their personal workloads was not lost on many SWAs at the start of their work.

Perhaps because of the week's training all the SWAs had received from the London Leadership Centre there was a commonality about how the advisers visualized their approach to the role. Many stressed their status as 'consultants', but were clear about their job of advising the Change Management Team, developing a change strategy, building confidence and challenging accepted truths. They also saw the importance of understanding the context of the school and gaining an appreciation of the strengths (or otherwise) of the Head and senior managers within it. Many (n = 7) saw the major hurdles as changing school cultures, placing teaching and learning at the centre of the change agenda, as well as shifting teacher workload. The training process was almost uniformly applauded by the advisers, although some commented that a more diverse range of models of change management might have been considered. For a third of the advisers – especially those who had not worked in schools previously – the learning curve was extremely steep.

Interestingly, a third of advisers felt that there might be issues of personal credibility within schools, despite being associated with a highly financed, Department-led project. Other advisers perceived that some headteachers were rather unwilling to face up to the changes that would be necessary for their schools to successfully address workload issues. In particular this manifested itself as an unwillingness to 'force' the pace of change, with certain headteach-ers concerned that their staff would not be willing to make radical changes, or be prepared to suffer the inevitable disruption that change brings. Headteachers who had previously dominated the thinking of schools also revealed nervousness about delegating some of the decision-making to change management teams.

When SWAs were encouraged to raise any further issues, beyond those directly pursued in the semi-structured interviews, five chose to talk about the role of the DfES in the TSW Project. Some responses were rather equivocal or negative, with advisers feeling that the Department had not helped in fully clar-ifying schools' perceptions of what the Project members were trying to achieve. In essence, these more critical comments about the role of the DfES focused on questions of establishing trust, encouraging schools to take legitimate risks and sharing the processes and models of change. In one case an adviser felt that schools were confused at the start of the Project because of the tight timescales and their lack of preparation – schools needed 'time to think', particularly if they were expected to 'think the unthinkable'.

A clear message from the SWAs was that the government needed to take a longer-term view of the change process, offer a real chance for the transforma-tion of the teaching profession and not be content with simply providing a 'quick fix' solution to issues of modernization and remodelling. The interviews with SWAs revealed some of the motivations, hopes and expectations of change managers involved with the agenda for modernization and remodelling of schools in England. Although they worked as part of a short-term (two-year) gov-ernment-funded project, their input was key to the emerging approach taken to modernize schools.

Conclusion

This chapter has considered the ways in which change agents external to schools act to support the processes of modernization and remodelling of working prac-tices in state schools in England. The issues surrounding the implementation of change, by both organizations and individuals from 'outside' schools, have been briefly explored culminating in a series of statements made by SWAs about their roles as change agents.

Collarbone (2005b) visualizes the positive impacts of networking, collaborating and establishing partnerships with external change agents as follows:

> The collaboration we have witnessed within and between schools, LEAs, social partners and others gives me enormous hope that we can realize the latent potential within the system . . . the secret, it seems to me, is in devolved leadership and full staff involvement. Our system is moving towards a new order of school. An order which foresees schools which are networked and collaborative and with leadership distributed within and between schools and other agencies.

This dovetails with the government's aim of bringing about cultural change in the ways in which schools, and indeed the entire education workforce, function. However, we need to be cautious. Just as the LAs were never centrally involved in the TSW Project from the outset, so they have only more recently been substantially drawn into supporting the remodelling of schools – arguably once the government realized that the task was too large and difficult without them. There is also a significant tension between the use of 'private' and 'public' agents of change, which Collarbone (2005b) seems to largely ignore. This is fundamentally an issue of whether local governance of schools, within the current system of elected representation in LAs, is allowed to be the 'prime mover' in the modernization process. Or whether the market – as typified by the contracting of paid consultants, advisers and change agents – is permitted to take the dominant hand in achieving educational reform. It seems that schools are sites where the privatization of educational change is being played out, with particular implications for how expertise is conceptualized and used. Striking an equitable balance between the roles of an elected body and private consultants often proves problematic, particularly when we consider how publicly accountable each of these agents is. In essence, the question is whether change in schools is properly achieved through a system which expects some public dialogue and debate, or through one which has a largely unproblematic view of policy implementation by private means.

The answer surely lies in observing what is currently happening in English schools. Undoubtedly, as the TSW Project revealed, there are schools where workforce remodelling is proceeding satisfactorily and at pace. In a number of such schools the need for employing external change agents is often negligible. Heads, senior managers and devolved leaders have already forged positive ways forward and are secure in their appreciation of the needs of their staff and schools. These leaders tend to have both a keen awareness and a clear appreciation of the current agenda for change – they also work effectively in the context of what is 'right' for their schools. Imposing additional external change managers, change agents or networks is unnecessary in these situations, as the schools have already done this for themselves to a degree they are comfortable with. Importantly the staff within these schools often have a much fuller understanding of their needs than any external agents. This is not to say external support and guidance are unnecessary – rather that caveats must be applied to their wholesale application.

Schools need to be able to recognize the extent of the changes required for them to successfully modernize and remodel. The TSW Project (and subsequent policy directives) has strongly indicated that, to effect change, state schools may need to seek assistance from external partners. The rationale has been that it is difficult to recognize the direction in which change should travel when one is embedded within the organization that requires change. In addition, there may also be difficulties in financing change. As a result, schools now embrace partnerships (or create networks) with other organizations, schools, LAs and advisers to seek the benefits that can accrue from working collaboratively in communities. But establishing clear, fair, representative and mutually agreed programmes of change is essential – particularly when these increasingly involve working with the private sector.

For some time, the New Labour Government has sought to increase diversity and choice within state schooling – but in so doing it is steadily shifting control and funding streams away from the public sector, LAs and higher education towards external private partners, consultants and sponsors. Indeed, there is now a clearly established belief in the efficacy of quasi-markets to drive educational reform and also release schools from LA control (DfES 2005a). The involvement of businesses and – in the case of the planned independent non-fee-paying state schools – religious organizations and charities to lead such reform has shifted both the power and resource streams away from the public sector. Such an extension of private control into state-funded schooling, where schools are now routinely using public money to purchase resources from the private sector, has clear implications for the integrity and governance of state schools. Public sector services and organizations – such as schools, hospitals and transport – increasingly find themselves tied into stringent financial relationships under public–private finance initiatives that are ultimately detrimental to the control, management and funding of their activities.

Part Three: Modernizing Learning

In this section we present three chapters where we are concerned to focus on the issues involved in 'Modernizing Learning'. The chapters specifically investigate the use of ICT in schools to bring about remodelling of learning. Considerable emphasis has been given to, and bold claims made about, the potential of ICT to revolutionize the learning environment, as well as to assist in the modernization and remodelling of schools.

The TSW Project (Appendix 1) and the ICT Test Bed Project (Appendix 2) exemplified the drive towards extending the use of technology in schools, the effects of which are considered here. Butt and Gunter present an overview of the main issues, and draw on a series of case studies to examine the realities of developing the use of hardware and software. Pilkington extends the arguments introduced in Chapter 8 by considering the educational rationale behind the further use of technology in bringing about changes in curriculum, pedagogy or learning. She suggests a range of 'ways forward', but is clear about the costs of managing change as she indicates a number of constraints, tensions and barriers. We conclude this section with a chapter by Selwood specifically focused on the issues that influence ICT-related change in schools – in essence, the management of ICT by school leaders and ICT coordinators.

Chapter 8

Remodelling learning – the use of technology
Graham Butt and Helen Gunter

Introduction

This chapter provides a perspective on the use of ICT to remodel learning in schools, from headteachers involved in the Transforming the School Workforce Pathfinder Project. It also offers a commentary on the main issues surrounding the introduction, or extended use, of technology in the learning environment. The TSW Project placed considerable emphasis on the potential of technology to assist in the modernization and remodelling of schools, establishing it as one of five key 'strands' for schools to consider as catalysts for change. Indeed, all schools were provided with funding for both ICT software and hardware as part of an incentive to join the Project – usually offered in the form of a laptop for each member of their teaching staff.

For some time before the launch of the TSW Project the UK Government had considered that schools were not using available technology in the most effective ways to advance learning and to alleviate problems of staff workload. However, this issue was framed more in terms of the potential of technology to reduce the impact of bureaucracy on teacher workload, rather than of the pedagogical gains of greater use of ICT in classrooms. In *Time for Standards* (DfES 2002a) it was stated that teachers were spending 20 per cent of their time on tasks which could be undertaken by other adults and that 'the potential of ICT in helping to reduce workload was not being fully exploited' (Butt and Lance 2005b, p. 403). In March 2001 the government announced a £35-million technology package to help schools reduce their internal bureaucracy, which was again envisaged as a major source of additional teacher workload. The scheme enabled schools to purchase new computers, software and training specifically to remodel their management and administration systems (DfEE 2001a).

A government-commissioned survey of teacher workload carried out by PricewaterhouseCoopers (2001) concluded that teachers could save between 3.25 and 4.55 hours per week through the effective use of ICT. As such, the application of technology has been conceptualized as a cornerstone of the modernization and remodelling process, both with respect to classroom practice and workload reduction. In their analysis of the PwC survey, Selwood and Pilkington (2005) comment:

PwC also noted that effective use of ICT in schools was inhibited by: lack of hardware for teacher use both in schools and at teachers' homes; skills gaps due to the lack of availability of hardware and questionable quality of ICT training they had received; and lack of central direction in schools concerning the strengths and limitations of ICT.   (p. 164)

The TSW evaluation undertaken by the University of Birmingham specifically addressed each of these issues through its whole-staff questionnaires and one-to-one interviews of a cross-section of teaching and support staff in each school. Some of the data from this evaluation are used here to provide a context to the comments made by headteachers later in the chapter.

The impact of using ICT in the classroom

As John and Sutherland (2005) accurately state, 'in recent years the emergence of new digital technologies have offered up the possibility of extending and deepening classroom learning in ways hitherto unimagined' (p. 406). There is now optimism, not least in government circles, about the extent to which technology can advance pedagogical practice – essentially expressed as a belief that digital tools will both transform the ways in which students learn and the outcomes of their learning. However, we may need to be reminded that 'in reality, learning is always distributed in some form between the technology, the learner and the context and there is nothing inherent in technology that automatically guarantees learning' (ibid.). Teachers and governments alike therefore need to be more critically aware of the limitations, as well as the potential strengths, of technology. John (2005) argues that school subject cultures tend to be built on deep traditions which need to be understood if the successful use of technology is to become embedded into the school curriculum. He particularly focuses on the need for policy makers and innovators – who he believes think in revolutionary, rather than evolutionary, terms – to consider how their expectations mesh with the pragmatism of teachers.

The degree to which the introduction, or extension, of the use of technologies in the classroom has been successful requires some framework for evaluation. The consequences of using ICT can be assessed by interpreting the tool itself, the assumptions it makes of the user, the activities it encourages and the ways in which it can either promote or constrain particular working practices (Woolgar 1991, cited in John and Sutherland 2005). In short, the technology and its potentialities shape the ways in which it tends to be used. As John and Sutherland (2005) explain:

this regulation of social practice (by technology) is not random or idiosyncratic, rather it is systematic in that the activities encouraged tend to envision the world in a certain way. To consider ICT in this way means focusing on the design of the application, the sorts of choices offered and those which are not.

It also means exploring the relationship between the software, the hardware, and the learning process as well as uncovering the sorts of pedagogical implications attendant upon that relationship. (p. 409)

Once introduced, and used successfully, technology tends to scaffold learning – particularly where it makes an activity or learning outcome possible which had previously been difficult to realize, or time-consuming to achieve. However, the essential element in the process is the teacher and the way in which he/she integrates and mediates the use of ICT in the learning experience, often according to their perception of the potential of the technology, its compatibility with their subject and the desired learning activity.

One of the most important considerations about teachers using technology is that the process of adoption of ICT is often slow. As John (2005) contends, when teachers extend their personal use of ICT, even under well-supported conditions, they often take substantial amounts of time to accommodate how the technology will fit into their teaching and learning. He believes that a new blending of technology and subject often has to take place which, for many teachers, highlights the centrality of achieving a 'pragmatic pedagogy'. Initial resistance amongst teachers to the use of technology is often high – Olson (2000) questions why teachers should move from the safety of their existing teaching methods towards the uncertainty of technology-based teaching; whilst Goodson and Mangan (1995), John and La Velle (2004) and Watson (2001) (all cited in John 2005) claim teachers accommodate, incorporate and assimilate ICT at levels corresponding to a complex mix of factors related to subject cultures (or sub-cultures), personal predilections, professional mores and levels of technical support. Many teachers have concerns about the encroachment of technology into their subject culture, about the boundaries that exist between subjects and technologies and the ways in which these may be successfully crossed. The centrality of the subject sub-culture in teaching, and the dominance of subject departments in schools, has meant that policies on the use of ICT end up being heavily mediated. This is particularly true within subjects where teachers feel that 'their core values are fundamentally at variance with ICT' (John 2005, p. 475). As Wenger (1990) argues, ICT tends to be used in subjects where its significance as a learning tool is recognized and its 'visibility' as an intervening tool is low – the reverse also tends to be true. The balance between these two factors appears crucial as to whether technology is employed in the learning process, or not. However, over time, teachers report a diminution in the distinction between their teaching styles and their use of ICT – such that they eventually noticed 'fewer differences between how they taught, the subject content and the use of technology' (John 2005, p. 477).

The capabilities of technology to mesh with the ways in which teachers want to teach (and want their pupils to learn) is important. For example, Counsell (2003) draws a distinction between situations where the ICT resource is intrinsic to the type of learning experienced and those where there is a lesser congruence between the technology and the learning activity – that is, where ICT is merely an additional tool. Self-evidently when technology is central to the process of learning, then learning would not be possible if the technology were not present. Interestingly, certain technologies, which might initially imply that a particular style of teaching and learning would occur, were not always used in the ways expected. For example, interactive whiteboards (IWBs), despite their name, often tend to be used in didactic ways by teachers – for whole-class teaching, presentations and display purposes rather than for interactive learning (John 2005; Smith *et al.* 2005).

Findings from the TSW Project

Perhaps surprisingly, the perceptions of teachers across all project schools about the potential of ICT to reduce their workload were initially equivocal, at best. Indeed, Selwood and Pilkington (2005) commented that in the section of the questionnaire that specifically asked teachers about their use of ICT: 'Given the potential of effective use of ICT to "streamline" paperwork and lesson planning through finding, preparing and sharing resources electronically we would have expected more mention of ICT' (p. 165). Unsurprisingly, given the emphasis on the use of ICT in one of the five main areas for investment in the Project, teachers found that their access to ICT – not least through being given their own laptops – had substantially increased. The ICT facilities in schools, for the use of teachers and administrators, had often improved substantially – with access to networked suites, interactive whiteboards, technical support, training and a range of software and hardware at levels only previously dreamt of. Nonetheless the reactions of teachers towards the possibilities that the new technology offered were not entirely positive, particularly within secondary schools.

Teachers were asked to provide some perspective on their personal use of ICT. Firstly, they were asked 'How many hours do you currently spend using ICT for your work each day?'. In 2002 the majority of teachers reported using ICT for between one and three hours each day, but by the end of the project in 2003 secondary school teachers were stating a daily use of 2.51 hours, primary teachers 2.46 hours and special school teachers 2.28 hours. This represented an increase of use on the previous year of 33 minutes, 65 minutes and 11 minutes per day respectively. Notwithstanding the additional time (and workload) necessary for teachers to learn how to use new technology, this would seem to be a positive directional change. Further questions posed to assess teachers' attitudes towards ICT, their readiness to use ICT applications, their belief in the value of ICT in reducing workload and the ability of ICT to increase productivity showed that by the end of the Project teachers (in the main) felt they were competent users of technology, that they had improved their skills, that using ICT would reduce their workload and that technology had made them more productive. However, in primary schools 37 per cent of teachers had not changed their opinions since the start of the Project, in secondary schools 42 per cent and in special schools 27 per cent. Clearly, a substantial proportion of teachers across all school types have not 'bought into' the potential of ICT to change their working practices.

Most important, from the perspective of this chapter, were the teachers' responses on their use of ICT to support teaching, learning, target setting and review, as well as in their analysis of performance data. With regard to the former the changes recorded from the start of the Project were very positive. In special schools 38 per cent, in primary schools 52 per cent and in secondary schools 31 per cent of teachers reported they were more positive about their own use of ICT to support teaching and learning. Across all schools teachers clearly agreed that ICT could be used to analyse performance data and for target setting and review, but were less confident in their personal abilities to do so. As Selwood and Pilkington (2005) report, teachers discovered a variety of ways in which technology could further support their work during the Project:

Although it is difficult from questionnaire data alone to gain an impression of exactly how teachers expected that use of ICT might have a more direct impact on teaching and learning, from interviews with teachers a number of recurring themes emerged including:

- The creation of reusable teaching materials saving preparation time;
- The sharing of teaching materials and lesson plans via an intranet, again saving preparation time and sharing ideas or good practice;
- Student access to materials out of hours via the intranet – helping to deliver support to the individual when it was needed;
- The production of better quality (multimedia) materials with more explanatory power and/or higher presentational clarity or visual appeal (teachers would not otherwise have time to produce these);
- Use of ICT in the classroom creating interactive and engaging lessons that would motivate disaffected students;
- The use of ICT to monitor attendance, progress and performance and to alert teachers, parents and students to the need for intervention or support. (p. 171)

Teachers across all sectors and types of schools felt that ICT would continue to have a positive impact on educational standards in their schools and that, in general, their personal use of ICT would increase. Most teachers recognized the issues surrounding implementing change during a one-year project and realized that any change in working practices incurs costs in terms of time and workload. It was particularly apparent that one of the major factors influencing teachers' use of ICT was their ease of access to the ICT facilities. However, perhaps the most significant point made by many teachers was that although they felt they were competent users of technology, only around 50 per cent believed they had been trained in *all* aspects of ICT necessary to their work. Training was clearly a problematic issue – particularly given the low levels of high-quality formal ICT training that the majority of teachers had received.

Increased access to ICT, and its successful incorporation into teaching and administration, was central to the Project. It was hoped that given greater access to technology, teachers would make fuller use of web-based learning and teaching resources, whilst the sustained use of technology in administration (such as the direct recording of pupil data onto ICT equipment) would reduce the time teachers spent on such tasks. While access to ICT improved for most teachers, their readiness to make full use of the technology was dependent on a common set of factors. Firstly, the perception of the user as to their computer competence was of major importance, as was their belief that technology would be able to assist their productivity. Secondly, access to high-quality training and support was seen by many teachers as being significant. As expected, their increased access to ICT – often through being provided teachers with their own laptops – meant that they were more likely to use ICT in working directly with pupils, and for 'other pupil contact' (such as registration, recording marks, etc.). It was clear that increasing the personal access of teachers to ICT, particularly through their personal use of laptops, was an important step in extending the overall use of ICT in schools.

Almost half the teachers interviewed stated that the provision of laptops to their schools' teaching staff had been a significant outcome of the Project, and that ICT had helped to improve their teaching and to streamline their planning, assessment and administrative work. However, they also noted that having instant access to information did not necessarily mean that they had the time to take immediate action:

> It [technology] speeds up work, but doesn't necessarily reduce it. It makes information available much more quickly, but also implies action should be taken more quickly. It is most beneficial in terms of teaching and learning. We now have more experience of using ICT, but the long term benefits for the school are still to be seen.
>
> (Teacher, Town School, Thomas *et al.* 2004, p. 50)

Nearly half the teachers, and three-quarters of support staff, identified developments in ICT use as having contributed to improvements in pastoral administration and attendance:

> Electronic registration has given much more information and has improved school systems. [But] it did increase workload at first.
>
> (Teacher, Suburban School, Thomas *et al.* 2004, unpublished data)

> The Project has improved attendance and our ability to track student behaviour, and therefore has probably influenced learning.
>
> (Teacher, City School, Thomas *et al.* 2004, unpublished data)

A case study of a consortium of four small primary schools involved in the Project specifically looked at their use of ICT across the curriculum. The principal developments were the use of interactive whiteboards and of computers to develop stronger contacts between schools. Other issues followed on from this, including an initial increase in workload and the need for additional training. The somewhat tempered enthusiasm that resulted regarding the increased use of technology is revealed by the following:

> ICT has increased workload. Some teachers weren't prepared and some aren't computer minded. The general feeling is that the money could have been better spent. We've been given computers in the classroom without preparation.   (Teacher, Border Schools' Cluster, Thomas *et al.* 2004, p. 72)

> The nature of using computers is that people need support in using the machines when they've pressed the wrong button. You end up with trying to teach the class and a group for IT. Stress levels go up.
> (Teacher, Border Schools' Cluster, Thomas *et al.* 2004, p. 72)

However, other teachers were very enthusiastic about the changes that technology had brought to their working practices:

> As a direct result of the Project we have whiteboards and broadband. This has made a huge difference to what we do. Finding resources off the internet, doing work at home rather than at school. It has massively reduced my workload but for staff without the expertise it has increased workload and stress levels. . . . The interactive nature of the whiteboard is fantastic.
> (Teacher, Metropolitan School, Thomas *et al.* 2004, unpublished data)

In the majority of TSW Project schools the additional ICT resources were viewed as beneficial, although the scale of impact during the short life of the project was relatively modest. One of the main outcomes was the importance of sustained support and training to accompany any influx of hardware and software.

The views of headteachers on ICT use in TSW Project schools

The use of ICT to enable remodelling and modernization of schools – largely with regard to teaching, learning and administrative systems – was a major strand of the TSW Project. Three years after the end of the Project we approached six headteachers who had been involved to ask them to comment on significant changes. Two spoke at length on whether the technology-related changes that had been implemented had been sustained. We also wished to ascertain how significant the impacts had been in terms of how the schools functioned. The particular focus reported on below is the use of ICT to enhance teaching and learning in a modernized school setting. An account is also provided, for comparative purposes, of a non-Project school which has modernized its pedagogy through the integration of ICT into all its teaching and learning.

Metropolitan School

Metropolitan School is an average sized 3–11 primary school in south London. Almost half the students speak English as an additional language, reflecting the cultural mix within the school's catchment area, with the majority of students coming from Black Caribbean, African or Chinese heritages. The percentage of students eligible for free school meals (55 per cent) is well above the national average, with many coming from economically deprived backgrounds. The school only records 16 per cent of its students as having special educational needs, although a higher percentage have moderate learning difficulties often related to literacy. It is a community school with above average value-added measures at transfer from Key Stage 1 to 2, compared to both the local authority and national averages. The school continues to perform at above average levels locally for performance in English, Maths and Science.

The headteacher, in concert with the Change Management Team, concentrated on a number of initiatives to instigate the remodelling of the school's workforce and administrative systems. One aspect of her vision was to update and extend the school's use of ICT and the range of such facilities available for teaching and support staff. To this end, all classrooms were fitted with interactive whiteboards and the school established an intranet that could be used both for teaching and administration. The headteacher is clear that the TSW Project provided the main impetus for the increased use of ICT within the school, and that without the additional funding which the Project afforded, these changes would not have been made so rapidly.

The provision of laptops, both during the Project and in the period immediately following, has helped teachers immensely – but these computers (and all IT equipment) are prone to breaking down and some of the technology now needs replacement. This raised an important issue about the sustainability of initiatives that may have a major positive impact on schools – at the same time raising expectations and standards – which cannot be maintained once funding and support dries up. The headteacher reported that finding well-qualified and competent IT support staff had been difficult and that such staffing appointments tended to be costly. Since the TSW Project, the school had been fortunate enough to employ an IT graduate, but funding this post in the longer term would prove problematic. There were also financial implications concerning funding the post of a manager for the IT systems. As such the TSW Project had provided an initial cash impetus of funding for the implementation of more ICT facilities but this had subsequently meant that a significant annual financial commitment had to be made to ICT from the school budget.

The increased ICT facilities, and their concomitant use amongst the school's staff, had resulted in measurable gains in terms of improvements in the standards of teaching and learning – as well as in the efficiencies of new administrative systems. Staff had reported that their work–life balance had been positively affected by being given laptops – one of the deputy heads indicated that as a senior manager having a laptop had meant that he could now organize his time more effectively between working in school and at home. The laptop had created the flexibility for him to avoid times of major commuter traffic flow, which previously had restricted the amount of time he could spend on school work in the evenings. Taking work away with him on the laptop immediately at the end of the school day and then working on both teaching resources and administrative work at home was a significant gain in time efficiency. This meant that his home life became less stressed as he was no longer reliant on being physically present 'in school' at times that would force him to travel home at the peak of the rush hour. Much of his managerial paperwork and lesson planning was now taken away with him on the laptop to be completed at more convenient times.

Country School

Country School is a larger than average 11–16 mixed secondary school in the north of England. It is a split site school – with the two campuses about one mile apart – currently with plans to merge into a completely new building on one site. Country School is a community school with below average value-added measures for transfer from Key Stage 2 to 4, compared to both the local authority and national average. Some 11 per cent of pupils have a recognized special educational need (which is above local and national averages) with the school performing at below average levels in English, Maths and Science. Absences, both authorized and unauthorized, are higher than the norm. Slightly over half the students are white British, with significant percentages of students from Bangladeshi, Pakistani, Kashmiri and Afro-Caribbean backgrounds. The catchment area of the school is relatively disadvantaged, with an above average proportion of children eligible for free school meals, and a high student turnover. The school has Specialist Technology College status.

The Headteacher believes that since the TSW Project the school has a more can-do culture and that his staff now see that change is a 'way of life' for schools facing the modernization and remodelling agenda. Apart from employing additional faculty support assistants and year managers, the school purchased 90 laptops and installed a wireless and administrative network during the life of the Project. This had proved successful, and the provision of laptops for teachers had subsequently been extended to include support staff (including the bursar and learning managers), such that there are currently about 110–120 laptops in the school. Staff changes have been integral to the school's modernization and remodelling – the employment of a network manager has been key, not only highlighting the necessity of having a single member of staff to oversee issues and day-to-day management of systems but also increasing levels of experience of technology. The headteacher reflects that the ICT facilities have developed well and that the school has also been able to employ a web page designer – who initially worked with the English department to develop teaching resources and then subsequently was attached to the Design and Technology department to help innovate teaching and learning resources.

The most significant technological development which has aided modernization has been the wireless network, the effect of which the headteacher describes as being 'liberating'. This has enabled all staff to work where they want to around the school campus, aiding flexibility and increasing the use of technology. It is now a common sight to see staff working on laptops around all the buildings. As a result, the ICT capability of staff has developed, but this has some drawbacks, for if the networked system 'goes down' then the dependence that staff have developed on the technology becomes very apparent. The wireless network has also helped in ways beyond supporting teaching and learning – for example, there is an events log on the network which cuts staff paperwork and keeps all staff updated with events. This facility is being used more and more, although there are still some 'pluses and minuses' associated with students logging into the system.

The school is moving forward with its agenda of modernization and remodelling. The original laptops which had been provided by the TSW Project in 2002 have now been replaced, highlighting the expense associated with running a technology-led school. However, this is viewed positively, as, without the initial investment into hardware, software and training, the significant changes witnessed would not have come about. The training of staff in the use of the new technology has been integral to the modernization process, such that things have moved in stages and people have grown in confidence. At the school's last OfSTED inspection in May 2005 it was reported how well ICT was being used to deliver lessons and support learning.

ICT is now an integral part of assessment and recording in the school. Registers are taken on the laptops, which also incorporate a photograph identification facility. Computer technology is also central to the generation of reports, target setting, recording of assessments and day-to-day student administration.

Estate School

Estate School is a large Midlands comprehensive school for girls aged 11 to 19, with a very small number of boys in the sixth form. Over two-thirds of students in the main school, and 86 per cent of students in the sixth form, are from minority ethnic groups. There are 1,753 students on roll. Over 50 per cent of students in the main school – rising to three-quarters of the students in the sixth form – have English as an additional language. A high proportion of students, some 39 per cent, are eligible for free school meals whilst 88 per cent of students in the sixth form qualify for the education maintenance allowance. The proportion of students identified as having special educational needs, or with statements, is below the national average. The school achieved Specialist Science status in September 2003 and has become a Training School in partnership with the local university. The school has a number of distinct features which have a direct and beneficial impact on staff and students and on the links with partner schools. According to its most recent OfSTED report the school makes excellent use of ICT to improve the quality of communication, administration, teaching, learning and assessment – indeed the Training School partnership specifically focuses on the use of ICT in the training of Postgraduate Certificate in Education (PGCE) trainees. All teachers and managers also make very effective use of the wireless network from within each of the separate school buildings and from outside the school.

The use of ICT within the school has been a cornerstone of the modernization and remodelling of Estate School. However, this is not a process that has occurred overnight – as might be the case with some of the Project schools – but one which has been integral to the school's forward planning for well over a decade. Senior managers within the school have always had a positive attitude towards the impact that technology could have on teaching and learning and have promoted policies to accelerate its implementation. This has been supported both by the granting of Specialist Science College and Training School status – which have brought financial incentives to purchase and incorporate technology – and by the employment of significant numbers of technology-proficient new staff. Indeed, the Training School activities which have focused on the further training and support of PGCE students in their use of computers have had a beneficial effect in bringing ICT-focused teaching into a number of subject departments in the school. The school's commitment to a future that has made technology central to learning in all curriculum areas is linked to its previous investment in substantial computer resources around the school and the establishment of an ICT 'hub' which has rooms with state-of-the-art technology within them. As such, a suite of rooms have been developed that have stand-alone computers, laptops, video-conferencing facilities, web cameras and a huge range of other hardware and software for the use of staff and students alike.

Each of these accounts provides a particular appreciation of the different approaches adopted by the schools in their attempts to use ICT to remodel teaching and learning. The contexts, and therefore the approaches adopted, are unique – nonetheless, there are commonalities and consistencies across each of the case studies. Headteachers noted the importance of the funding provided by the Project in enabling the initiation, or continuance, of ICT-related changes. In each case the improvements to teaching and learning were tangible and closely linked to a change in the working culture of the school. However, they also commented more critically on sustainability and staffing issues.

The inclusion of the third case study, from Estate School, illustrates how a school that was not involved in the Project could also achieve similar results, despite the lack of additional and targeted funding (although other significant funding streams accessed by the school have created the possibilities for change). Estate School has made ICT central to the remodelling of its teaching and learning for many years, with senior managers all having faith in the use of technology to improve pedagogy. By comparison, the school has taken longer to modernize and remodel learning – but has achieved this in a more 'secure' fashion, having established more permanent funding streams and staffing levels. Estate School therefore exhibits a longer-term and more ingrained culture of change, with virtually all staff being both confident and competent in their use of technology within the classroom.

Conclusion

As John (2005) observes, technology is most successfully integrated into day-to-day teaching when 'teachers maintain[ed] their professional control over the technology using their pragmatic professionalism' (p. 487). The boundaries and frontiers between the subject sub-culture and the technology are very significant.

As such, the most successful examples of modernization and remodelling using ICT to enhance teaching and learning exist where teachers see the real benefits that technology can bring to their practice. However, a number of significantly sized hurdles need to be crossed – many subjects have a sub-culture which provides resistance to the use of ICT, as the teachers do not perceive the benefits that technology can bring, or feel that its use does not 'fit' within the teaching of their subject. This is often related to a lack of awareness of what the technology can do within their area of the curriculum. Training in the use of hardware and software is also a major issue, with around 50 per cent of teachers reporting that they had not received the training necessary to use ICT competently, and most teachers having learned how to use technology informally through contact with other teachers who have greater competence, knowledge or understanding of its use. Perhaps one of the biggest hurdles is the investment of additional time and effort that using ICT implies for the classroom practitioner. Ironically this will initially increase teachers' workload, although the longer-term gain should be a reduction of the time spent at work.

It is worth briefly considering the role of technical support and training in the enhanced use of ICT in schools. Many teachers interviewed during the evaluation of the TSW Project mentioned how essential they felt enhanced technical support would be to their continued use of technology within the classroom. This was an issue not only of updating the teachers' professional competence in their use of ICT and awareness of new software, but also of the technical support and maintenance of machines. The levels of staffing of technicians afforded by the Project were often high in many schools; however, the real concern that this staffing would end at the culmination of the Project was tangible. Affording the 'space' for teachers to experiment with software and teaching approaches in a supported environment was considered important.

This chapter has been concerned to present an overview of the issues involved in modernizing schools through the development of ICT. The experiences of schools both inside and outside of the Project have shown different aspects of the ways in which ICT can be used to remodel and modernize teaching and learning in schools. There are important themes around the relationship between innovation and sustaining resources for the constant update of hardware and software, as well as training needs. Attention has also been given to the significance of subject sub-cultures and the effects these can have on departments either embracing or rejecting the use of technology. Two important themes arise from this chapter that are now explored further: first, Pilkington in Chapter 9 examines the pedagogic and learning potential of ICT, and notes how innovations are creating interesting and dynamic opportunities to develop learning. The school will look different as a result of this, but she goes on to show that investment will be essential in constructing the type of future school we would want to achieve. Second, Selwood in Chapter 10 focuses specifically on the management of ICT in schools, concluding with a discussion of the leadership styles that have proved most effective in supporting remodelling and modernization in this context. Here a common vision, strategic leadership, appropriate infrastructure, training and planning have, perhaps unsurprisingly, been found to be central to the effective use of ICT.

Chapter 9

Learning and ICT

Rachel Pilkington

Introduction

Technology has revolutionized the way we work and is now set to transform Education. Children cannot be effective in tomorrow's world if they are trained in yesterday's skills. Nor should teachers be denied the tools that other professionals take for granted. That is why, two years ago, I said a Labour Government would connect every school in Britain to the information super-highway. . . .. Last year I announced that we would create a National Grid for Learning to provide the content that would make these networks come to life . . . . (Blair 1997, pp. 1–2)

The National Grid for Learning (NGfL) proposed above was created forming a portal to online content aimed at helping teachers to exploit ICT for learning. The period between 1997 and 2004 saw unprecedented investment in ICT in schools, including investment in infrastructure to connect schools to the Internet and to develop online resources that could be accessed through such networks and portals. The NGfL portal closed in April 2006. The British Educational Communications and Technology Agency (Becta) is taking over responsibility for reorganizing/rationalizing its content with existing services. It seems a good time to reflect on what has been achieved through the wider drive to embed ICT in the school curriculum which it was part of. In doing so I want to explore visions for the 'future school' (Walsh 2002; Andres *et al.* 2003), the progress toward such visions and the barriers to change.

A central vision for the 'future school' was that of a hub or learning centre connected by the superhighway to a community of between 5 and 20 other schools – all with online access to learning content through the NGfL. Part of this vision was that online access to content and local experts would enable changes to the school day with additional benefits for learning. The home could connect to the hub, making learning 'through the bell' and beyond the class-room walls possible. This in turn would require changes to the roles of staff in schools. Adults in learning centres would be teachers, but there would also be other para-professionals and business people working alongside volunteers in teams. Walsh concluded in 2002 that some schools were already moving fast toward this vision. Some aspired to do so, whilst others did not.

In evaluating the extent to which such visions have shaped change and impacted upon learning I will compare and contrast experiences from the Transforming the School Workforce Pathfinder Project and ICT Test Bed Project schools (Thomas *et al.* 2003a, 2003b, 2004). In particular, I will weave into the discussion the voices of teaching staff, teaching assistants and support staff, headteachers and IT coordinators from three 'case' example schools; one secondary school (Field School, see Thomas *et al.* 2003b) and two primary schools (Road School, see Thomas *et al.* 2003b; and Metropolitan School, see Thomas *et al.* 2004).

Positive rhetoric or realizable goals?

In 1997 New Labour was committed to using ICT to improve teaching and learning. A range of initiatives, collectively described as the National Grid for Learning, were introduced to provide the necessary infrastructure and resources. NGfL had received £1.5 billion in investment by 2002 (McMullan 2002). Education Action Zones alongside a range of policies including Specialist Schools were also driving investment in ICT. Acquiring Specialist School status had major funding implications. In the ICT Test Bed Project the headteacher at Inner City School commented, 'as soon as we got Specialist School funding we put in a lot of ICT – 60–70% of the money was spent on ICT'.

Reynolds *et al.* (2003, p. 151) describe claims for the effectiveness of ICT as 'optimistic rhetoric' that have led successive British Government initiatives to spend billions of pounds without first establishing through research whether ICT improves learning. At Road School, only 48 per cent of teachers believed students would learn more when using ICT. In contrast, 71 per cent of teachers at Inner City School agreed with this statement. The headteacher at Inner City School was convinced that dramatic improvements in the number of children gaining A to C grades at GCSE were due to investment in ICT, investment which Road School had not yet benefited from. An acknowledged difficulty for both advocates and sceptics is finding hard evidence for the impact of ICT on learning where ICT is just one factor in a large complex of factors. End-of-year exams are, at best, a crude way of judging the role of ICT. Moreover, as *IMPACT2* (DfES 2002b) acknowledged, 'good teaching' remains the most important factor, whether or not the teacher is using ICT. However, some consensus is emerging concerning the properties of ICT that can be beneficial for learning, plus evidence associating ICT with changes in pedagogic approach that improve learning. In the next section this pedagogic rationale is discussed further.

The educational rationale and drive for change

Society is changing from an industrial to an information society (European Commission 2002; OECD 2004; Voogt and Pelgrum 2005). Thus, we are told, one important driver towards embedding ICT in the curriculum is what Coutts *et al.* (2001) call an economic and social imperative – we must train tomorrow's workforce to be competent in ICT if the UK is to perform effectively in the global marketplace. However, New Labour's modernization agenda – according to Fergusson (2000) – is not just about 'garnering the power of mass computer literacy to exploit the potential of information technology' (p. 205), it is a longer-term strategy to allow 'maximum talent to rise from the largest possible pool' (ibid.) by providing effective teaching for children in historically poorly performing schools. The argument for embedding ICT is not just to acquire a new set of skills ('IT skills') to prepare children for the workplace, but the exploitation of properties of ICT to raise learning standards and to re-engage the disengaged. Moreover, the competencies to be learned are not just IT competencies but 'lifelong learning competencies' that anticipate the need to reskill throughout the lifespan (Voogt and Pelgrum 2005, p. 158).

What might a pedagogy for lifelong learning look like? Principles of Knowles' (1970) theory of adult learning, together with the work of other social and constructivist learning theorists (e.g. Vygotsky 1978; Schön 1983; Kolb 1984; Lave and Wenger 1991), suggest that as we develop and become adults, increasingly we need to be able to take responsibility for our own learning, to be involved in planning, negotiating and personalizing our learning and ensuring its relevance to our aptitudes, vocation and interests. Approaches that are thought to scaffold this kind of autonomy emphasize the importance of sharing experiences through collaborative inquiry and authentic problems or tasks that involve joint constructive activity. Most importantly, such approaches give plenty of opportunity for discussion and reflection on experience. Reflection is important for developing deeper conceptual understanding and developing an understanding of the relationship between theory and practice (Scardamalia and Bereiter 1991; Cognition and Technology Group at Vanderbilt (CTGV) 1992; Savery and Duffy 1996; Edelson *et al.* 1999).

Common to these approaches is an emphasis on the need for the tutor's role to change from a 'sage on the stage' to a 'guide on the side'. The teacher becomes a facilitator of learning. Thus, the ability of the tutor to use facilitation skills can be an important determinant of success in developing students' reasoning skills (including problem solving, meta-cognition and critical thinking) and in helping them to become independent, self-directed learners (Barrows 1992; Savery and Duffy 1996). Key facilitating skills include probing, clarification and justification questions that elicit explanations (Palinscar and Brown 1984; Rosenshine and Meister 1994; Pilkington and Parker-Jones 1996; Pilkington and Walker 2003).

What has this to do with ICT? Paradoxically, many believe a positive aspect of ICT is that it encourages a shift in pedagogy toward more facilitative or socio-constructivist models of learning (Crook 1994, 1997; Silverman 1995; Wegerif and Dawes 1998). The computer screen around which students often work in pairs, or in rows side by side, becomes a new focus of attention. New conversations occur around the computer as students interact with it. The tutor and blackboard are no longer the single focus of attention nor are they the sole source of feedback. Interaction is at least three-way (student–computer, student–student and student–teacher). The tutor must find new ways of engaging with students as a consequence. The Deputy Headteacher at Inner City School echoes this: 'ICT makes you become a facilitator of learning. . . . [It is] no longer a didactic approach but orchestrating and guiding'.

But as Barrows (1992) suggests, there is nothing automatic about becoming a good facilitator. Coutts *et al.* (2001) describe the teacher hovering in the background uncertain of what to do as pupils engage with computer software. Moreover, some technologies such as the use of PowerPoint on the interactive whiteboard support teachers in continuing with traditional whole-class 'sage-on-the-stage' delivery methods. Ideally, student activity at the computer holds their attention, releasing the teacher to give more personalized support – to facilitate. However, this requires considerable skill (Walsh 2002; Gipson 2003). ICT can, therefore, both challenge and change practice, but this is not automatic.

Additional claimed benefits for using ICT include the development of resources that can be accessed 'any time any place', increasing opportunity for independent revision/reflection or constructive activity 'through the bell', i.e. across and between lessons, in the school day and at home. Students can make their own connections between subjects and continue to refer to, and reflect on, material from one lesson in another lesson, or at home (using the Internet or mobile technologies). In this way it is also possible to create interdisciplinary project work using creative software such as word processors, web-editing, movie-making and graphical design tools.

Exploiting messaging and other communication technologies can also increase opportunities for new kinds of discussion within and beyond classroom hours. Text-based and asynchronous communication creates opportunities for more individual and reflective constructions that can help develop language and debating skills. Synchronous computer conferencing creates the opportunity for collaboration and immediate feedback without the need to travel. Such software, particularly text-based conferencing, has also been shown to encourage students who are not often vocal in face-to-face discussion (Herring 1996; Preece 2000; Pilkington and Walker 2003).

Use of interactive multimedia, in addition to providing alternative ways of presenting information to meet the needs of learners with a disability, can enhance learning for all learners by providing richer resources that engage an additional perceptual channel to encode and retrieve information. This benefits both initial understanding and recall. Moreover, for understanding particular kinds of processes the dynamic qualities of video and animation with explanatory narration can improve learning (Paivio 1991; Mayer and Anderson 1991; Najjar 1996). Simulations additionally enable students to experiment with the consequences of action in situations which would otherwise be too expensive, complex or dangerous (van Joolingen and de Jong 1991; Steed 1992). Moreover, for many students, interacting with computer-based learning materials can improve motivation to learn (Passey *et al.* 2003).

Progress in embedding ICT in the curriculum

Voogt and Pelgrum (2005) conducted a case-study analysis of pedagogic practice in 28 countries and concluded that those choosing to innovate with ICT in the school curriculum do generally evidence a new vision for teaching and learning emphasizing collaborative and metacognitive skills and lifelong learning. They also argue that one can see a shift in pedagogic practice when industrial and information economies are compared and contrasted: in the latter the learner is more likely to be actively engaged in both self-directed (independent) and collaborative problem-based activity; more likely to be in smaller more heterogeneous groups and to be exposed to teams of teachers and para-professionals, rather than individual teachers.

However, different goals or visions for exploiting ICT were also evident. These differences echoed those suggested by Coutts *et al.* (2001): some seek to use ICT in the classroom in an instrumental fashion to deliver the existing curriculum; some seek to enhance curriculum and pedagogy through using ICT (whilst accepting some contradictions with existing structures and procedures, e.g. the timetable, classroom space or assessment methods); and there are those who see the transformational power of ICT to be too important to be constrained by present organizational structures. For the latter, ICT in the curriculum can be a 'Trojan horse' to revolutionize the way in which the school as a whole is organized for the greater good. In the next section I will revisit these different visions, comparing progress toward them at the three selected case schools.

Delivering the existing curriculum

Pelgrum and Anderson (1999) found that, despite major investment in ICT in education, embedding ICT in the curriculum was disappointingly slow. Similar conclusions are drawn by Gipson: 'the investment in the implementation of ICT in education in the UK has been significant . . . but little systematic impact has been made in genuinely transforming the teaching and learning environments of individual classrooms' (Gipson 2003, p. 26). Voogt and Pelgrum (2005) in looking at their international case studies concluded that the majority of teachers hardly changed their practices when using ICT. ICT was used to create more attractively presented worksheets, to save time in collating test scores and printing out timetables (Coutts *et al.* 2001), but the transformational power of ICT was rarely fully realized.

In general, ICT Test Bed Project baseline data would seem to bear this out – the predominant ICTs used were word processors, web browser and email tools. Use of ICT for teaching and learning reflected the tools teachers were using personally – other technologies were used rarely and email was not generally used for interaction with students. However, the majority of teaching staff had used some CD-ROM or multimedia software with learners, at least for drill and practice activity. Across all ICT Test Bed Project schools teachers had rarely used ICT to improve visual understanding, for problem-solving or for discussion of alternative viewpoints (Thomas *et al.* 2003a). One teacher at Road School describes their use of IT to raise the quality of resources and looks forward to the day when he has an interactive whiteboard in his class as a result of the ICT Test Bed Project:

> [Main benefits of IT are] efficiency – speed mainly, improves quality and number of OHPs [we can use, we use the] word-processor and copy onto transparency – the clarity is better. Visual cues/diagrams, pictures, flow-charts, tables are all clearer and used more often. . . [we will be able to] extend [this] to PowerPoint in the future or Whiteboard if [we] could use this.
> (Teacher, Road School)

This does suggest that some of the properties of ICT for handling multimedia were being exploited to aid clarity and quality of resource and probably, therefore, also to aid understanding.

However, the most frequently mentioned examples of use of ICT to support learning at Road and Inner City Schools were to support the learning of literacy, numeracy and basic IT skills. This reflected a general pattern across all ICT Test Bed Project schools (Thomas *et al.* 2003a). The Independent Learning Suite (ILS) software used at Road School included software that highlighted words as the computer reads them (talking text), enabling the matching of sound to text to improve reading fluency. A range of different spelling games were also used and it was reported that these motivated children. These kinds of software were said to boost self-esteem whilst helping support learning of basic literacy and IT skills. Such software has been accused of delivering the *status quo* rather than enhancing the curriculum. The pedagogic model underpinning its design has been said to be that of the behaviourism of the 1960s. Such 'programmed learning' may have a useful role to play in drill and practice but lacks the capability to help students learn deeply or understand concepts. However, Coutts *et al.* (2001) argue that modern software can be effective in teaching children aspects of Mathematics and English, particularly where there are clear 'right' and 'wrong' answers. In these situations it can provide a differentiated response according to the actions of the learner, giving more opportunities for individual feedback. Moreover, whilst students are interacting with software, teachers are free to circulate and give individual attention to those who need it.

At Road School there were problems with using the ILS to deliver the curriculum. Software was most often used by one or two children sharing the computer in the classroom rather than in the ILS, due to technical difficulties in using the suite and logistical difficulties in moving the class to it. Moreover, there was a poor software/curriculum match for teaching literacy as one teacher commented:

> The numeracy software was fantastic for numeracy, however, literacy software did not fit – the literacy hour is so specific in what you teach and when you

teach it that the software was not right for the literacy hour . . . and the room was too small for a class. Plus only one class at a time when all numeracy and literacy is held at similar times.   (Teacher, Road School)

Enhancing curriculum or pedagogy

An intermediary stage in using ICT in a transformational way is to enhance the existing delivery through exploiting the new properties of the technology. Examples of this kind of use of ICT include exploiting multimedia.

At Road School a Science teacher had used Computer Assisted Design (CAD) software in project-based work with children. The software had been used to help with difficulties in visualization, particularly in rotation of nets. The children had found this both motivating and helpful in understanding underpinning concepts.

A teacher at Inner City School explained the way in which ICT enhanced the curriculum by enabling students to improve their design skills:

Many don't have a good 'making' skills-base. Physically making things can be difficult. [They] can access design technology and art in a different way through ICT. The machine 'makes' what they design. [IT] works for both SEN and high achievers . . . can do things that would take you seven years to learn to do by hand.

In addition to exploiting features of multimedia, the independence of time and place could be exploited to enhance the curriculum. At Inner City School, in collaboration with partnered schools abroad, email was used to extend opportunities to communicate authentically by writing in the target-language and video-conferencing was similarly used to converse authentically with native speakers.

Coutts *et al.* (2001) also cite the example of using computers to help marginalized or excluded students access the curriculum when they otherwise would not be able to do so. For example, the TOPILOT (1996) Project was designed to meet the needs of travelling families, allowing them to use the technology to receive education on the move – this kind of approach, whilst not revolutionizing schools, does start to meet the specialist needs of groups who may be disadvantaged by traditional delivery methods.

ICT also re-engaged the disengaged, or those otherwise marginalized by special educational needs at Inner City School. A teaching assistant commented:

It holds their attention – weak kids, fascinates kids with learning difficulties. Helps students with second language and naughty kids are model pupils on the computer.

An alternative way to enhance the curriculum through the use of ICT is to use tools across the subject boundaries to create interdisciplinary projects that extend learning across lessons. This type of learning was referred to earlier as 'through the bell' learning. Coutts *et al.* (2001, p. 229) cite Gatto (1992) and the negative message the lesson bell can implicitly give that no work is worth finishing. They also describe the ACOT Project in which pupils worked across Environmental Studies, German and English lessons to produce multimedia project work on litter. Although examples of this cross-subject and 'through the bell' working were rare, the same teacher at Road School who used CAD had also engaged students in digital video work. Children learnt to operate the video camera, training and sequencing shots, scripting and planning their own film. As well as learning design skills, children learnt to collaborate and to peer-review each other's work. This is an example of a deep-learning approach that should encourage development of metacognitive and lifelong learning skills with inter-disciplinary learning objectives. Project work was not, however, conducted in different subject lessons – for this a more revolutionary approach to curriculum design and/or organization of the school day would be required.

Revolutionizing learning

An alternative vision for ICT in the 'future school' has been described as a 'Trojan horse' in transforming the school as a whole. At Inner City School the Headteacher had this kind of vision concerning ICT as part of an overall strategy to transform the school:

> ICT [can be seen as] a Trojan horse for changes in pedagogy and practice generally – a Trojan horse to change all sorts of things – views on pedagogy, assessment . . . .Use of ICT is a strand in the school development plans – a strand throughout planning, not a separate strategy.

Walsh (2002), in comparing four case-study schools, identified King's College as an example of a school engaged in this kind of transformation: a previously failing school was redesigned internally to allow for curriculum delivery that integrates ICT and was granted Specialist School status. To achieve changes at King's College, Walsh says the Headteacher adopted a flat management structure, introduced a continuous school day with no bells and longer lessons, redesigned the learning spaces, introduced a modular curriculum, and created a learning intranet and time for independent learning in the Learning Centre. In this 'revolutionary' model it is not really possible to isolate the precise contribution of ICT alone, since changes were made at an organizational level which enhance the ways ICT can be used for learning – they are interdependent.

This is very much the sense in which the Headteacher at Metropolitan School saw the role of ICT – as part of a whole process of school reform. At this school the central change has been to the school day and timetable, enabling staff to use the afternoon session for extra-curricular activity. The afternoon session finishes at 2.30 and clubs run until 3.30. Teaching assistants, parents and volunteers supervise many of these activities, releasing teachers for planning, preparation and assessment activities which they do not need to do at school. The Headteacher commented:

> Laptops mean we can finish school earlier. They enable a different mind-set, such that people now feel guilty if they stay in the building! The question is 'do you have to do your work here?'. We now have 2 hours of non-contact time for paperwork, planning and assessment and can e-mail assessments.

Higher confidence in ICT is often inspired by personal ownership, and this confidence was helping teaching staff improve the quality of resources for classroom teaching by preparing them in advance on their laptops. Metropolitan School was also using TSW Project funding together with changes to the role of support staff to raise the quality of content resources in other ways. One of the support staff commented:

> A resource room was built for teachers and support staff. Computers were put in, as well as photocopiers and other equipment – everything that was needed to make resources. The reprographics room now has space to spread out and make displays.

The Headteacher and ICT coordinator felt the new timetable and the ICT equipment had worked hand-in-hand to enable the school to involve parents and support staff in broadening the curriculum (e.g. drama, sport and martial arts), giving children more learning choices. One of the support staff commented:

> The flexibility in timetabling and structure of the school day has impacted on pupils' learning. This has enabled us to try new teaching styles, to identify where kids are at, and to focus more on planning for the children themselves and for teaching and learning. ICT has had a big impact.

This observation is echoed by a class teacher at the school who commented on the retimetabling giving greater scope for individual or personalized learning:

> The TSW Project is also helping children in other ways. It has meant extra-curricular activity trips out, which help to develop a well-rounded person – not just one who is academically developed. More has been done to cater for pupils as individuals and to nurture their specific talents and abilities.

This links to a key strand of the vision of the 'future school' (Andres *et al.* 2003; OECD 2004), that of individualizing learning. Andres *et al.* suggest the 'future school' will achieve high learning standards in part by realizing the diverse aspirations of students, from 'jazz piano' to 'dominating the midfield of the soccer pitch' – schools need to recognize the individual and work with them to realize their learning potential.

Managing change: constraints, tensions and barriers

In the majority of schools, change involving the embedding of ICT to support learning has been aimed toward delivery of the existing curriculum, with few examples of using ICT to enhance or extend the curriculum and even fewer of the use of computers to reform the organization of learning in the school in 'Trojan horse' style. Why had comparatively few schools opted for this more radical change? Gipson (2003) suggests that issues include: infrastructure and inconsistent opportunities for ICT connectivity; lack of equity in access and, paradoxically, an overemphasis on equity instead of pedagogy; and a shortage of trained teachers. These barriers to rapid progress were also evident in the three case-study schools. In particular, staff identified problems due to lack of infrastructure, training and local autonomy.

In relation to infrastructure, McMullan (2002) concluded that there had been good progress in meeting 2002 targets for computer:pupil ratios of 1:11 in primary and 1:7 in secondary schools. However, whilst 99 per cent of schools were connected to the Internet in 2002, most did not have broadband. McMullan also concluded that where schools did have broadband, the bandwidth was often below that required to fully embrace a digital curriculum. The McMullan report makes a number of recommendations including investment in regional hubs and, to create confidence in the content development sector, a long-term commitment to resource schools in a sustainable fashion along commercial lines.

At Metropolitan School there had been mixed progress toward a transforming curriculum as the school still lacked networking. This limited the rate at which they could proceed toward linking the school with the home and the wider community. The potential of networking was recognized by the independent IT consultant at Road School who was then involved in a £22 million project to link Learning Centres and schools in the local area. At Road School the Headteacher also indicated that even with broadband access in the school they were limited in their ability to expand community links due to the children not having access to a networked computer at home. Moreover, ongoing problems discouraged staff from using the Internet and email communication including: accessing the network (log-in authentication); maintaining a link without 'crashing' the machine; and lack of on-site technical support when problems occurred. These problems were also preventing the sharing of information via email attachment of documents and using a shared access area to share content files. Although Inner City School had a high input of resources due to Specialist School status, and was further along the way toward the vision of a 'future school' with an associated Learning Centre, even here the network facilities were still limiting. A teacher commented: '. . .compared with most schools [we have] good access, but appalling by comparison with industry . . .[we need] a decent network and decent support'.

Another barrier was that of maintenance of existing equipment. In primary schools the IT coordinator was often one of the teaching staff with their own teaching responsibilities who was constantly interrupted by other staff when their computer had 'gone funny' (McMullan 2002). McMullan adds that in 2002 of 1 million computers in schools less than 10 per cent were covered by a managed service contract. At Road School Primary one teacher put it this way: 'Initial capital investment was not backed by the insurance of rolling mainten-ance provision', things broke down and no one could fix it.'

Most teachers were not using the ILS, due to persistent problems. As one teaching assistant commented: 'ILS people complain. It is right for two days and then [it's] three weeks before it is back online. This disappoints the children. Raises their hopes and then it doesn't work'. A teacher added:

> [The] physical disruption of the class of moving children to suites is a disin-centive – especially when [the network] often doesn't work. Small groups used the Internet to research things – but unreliability of the network puts people off.

The issue of technical support is an important one, as those who find technical support close at hand when problems occur also enjoy higher confidence and are more likely to continue to use equipment. A senior teacher at Inner City School commented: 'If training has been successful then back-up from school technicians is crucial'.

Of all the issues that impact on the ability to improve the quality of teach-ing and learning using ICT, McMullan (2002) suggests that the most impor-tant is the ability of teachers to use it. Gipson (2003) argues that one of the keys to ensuring significant take-up of ICT in the classroom comes from empowering teachers with the skill, knowledge and understanding to trans-form learning using ICT. Lack of confidence, variable quality training and teacher scepticism in relation to ICT have all been suggested as reasons for inertia in embedding ICT across the curriculum (Dawes 1999; OfSTED 2002; Gipson 2003; Gray *et al.* 2005). Many writers in the field have recognized the need for staff development if ICT is to be used effectively in the classroom (OfSTED 2002; McMullan 2002; Gipson 2003; DfES 2003b; Voogt and Pelgrum 2005). Despite government initiatives such as the New Opportunities Fund training, a skill and confidence gap remained for many teachers (OfSTED 2002). Dawes (1999) commented that the apprenticeship model of Lave and Wenger (1991) cannot entirely deal with learning to embed ICT in the curriculum because of the rapidity of change and the scarcity of 'old timers' to pass on their knowledge. Importantly, the nature of that training should not be restricted to basic IT skills for personal use. Training needs to relate to the pedagogic context of use, i.e. for learning as well as teaching pur-poses (Kennewell 2001). One of the key issues for teachers at the three case-study schools was that many centralized training providers delivered training for tools teachers did not have personal access to, or delivered training without reference to the pedagogic context. For example, basic instruction on how to use a spreadsheet or word processor was not what they felt they needed: what they needed was inspiring ways to integrate use of these tools into school work to support learning.

Additionally, Voogt and Pelgrum (2005) argue that in many situations the innovations which schools can make are limited by their lack of autonomy, particularly their lack of control over changes to the curriculum. They suggest that governments must play a role in promoting the kinds of change necessary at the content level to realize more radical 'through-the-bell' visions for the kind of pedagogy and curriculum required for the information society. However, it has been argued that this is against current trends which have seen increased centralized control of the curriculum in contradiction to greater autonomy in managing schools (Walsh 2002).

In the Creative Waves project, Andres *et al.* (2003) looked at five case studies of school leadership on five foci (or 'future visions') and concluded that the potential of ICT is limited by the degrees of freedom the school's management team have over the direction of the school, including: the timetable, design of spaces for learning and the curriculum; staff responsibilities; the mix of staff and the ability to redefine roles; and the relationship and nature of partnership between schools, community centres, parents and staff.

Summary of emerging issues

In the work of Walsh (2002) and McMullan (2002), and in the examples and illustrations from ICT Test Bed and TSW Projects, many of the barriers to meeting goals and targets for transforming schools by exploiting the power of ICT have been identified. Some of these issues are difficult for individual schools to address in isolation, particularly infrastructure issues relating to connecting schools with high-quality broadband through regional hubs and learning centres. Delays in rolling out this infrastructure had knock-on effects for the development of commercial and high-quality content resources to meet the needs of the curriculum. Some schools were tackling this problem by using support staff to help create content resources which could be shared and reused by other staff. There was a desire to build up an intranet of shared resources. However, the sustainability of the existing ICT resource and meeting the long-term cost of maintenance was an issue.

A further issue identified was the lack of a common vision for how ICT might transform teaching and learning. For school leaders, a concern was raising awareness of how ICT could be integrated with the strategy for transforming or improving the school (not just delivering the existing curriculum in didactic style) and how to communicate this vision. Opportunities to learn about ICT were seen as a key part of this strategy. There was a need for training, particularly pedagogic training, that went beyond basic IT skills for personal computer use.

However, there were some major positives in moving toward the 'future school'. I have illustrated some examples of teachers increasing their confidence in using ICT for personal use: to save time in preparation and report-writing, but also to create higher-quality reusable resources for use in classroom teaching. There were examples of using multimedia to improve and extend the curriculum in art and design, modern foreign language teaching and science classes. These examples went beyond basic improvement of handouts and over-heads and used ICT across lessons in authentic and collaborative problem-solving tasks, or in ways that accord with the vision of OECD (2004) for developing lifelong learning skills. These uses encouraged greater autonomy amongst learners. There were also examples of extending the curriculum to help engage the disengaged or those with special needs.

Particularly at Metropolitan School, more radical reforms at organizational level, supported by the introduction of laptops and changes to staff roles, included changing the school day to create time in the afternoon for extra-curricular activity. This brought closer links between parents, the school and the wider community. This in turn helped to personalize learning to meet children's individual needs and learning aspirations.

Revisiting Inner City School more recently, the introduction of interactive whiteboards throughout the school has had a huge impact on the use of ICT both to deliver and enhance the curriculum: teachers there continue to become more confident and innovative in their integration of ICT. Thus, whilst at first teachers might use PowerPoint on the interactive whiteboard without changing their approach to delivery, later more sophisticated use of images and text to create multimedia resources and collaborative team games that re-engage the disengaged emerge – with resulting benefits for language development (Pilkington and Gray 2004; Gray *et al.* 2005).

However, more generally, in 2003–04 the vision proposed by Walsh was not yet apparent: although most schools are now connected to the Internet and many are connected to learning centres, the nature of that connectivity (bandwidth) often does not meet needs and expectations and there remain problems in terms of a lack of roll-out of laptops and wireless networks to really exploit the poten-tial of mobile technologies for 'anytime anywhere' learning. This limits the inte-gration of ICT in the classroom – it is not yet as hassle-free and unconscious to use (by both teacher and students) as the pencilcase or blackboard.

Conclusion

Where to next? The future is wireless and almost certainly includes the provision of a laptop or tablet for every child as well as every teacher. At this point, tool use is likely to evolve and become more natural and unconscious. Students will be able to 'show and tell' their individual work to the whole class on the interactive whiteboard, to each other, in the homework club and to parents. They will be able to share individual and joint constructions with teachers and peers seamlessly and across lessons. The intranet will enable staff to locate and share reusable content and templates for the construction of 'learning objects' – reusable activities designed by themselves, or with the help of the resource team. These will include examples/illustrations, exercises and templates. Reusable learning objects can be downloaded 'anytime anywhere'. Management of information will become increasingly sophisticated and will be combined with the use of mobile messaging and conferencing facilities to enable virtual learning spaces in which students and tutors can collaborate and construct. However, exploiting these new learning opportunities will depend upon resources, local autonomy to implement the organizational changes required, awareness of the possibilities and the vision espoused. As chapters by Selwood (Chapter 10) and by Gunter and Butt (Chapter 1) also illustrate, these themes resonate with those seeking to change other aspects of school culture and organization, not just those seeking to embed ICT for learning and teaching purposes.

Leading and managing ICT

Ian Selwood

Introduction

The introduction and/or extension of the use of ICT in school settings is usually considered as core to the remodelling process and the wider modernization agenda in schools. In England, education with and about computers (ICT) and the use of computers for educational administration can be traced back to the mid-1960s. However, even though massive investments had been made over the years, the Stevenson Committee (1997) concluded that the state of ICT in UK schools was 'primitive' and 'not improving' and that it should be a national priority to increase the use of ICT in schools. Undoubtedly, since the publication of the Stevenson Committee's Report, progress has been made (OfSTED 2004b and c). However OfSTED (2005) reported that there was wide variation in the extent to which ICT was embedded in the work of schools, even though ICT as a tool for learning was expanding in all schools. Additionally, even though teaching and learning were being affected by ICT in some subjects and some classes, pupil use varied between subjects and year groups, and ICT was yet to become integral to teaching and learning, or become a driver for school improvement (OfSTED 2005).

Bearing the above in mind – as well as considering that remodelling does not begin with teaching, learning and the ways in which ICT can enable them to develop, but focuses on organizational effectiveness – this chapter analyses the issues that influence ICT-related change in schools. The management of ICT is the focus of this chapter, drawing upon the available literature and the Evaluation of the Transforming the School Workforce Pathfinder Project (Thomas *et al.* 2004).

Factors that influence the uptake of ICT by teachers

The reasons for the lack of progress in integrating ICT into all aspects of education are complex, but recent research studies have highlighted barriers (Jones 2004) and enablers (Scrimshaw 2004) that influence teachers' uptake of ICT. In his review of the research literature Jones (2004) noted a number of potential barriers to the uptake of ICT including:

1. lack of access to appropriate ICT equipment;
2. unreliable equipment and lack of technical support;
3. lack of institutional support from leaders, and involvement of teachers and managers in implementing change;
4. teachers' lack of ICT confidence as this is a significant determining factor of usage;
5. teachers' lack of will to change their teaching practices;
6. teachers' lack of realization of the advantages of ICT; and
7. lack of time for training, practice, preparing and researching materials for lessons.

Similar issues were highlighted in PricewaterhouseCoopers' (2001) *Teacher Workload Study.*

I would argue that the first two of these barriers relate to ICT infrastructure; barrier three to management practices and style; four, five and six to teacher continuing professional development (CPD); and the final point to teacher workload. Without investment in appropriate ICT infrastructure (hardware, software, networking) it is apparent that progress will be limited. Nevertheless, infrastructure alone will not guarantee the integration of ICT. For example, the provision of adequate technical support has been highlighted as a significant issue for enabling successful use of ICT (Leask and Pachler 1999; Scrimshaw 2004). Furthermore, it is apparent that many of these potential barriers can be addressed by appropriate professional development that accommodates the needs of 'all staff individually and as a whole' (Scrimshaw 2004, p. 5). However, this raises the issue of lack of teacher time and teacher workload, particularly lack of time for training and practice. Thus it is further apparent that the barriers to ICT uptake are inextricably linked. Overcoming such barriers is a management issue and the role of school leadership is central for success (Scrimshaw 2004). Indeed OfSTED (2005, p. 6), stressed that 'the most critical factor in good ICT leadership was the involvement of senior managers, especially the headteacher'. Scrimshaw (2004) also noted the importance of planning, including the need for an ICT vision statement, a needs assessment and an ICT school development plan.

In the remainder of this chapter these factors that influence the uptake of ICT by teachers are analysed by examining some of the literature concerned with ICT leadership styles and vision, ICT coordination, ICT planning and ICT CPD. The second part of the chapter examines the data from the Evaluation of the TSW Project (Thomas *et al.* 2004) which serve to illustrate the effects of an intervention strategy on ICT uptake.

The role of school leadership

Bosley and Moon (2003) highlight the importance of the support of senior management for implementing new practices and addressing the financial implications of change. In a Canadian study, Sheppard (2003) identified three different groups of schools, which corresponded to three different styles of leadership, and this in turn related to the schools' success in integrating ICT into teaching and learning. In the schools deemed to be most successful in integrating ICT, the leadership was collaborative, supported innovation and risk-taking and included classroom teachers, parents and others. There was considerable dependence upon teacher pioneers, but 'regular' teachers were increasingly comfortable with the use of ICT. Morale was generally high across the schools and team leadership was apparent. Teachers, students and parents from these successful schools were excited about the extent of learning in their school, and eager to share and utilize their experiences and new knowledge.

In the least successful schools, Sheppard found that the leadership style tended to be traditional and hierarchical, and although committees existed it was a common expectation of teachers that the principal was responsible for bringing about change. Even the existence of a formalized school improvement process, focused on the implementation of ICT in the classroom, had not guaranteed success. In these schools Sheppard noted that there appeared to be limited vision of the potential of ICT, and therefore there was practically no awareness of the need for change. Even though one or two teachers with a special interest in ICT had initiated several projects integrating ICT into the curriculum with their own classes, they had not been encouraged to share their new knowledge with others. If teachers perceived backwardness in ICT they tended to blame this on external factors.

In addition to leadership style, other factors are considered important in the literature relating to the leadership and management of ICT, including the actual processes of leading and managing ICT. OfSTED (2005), as well as noting the importance of the involvement of the headteacher for good ICT leadership, stressed that it is critical that leadership should be complemented by effective coordination of ICT (an issue that will be discussed later). Moreover, Becta (2003) stressed that when senior leaders are enthusiastic and visionary about ICT they can give a positive lead and raise the profile of ICT for management, and teaching and learning. Furthermore, by learning with staff and leading by example, headteachers can inspire their staff in the use of ICT, as evidenced by the evaluation of the New Opportunities Fund's (NOF) ICT teacher training programme (Preston 2004). Senior leaders and headteachers in particular need to use the school's Management Information System (MIS) effectively for planning and evaluating the performance of their schools. The use of the data available within the school's MIS can improve the strategic decision-making within schools and reduce the time spent on administrative tasks. However, to use MIS effectively, senior leaders need training and advice (Selwood and Drenoyianni 1997).

As noted above, Scrimshaw (2004) stressed that if schools are to meet the challenge of implementing ICT effectively they must have a clear ICT vision statement, and this should be clearly articulated and shared (OfSTED 2005). Vision is seen by Becta (2004) as the first stage in the cyclical process of school improvement and it suggests that leadership teams need to develop a vision of where they wish to go, audit where they currently are and then plan how to get there. Once implemented the plan must be reviewed to determine how the school is progressing. This approach to change management has been suggested by many other authors (Holly and Southworth 1989; Hargreaves and Hopkins 1991; MacGilchrist *et al.* 1995) and is often referred to as development planning. Moreover, the White Paper *Excellence in Schools* (DfEE 1997a) emphasizes the need for schools to produce effective development plans to support and promote school improvement. As noted above with respect to MIS, senior leaders need continuing professional development and support if the change process is to be effective. Indeed, in two major Department for Education and Skills (DfES) projects, the ICT Test Bed Project (Somekh *et al.* 2006) and the Transforming the School Workforce Project (Thomas *et al.* 2004), schools were provided with specialist support in change management.

The role of the ICT coordinator

Having examined the role of senior leaders with respect to ICT this chapter now examines briefly the extremely important role of the ICT coordinator (formerly IT coordinator). Due to the nature of ICT in schools, a middle management role, the ICT coordinator, has developed over the years. As long ago as 1972 the need for an 'ICT co-ordinator' in schools was evident (IFIP, 1972); more recently Evans (1989), North (1990) and the National Curriculum Council (NCC 1990) discussed and defined the crucial role of the IT coordinator. The importance of this role remains central to ICT as can be seen by the fact that texts concerning it continue to be published (Tagg 1999; Crawford 1997; Becta 2002; Fox 2003). The ICT coordinator is required to combine a daunting number of roles and skills including provision of CPD and cross-curricular support for colleagues, technical expertise, curriculum planning and whole-school resource management. Few other roles can vary as much from one school to another, or can be filled by staff with such varied backgrounds. Furthermore, there is anecdotal evidence that many teachers with long experience in specialist IT teaching are seen by their headteachers as unsuited to the role of ICT coordinator. In their research, Kennewell and Selwood (1997) identified six major areas of responsibility for ICT coordinators: resource allocation; system maintenance; staff training; coordination of ICT across the curriculum; classroom support for staff; and teaching ICT (IT) as a separate subject. These areas were recognized by two-thirds, or greater, of the respondents. At first sight this may not appear to be such a daunting array of tasks. However, Selwood and Kennewell (1999) elaborated on each of these areas of responsibility; for example, coordination of ICT across the curriculum was seen to include: chairing the ICT committee; carrying out ICT audits; production of ICT policy and development plans; assisting heads of department/subject leaders in producing their policies and development plans (to ensure integration of ICT); ensuring that ICT (IT) capability is developed in line with National Curriculum requirements; advising senior management on progress of the ICT policy and development plan; reviewing the ICT policy and development plan; and ensuring that assessment of pupils' IT capability takes place, and is appropriately recorded.

Similar analyses of the other five areas of responsibility are given by Selwood and Kennewell (ibid.), and demonstrate the enormity of the role of ICT. To resolve this problem, Selwood and Kennewell suggested that responsibility for ICT should be shared between a Network Manager, ICT subject leader (to take responsibility for the teaching of ICT skills and concepts) and the ICT coordinator (to coordinate ICT across the curriculum). Indeed, more recently, Becta (2002) noted that many schools have moved away from the idea of having a single ICT coordinator to a sharing of responsibilities, with various members of staff managing the different aspects. The National Agreement between the government in England and teachers' unions (DfES 2003a) meant that no teachers should routinely carry out 'ordering, setting up and maintaining ICT equipment and software' (NASUWT 2003) thus reducing the role of ICT coordinator, implying the need for school-based ICT technicians and allowing ICT coordinators to spend more time on their core role.

OfSTED (2004b), when reviewing the effects of government initiatives, highlighted the importance of ICT coordinators, noting that when headteachers worked in partnership with their ICT coordinators there had been improvement in the understanding of and rationale for the use and development of ICT. Furthermore, they stressed that the best planning occurred when subject coordinators worked with the ICT coordinator and took responsibility for ICT in their own subjects. Moreover, with respect to the role of the ICT coordinator, OfSTED (2004b) noted that ICT coordinators influence practice by 'leading staff meetings, providing lesson demonstrations and working closely with other coordinators to develop and implement policy and practice' (OfSTED 2004b, p. 11).

ICT and planning

The importance of planning was highlighted above and ICT can be involved in development planning in two ways. Firstly, ICT is needed for whole-school development planning to help in the collection and analysis of the large amounts of data available in schools. Data can be used for analysing 'where the school is at', and once analysed the derived information can be used for decision-making and development planning. Many MIS systems contain a number of applications that are designed to be used specifically for development planning (e.g. SIMS, see Wild and Walker 2001). Secondly, and perhaps more importantly from the point of view of this chapter, schools need to use development planning to effectively implement ICT. A good deal has been written about developing an ICT plan (e.g. North 1990; NCET/NAACE 1997; Harrison 1998; Becta 1999; Tagg 1999). Indeed schools have been required to produce a development plan for

ICT to qualify for funding under various government initiatives, notably the National Grid for Learning (DfEE 1997b).

Planning for ICT is, however, perhaps more problematic than for most other changes in education due to the rate of technological progress. Who would, for instance, five years ago, have foreseen the massive investments that schools have made in electronic whiteboards? Government policy and funding support for ICT also changes at the whim of ministers – all too often central initiatives are announced and expected to be responded to and implemented within months, rather than years. Therefore planning for ICT development is perhaps differ-ent in that it needs to use shorter planning cycles and possibly be more detailed than planning for other educational change. The need for, and nature of, an ICT vision statement has already been discussed. Following the creation of a vision statement, schools need to develop an ICT policy. However, there is some confusion in the literature with respect to ICT policies, with some authors (North 1990) suggesting that ICT policies should include an action plan for the following year(s), while others make a distinction between the ICT policy and the ICT development plan (Fox 2003). It is my belief that these should be two separate documents, with the ICT policy setting out the ICT vision statement and the general parameters within which the school works. On the other hand the ICT development plan should address how changes in ICT are going to be implemented in the coming year in order that the ICT policy and vision state-ment can be achieved.

According to Freedman (2005), the ICT policy should not be a bulky document ('no more than five pages'). Additionally Freedman suggested the ICT policy should contain statements concerning: equal opportunities; delivery and assess-ment of ICT capability; ICT purchasing policy; ICT equipment maintenance and replacement policy; role of ICT committee; ICT in-service training (INSET), soft-ware copyright, antivirus, data protection, Internet access policies; and how the ICT policy is reviewed and monitored. Though this list appears comprehensive. I believe several important issues are missing regarding the role of ICT in sup-porting teaching and learning, school administration and management.

ICT development plans should build on both the vision statement and the ICT policy, but they also need to start from 'where the school is at' and address how changes in ICT are going to be implemented in the coming years. This brings us to the first stage of the development planning cycle – auditing or reviewing the state of ICT. Auditing ICT can cover a whole range of related factors or issues including hardware, software, staff ICT use and capability, pupil ICT use and capability, curriculum coverage, progression, continuity and coher-ence. Methods of conducting audits are as numerous as the areas which they cover and can include: paper-based questionnaires; interviews; diaries; com-puter logs; and online tools, e.g. the Self-Review Framework (Becta/NCSL 2006). The practicalities and desirability of a full ICT audit are perhaps debat-able as the purpose of carrying out such an audit is to produce a development plan. Moreover, many authors, when writing about development planning, note that plans should be credible, manageable and sustainable (Fox 2003), and to achieve this it is it is necessary to take strategic decisions concerning priorities for action. With limited resources it is highly unlikely that all ICT areas requiring development can be addressed within one cycle of development planning. Thus, school development plans will vary greatly from school to school. However, what should be common across them is their overall structure. For each strand of the plan, the objective of the strand, where the school is at currently, strategies to be used, personnel involved, time scale (including completion date), resource implications, success criteria and costs involved should all be detailed. Such structured planning that allocates responsibilities and success criteria should lead to effective implementation, evaluation and the next cycle of development planning.

Continuing professional development

Three of the seven potential barriers suggested by Jones (2004) and discussed earlier can possibly be overcome by ICT CPD. If ICT is to be used effectively, becoming central to the remodelling and modernization process, then teachers must be confident and competent in its use. This confidence and competence must not only support the teaching and learning of their pupils, but also their other professional activities. In the UK, the Stevenson Committee (1997) highlighted the need for training teachers in ICT and this was supported by statistics produced by the DfEE (1999). Two initiatives were introduced in 1998 to meet this need, which can be seen as major attempts to update teacher ICT skills and as the start of remodelling with respect to ICT. From September 1998 a National Curriculum for ICT in teacher education became a mandatory part of initial teacher training (TTA 1998a). Then, in the summer of 1999, a £230-million lottery funded NOF scheme to provide training or retraining for all 500,000 practising teachers and school librarians began. As the NOF programme was intended to bring all full-time classroom teachers up to the standard expected for newly qualified teachers (Preston 2004), the curriculum for initial teacher training and the expected outcomes of the NOF training (TTA 1998b) were, as one would expect, extremely similar.

The NOF training programme was imaginative and bold, but possibly misguided and overambitious. It used a combination of teaching methods including e-learning, with the emphasis very much on developing pedagogy rather than ICT skills. Though the focus of these schemes was on developing teacher competence in 'The use of information and communications technology in subject teaching', administration and management were not ignored. As such, one of the intended outcomes of the NOF programme was that: 'Teachers should know how to use ICT to improve their own professional efficiency and to reduce administrative and bureaucratic burdens . . .' (TTA 1998a, p. 13).

According to the Mirandanet Report on the NOF training for the TTA (Preston 2004), there was an intention that schools should update their ICT skills before embarking on the NOF programme, but this was not realized. In fact this intention was never widely publicized. Other problems highlighted by Preston included: lack of skilled trainers at the start of the programme; senior leaders not trained in the management of ICT in schools; schools choosing trainers who were good at marketing, rather than being suitable for the school; and the fact that the training had to be treated as optional, as supply cover was not funded in the scheme. To overcome some of these problems, training providers were encouraged to modify the programmes that had previously been approved by the TTA.

The Mirandanet Report is somewhat more positive regarding the effects of the NOF training than OfSTED (2004b), who reported that the expected outcomes had been met by only about a third of all primary schools, and that in another third they had not been met at all. The schools that were most successful in achieving the NOF expected outcomes were those that had good strategic leadership, collegiate work patterns, good technical support and encouragement from senior leadership (Preston 2004). These findings add support to the views of Sheppard (2003) (discussed earlier) regarding leadership styles in schools that successfully implement ICT. OfSTED (2004b) suggested that: 'a combination of in-house training, LEA courses and independent providers combined with improved resource provision, has generally had greater impact' (p. 13).

Even if the NOF training had been 100 per cent successful, it is apparent that changes in technology (e.g. interactive whiteboards, Tablet PCs, PDAs, etc. and advances in e-learning (e.g. developments in virtual learning environments (VLEs) and managed learning environments (MLEs), Wikis and Blogs, etc.) will mean that ICT CPD must remain high on each school's agenda.

Findings from the TSW Project

In the final section of this chapter, we present some of the findings from the TSW Project that relate to the issues discussed in the first part of the chapter. We explore issues surrounding ICT and modernization by examining the changes in teachers' views of ICT and their use of ICT over the year of the Project (see Thomas *et al.* 2004 and Appendix 1 for details of this project. A detailed analysis of the data concerned with ICT can be found in Selwood and Pilkington (2005)). In this chapter, the emphasis is on responses relating to ICT in the 2003 survey and on the changes that had taken place since the 2002 survey. This is supplemented by interview data.

Factors influencing ICT use

A key component of the TSW Project had been to increase the role of ICT in schools both in terms of learning and teaching and in support of administration. In both surveys, teachers were asked to report on the factors that were likely to influence their use of ICT. These were access to ICT resources at home and at school, their views on ICT resources available, the training they had received in ICT and their attitudes towards ICT.

When teachers were asked about their access to ICT at home in 2003 little change had occurred with respect to access to desktop machines, with 71 per cent of special school teachers, 83 per cent of primary and 77 per cent of secondary school teachers reporting positively in 2003. The most striking and substantial change was in access to a laptop computer at home. In 2003, home access to a laptop was available to 91 per cent of teachers in special and primary schools and 74 per cent of teachers in secondary schools. This equates to rises of 51 per cent, 64 per cent and 49 per cent respectively over the year, and these levels of change undoubtedly reflect the investment in laptops that was part of the Project. Access to other forms of technology at home also increased (digital cameras and Internet access) but these changes probably represent changes in wider consumer expenditure patterns rather than a consequence of the Project.

In both years, teachers were asked to report on their access to ICT facilities at school under the following headings: no access; access shared with pupils; access shared with staff; and sole access. The figures for 2003 demonstrate quite clearly that the schools had invested in interactive whiteboards. When reviewing the data on sole access, in 2003, there were now very high levels of sole access to laptop computers: 86 per cent in special, 78 per cent in primary and 74 per cent in secondary schools. In analysing the data on change between 2002 and 2003, teachers who replied in both years were compared. Sole use of laptops had also increased for all categories, i.e. those who had moved from shared access to sole, from no access to shared and from no access to sole access. Summing the three categories of response, 45 per cent of special school teachers had benefited from this change, 75 per cent of teachers in primary schools and 73 per cent of teachers in secondary schools. Sole access to desktop computers had grown by 4 per cent for teachers in special schools and it had increased by 12 per cent and 19 per cent in primary and secondary schools. In the special and primary schools, there had also been a significant growth in access to a curriculum network. There had also been significant growth in access to computer networks for administration in all three types of school.

Teachers were also asked their views with respect to hardware, software and technical support. In 2003 teachers from special and primary schools showed clear agreement that the hardware, software and technical support available to them in school met their needs. With respect to change in the views of those who responded in 2002 and 2003, about half the ratings of teachers in primary and special schools had moved towards a more positive view of the resources. However, in 2003 teachers in secondary schools were also satisfied with the facilities and support, but less so than other teachers. Although the views of secondary school teachers had also become more positive, the change was less marked.

With respect to teachers' views on training, they were asked about the quality of the training they had received in the last 12 months and if they felt they had been trained in all aspects of ICT necessary for their work. The responses to both questions were mixed in 2003: the means for each group of teachers were on the margin of 'agreement' and 'disagreement', with the means closer to 'agreement' – except for secondary teachers, who were closer to 'disagreement'. This was, however, an improvement over the responses collected in the previous year.

Attitudes towards ICT have an effect on teachers' readiness to use ICT. Teachers were therefore asked their views concerning their competency; whether they believed their skills had improved in the preceding 12 months; and their beliefs concerning the value of ICT in reducing workload and contributing to productivity. In 2003, the responses to all four statements show the large majority of teachers agreeing with each statement, i.e. they were competent users of ICT; their skills had improved over the previous 12 months; that using ICT would reduce their workload over the next 12 months; and that their use of ICT made them more productive. Comparing the 2002 responses with the 2003 responses, about half of all those who replied in both years had scored the same point on the response scale, but more registered an increase in all four categories.

Changes in teachers' use of ICT

An important aspect of the use of ICT in schools is whether and how teachers use ICT to support learning and teaching and, related to this, whether teachers have confidence in using ICT to analyse performance data, and use data with pupils to support target setting and review. Given the extent of data on pupil performance now available to schools, the ability of teachers to use this information confidently and reliably is of increasing importance. Generally teachers were confident in their ability to use ICT to support teaching and learning, and, over the period of the study, teachers' belief improved, with 38 per cent of teachers in special schools, 52 per cent of primary school teachers and 31 per cent of secondary teachers responding more positively. However, the teachers were less confident with respect to their ability to use ICT for analysing school and pupil performance data. Nevertheless, the change since 2002 was encouraging, with 38 per cent of teachers in special schools, 48 per cent in primary schools and 33 per cent in secondary schools registering greater confidence.

Across all the school types, teachers clearly agreed that they could use data for target setting and review, with an agreement level of 84 per cent in special schools, 86 per cent in primary schools and 81 per cent in secondary schools. In terms of a change of view between the two survey points, 44 per cent of teachers in special schools had moved towards more agreement with the statement, while change among primary and secondary school teachers was more evenly distributed. The majority (56 per cent) of teachers had not changed their opinion.

The use of ICT for management and administration was an area where it was hoped that there could be an important shift in the nature and extent of use of ICT. A number of questions in the surveys directly addressed the use of ICT to support management and administration, and these are examined in this section. At the end of the TSW Project, 85 per cent of teachers in special schools agreed that they used 'ICT appropriately to support administration and management', compared with 80 per cent in primary schools and 79 per cent in secondary schools. Comparing the data for the two surveys it would appear that in primary schools almost half of the teachers had increased their use, whilst in secondary and special schools over a third had increased their use.

Four areas of 'current use' were investigated in the two surveys: other pupil contact as opposed to working directly with pupils (e.g. contacting parents by email, registration); school/staff management (e.g. timetable, planning, finance); general administration (e.g. department/school records; organizing resources such as building, books, equipment; clerical work, that is word processing); individual/professional activity (such as training other staff, being trained, e-learning). In analysing the data, it was apparent that some of the cells in the matrix used represented very small numbers, particularly for special schools. However, when reviewing the data there was a clear shift showing increased usage of ICT in all four areas.

Workload and ICT

At the end of the questionnaire an open-ended question asked teachers about their views on workload in general. From the 86 teachers in the four special schools who responded, a range of factors were cited as the main causes of excessive workload. Nearly half (40) of these teachers cited bureaucracy and paperwork (marking, monitoring, record keeping, planning, form filling), and did not elaborate on this view. A further 16 cited demands created by work linked to creation of resources and the need to produce differentiated learning programmes of work. The 206 primary school teachers and 702 secondary school teachers who responded to this question identified similar issues to these. One hundred and twenty-eight primary and 317 secondary teachers cited paperwork and administration, including record keeping, planning and form filling, as the main cause of excessive workload. Most of these issues could be addressed at least in part by increased use of ICT. Interestingly, 33 secondary teachers identified the time involved in ICT take-up and systems conversion from paper to emedia as a cause of excessive workload. This highlights that changes in working practice themselves incur initial costs in time and resources and that the benefits of such changes may not be reflected immediately by a reduction in reported workload. However, efficiency gains may produce a net gain at a later date.

Prospective uses of ICT

When asked directly about whether ICT could reduce their workloads a large majority of teachers expressed the view that it could. This issue was further investigated and teachers were posed two questions about their views on the potential of ICT to reduce workload in areas related to teaching and supporting learning. There were quite high levels of agreement regarding the potential of ICT to reduce workload in relation to teaching (e.g. lesson planning), but the responses were markedly higher for the potential of ICT to reduce workload for activities such as accessing pupil records or writing reports. In special schools, 73 per cent of teachers agreed that in the future ICT could reduce their workload in teaching and 95 per cent agreed that ICT would reduce their workload in supporting learning. In primary schools, the rates were very similar (74 per cent and 90 per cent) while in secondary schools they were somewhat lower (69 per cent and 86 per cent). There was very little change between the two survey points.

Although it is difficult from questionnaire data alone to gain an impression of exactly how teachers expected that use of ICT might have a more direct impact on teaching and learning, from interviews with teachers a number of recurring themes emerged including:

- the creation of reusable teaching materials saving preparation time;
- the sharing of teaching materials and lesson plans via an intranet, again saving preparation time and sharing ideas or good practice;
- student access to materials out of hours via the intranet – helping to deliver support to the individual when it was needed;
- the production of better-quality (multimedia) materials with more explanatory power and/or higher presentational clarity or visual appeal (teachers would not otherwise have the time to produce these);
- use of ICT in the classroom creating interactive and engaging lessons that would motivate disaffected students;
- the use of ICT to monitor attendance, progress and performance and to alert teachers, parents and students to the need for intervention or support.

The four questions concerning 'current use' of ICT for administration and management were rephrased slightly to ascertain teachers' views on the potential of ICT to reduce their workload in the future. In their responses teachers showed a positive view, but this was not quite as strong as their views on the potential of ICT to support learning. Across the four statements, the average level of agreement was 70 per cent in special schools, 67 per cent in primary schools and 72 per cent in secondary schools. On the individual statements, the lowest level of agreement was the response to the statement on the potential of ICT in relation to pupil contact, such as contacting parents by email or its use in pupil registration; here the agreement rates were 57 per cent (special), 46 per cent (primary) and 67 per cent (secondary). The highest level of agreement was in response to the statement on general administration where the agreement rates were 74 per cent (special and primary) and 72 per cent (secondary).

Conclusion

It is generally recognized that the introduction and/or extension of the use of ICT in school settings is usually considered as core to the remodelling process and modernization agenda in schools. However, the issues are obviously far wider than this. Also it is apparent that supplying ICT infrastructure (computers, software, communications networks, etc.) on its own will not be effective. In the first part of this chapter the inhibitors to, and enablers for, effective ICT implementation in schools were briefly discussed. This led to a discussion of what styles of leadership were most effective. Sheppard's work (2003) highlighted the importance of collaborative leadership supported innovation, risk taking, high morale across the school, team leadership and a sharing culture for successful implementation of ICT. The importance of senior leaders is also supported by Becta (2003) who stressed the benefits of senior leaders who are enthusiastic and visionary about ICT. OfSTED (2005) also noted the importance of the involvement of the headteacher for good ICT leadership, but stressed that it is critical that this should be complemented by effective coordination of ICT. Thus the importance of the role of the ICT coordinator was discussed. However, together with good leadership it was suggested that effective planning involving the production of an ICT policy statement and development planning was essential for effective integration of ICT. Moreover even this is insufficient, for effective integration and effective ICT CPD is needed and this involves good strategic leadership, collegiate work patterns, good technical support and encouragement from senior leadership (Preston 2004). OfSTED (2004b) believed a good combination of in-house training, LEA courses and independent course providers combined with improved resource provision was the most effective way forward with ICT CPD. I would also emphasize the importance of provision that meets the needs of teachers and their schools.

From the literature discussed above, it is apparent that a major factor influencing teachers' use of ICT is their access to ICT facilities. In the Evaluation of the TSW Project, probably the most important and striking change during the Project was in teachers' access to a laptop computer at home. In 2003, home access was available to 91 per cent of teachers in special and primary schools and 74 per cent of teachers in secondary schools, a substantial increase from 2002. This 'ownership of laptops' was obviously reflected in terms of sole access at school, where there were also very high levels of sole access to laptop computers reported in 2003: 86 per cent in special schools, 78 per cent in primary and 74 per cent in secondary. Increased access to the Internet and email was also evident in 2003. Also striking was the amount of money that the primary schools had invested in interactive whiteboards during the Project, to a level where 85 per cent of teachers had some access. Increased availability of ICT is not necessarily reflected in greater use. However, over the course of the year, teachers reported additional daily use of ICT and increased usage of ICT for management and administration tasks. Views of teachers on access to hardware and software that matched their needs were positive and had been strengthened during the Project.

The increased usage and more positive views of ICT may also be due in part to the more proactive roles that leadership were encouraged to take in the project. Leaders were encouraged to devise an action (development) plan and to work within a change framework supported by their school workforce adviser. With the provision of change management training, they largely complied with this directive.

Teachers believed they were competent users of ICT, but aspired to higher levels of competency, as only approximately half felt that they had been trained in all aspects of ICT necessary for their work. However, training appeared to be problematic in that there appeared to be low levels of formal training. Additionally, with respect to the quality of training, levels of satisfaction among teachers were not high. However, during the year of the Project there had been a shift towards a more positive view. More specifically with respect to teachers' confidence, the majority of teachers felt confident in their ability to use ICT appropriately to support teaching and learning. Nonetheless, teachers were less confident in their ability to use ICT for analysing school and pupil performance data. Finally, teachers believed ICT could assist in reducing their workload and in making them more productive. During the year, these views had become more positive. However, as pointed out by some of the teachers in the Project, the benefits of the Project were 'yet to come' as the nature and complexity of the changes would take time to have their full effect. This is particularly true where the use of ICT is involved.

To conclude, the introduction and/or extension of the use of ICT in school settings is usually considered as core to the remodelling process and modernization agenda in schools. From the literature, it would appear that effective ICT implementation is linked to adequate infrastructure and support, leadership style and coordination, effective planning and continuing professional development in ICT. The findings from the TSW Evaluation Project appear to support this view.

Part Four: Modernizing Change: Strategic Perspectives

The final section of the book contains five chapters from international authors who are keen to explore the ways in which modernization and remodelling are playing out. These are invited chapters where our co-authers are stimulated to think about modernization in England and their own setting, and to develop an individual take and a distinctive interpretation of the task we set them (see Chapter 1). These chapters are followed by a concluding chapter by Gunter and Butt which returns to the four 'key questions' posed in the opening chapter. Berkhout engages with the transformation agenda in South Africa and considers the extent to which policy development in other countries has influenced change in the national context; Fitzgerald explores the remodelling of schools and schooling from the perspective of New Zealand, illustrating similarities with the situation currently being experienced in English schools; Smyth and Broad take a historical perspective on the modernization of teacher education in Canada, through a case study of programmes of teacher education in Ontario, to illustrate impacts on the identities of teachers and the creation of new forms of professionalism; Vidovich uses an analytical lens to look at globalization and how the forces associated with this have impacted on education in Australia and elsewhere, affecting teachers' professional identity, teaching and learning, and the need for modernization; whilst Malet continues the globalization theme through an exploration of the educational policies of France and England from a comparative perspective.

Gunter and Butt draw together the themes which have emerged from the preceding sections by asking the fundamental question 'Whither modernization?'. Here the major political claims made for the gains that will accrue from modernization and remodelling are considered against the evidence amassed from schools, teachers, support staff, parents and students. We conclude by asserting that although considerable gains may have been made at the local level in schools, these do not necessarily suggest an overall national system of education and change which is secure.

Chapter 11

Democratization and the remaking of teachers in South African schools

Sarie J. Berkhout

Introduction

The aim of this chapter is to critically engage with the transformation agenda in South Africa and the challenges this poses for teachers and educational leadership. Although initiated in the service of democratization, the transformation agenda has increasingly become influenced by policy development in other countries and imbued with a global marketization and managerialist discourse. The link between the idea of modernization as 'a condensate concept that abridges a range of things to be done: new roles, new work, new power relationships, new values and new employment . . . underpinned by narratives regarding the change imperative, which recognise a need to challenge and abandon practices that no longer meet expectations about the future' (Chapter 1) and transformation will be explored in the first section.

This will be followed by a contextualization of policy-initiated educational transformation in South Africa and an exploration of the growing disjunction between policy texts and education practice. Instead of the anticipated participatory democratic reconstruction of education, teachers that are enmeshed in the habitus of particular contexts and its related power relations (fields) are increasingly seen to be in need of *remaking*, or of being *equipped with skills* to enable the standardization of provision. The notion of remaking teachers derives from what Carrim (2002) sees as the 'new State's desire to cast teachers as constructors of the new democratic order' (p. 317). South African teachers have gradually become recast from being viewed as 'liberators', to being seen as 'facilitators' and eventually 'regulated performers' in terms of the so-called Norms and Standards that describe the seven roles of 'educators' (Jansen 2002, pp. 123–4). These are 'new modes of describing what we do', as teachers learn to talk about 'themselves and their relationships, purposes and motivations in these new ways' (Ball 2003, p. 218).

The initial expectations of democratically constituted school governing bodies (including learners) powerfully contributing to the transformation process are changing, as both teachers and principals gradually learn to experience themselves in terms of new 'scripts'. Teachers find themselves with less real power and increasingly function as part of the top-down chain of decision-making – reduced to acting out their respective roles.

Some of the tensions inherent in the transformation of the education system and the challenges it poses for education leadership will be explored in the final section. Fundamental to the challenges that education leadership faces is the discourse of the modernization of the public sector, where education is seen as part of a fairly general problem with regard to policy delivery. Apart from the legacy of apartheid the public sector is struggling with the delivery of policy change.

Against the background of dynamic change, complexity and diversity, deliberative democratic engagement would seem to be much more conducive to ensure equity in accountability. Managerialist control systems – predominantly based on measureables – would reduce accountability to hierarchies of achievement and deepen existing inequities.

Linking transformation and modernization

Transformation for me initially had a meaning different from modernization, as I saw it embedded in a different basic assumptive set or paradigm. It was very much related to the English restructuring of the 1960s which was underpinned by values of equity and democratic development and aspired to deliver the comprehensive ideal. Transformation in South Africa, contrary to the pre-democracy notion of education renewal (RSA 1992, p. iii) that identified problem areas that required managerial solutions and the determination of the financial implications, symbolizes the quest to build a nation, reconcile its diverse peoples, stabilize the economy and cultivate its newly founded democracy (Waghid 2004a, p. 191).

This notion of transformation was born out of the African National Congress' (ANC 1994) commitment to 'democracy, ensuring the active participation of various interest groups, in particular teachers, parents, workers, students, employers, and the broader community' (p. 4). The governance structures would aim at 'nation building and the eradication of racialism, tribalism, ethnicity and gender considerations as the basis of educational organisation' (ibid., p. 22).

The forerunner to the draft policy framework of the ANC, the National Education Policy Investigation (NEPI 1993), set the scene for a transformative process that would be consultative, participatory and accountable. Waghid (2004a) identifies the three central pillars of transformation as 'increased and broadened participation, responsiveness to societal needs, and partnership and co-operation in governance' (p. 293). He furthermore links the notion to the spirit of democracy and the central precepts of the constitution of respect for human rights, justice, equality, freedom, nation-building and reconciliation (Waghid 2004b, p. 526).

Modernization, for me, referred to a stage in the 'evolution' of humanity embedded in meta-theories of a sequence of phases in social development. Linked to the institutionalization of modern forms of life that characterized the second half of the nineteenth century in Europe it became a rather thorny concept in an ex-colony/developing country with vastly diverse communities and deep social divisions. The concept became associated with essentialist notions of development and *deficit hypothesis* analyses that disparage those institutions and communities not concomitant to modernity, or what Giddens (1991, p. 2) describes as the profound reorganization of time and space that prise social relations free from the hold of specific locales. Modernization is, however, also a concept born of the enlightenment discourse and Kantian notions of enlightened, critical, progressive citizenship aiming at extending the 'public sphere' of participant debate as far and as wide as possible. It encompasses the Habermasian critical ideal that sees modernity as the way that would enable us to work towards the truly democratic society (Norris 2000, p. 27). And in this sense it is closely linked to the transformative ideal of a South African democracy in which schools are expected to play a central role, albeit only after having been themselves transformed to ensure the redress of the legacy of the past. Teachers are expected to abandon cultures and practices of the past and reform their identities in the image of the modern global citizens, or 'universal subject', (Mattson and Harley 2002, p. 284) and educate learners to become citizens of a growing economy. Schools and teachers are, however, enmeshed in habitus and fields of power relations embedded in the past.

Apart from the struggle between tradition and espoused modernity, the economy is increasingly linked to the vagaries of a global free market and the neo-liberalist discourse that creates new tensions. The foundational notions of social participative democracy are increasingly undermined by neo-liberal discourses of competition and efficiency. As Codd (2005a, pp. 195–6) affirms, the 'institutional embodiment of the struggle for citizenship rights: that is to health, education and employment opportunities within a social environment of collective responsibility and national identity' also contrasts in South Africa with 'the emphasis on individual rights to property ownership, legal protection and market freedom, within a social environment of enterprise and competition'. Rather than social justice, global economic competitiveness and skills development are becoming the driving force that shapes educational transformation. Both transformation and modernization have thereby become part of a similar policy development whereby 'global economic success with a measure of social justice' (Fergusson 2000, p. 207) constitute the main fare of the progressive agenda in education.

Modernization, shaped by the need for redress and extensive policy development, has evolved around this notion whereby not only economic redress but also educational redress determines the discourse. Similar to the word 'modernization' that has become a hype phrase in England, 'empowerment' has become the shaping force in the local discourse in South Africa. It is a concept, however, still very much underpinned by notions of substantive power, rather than reflecting an understanding of the relational dimension of power. This shapes the discourse to focus on what could be 'given' or done by the state rather than as the active engagement of policy actors. Olssen *et al.* (2004), in their Foucauldian approach to education policy studies, argue: 'power is not a substance, nor a mysterious property, but a certain type of relation between individuals, and the source of the constitution of their subjectivity' (p. 24). This, as will be argued, is increasingly becoming visible in the tensions created by the way education governance, the curriculum and assessment are being 'transformed' and the need to 'remake' teachers. In a country with a vast array of different locales and contexts, from urbanized, highly competitive, school environments to rural traditional schools with poorly qualified teachers and resources, this poses major challenges for leadership on all levels of the system.

Policy change in South Africa – contextualizing modernization

The past 12 years have seen the major restructuring of the formal structures of the South African education system. Expectations built on notions of an all-powerful apartheid state that constructed an unjust education system were transferred to the new state and its promise to transform society into a more just and equitable system. Restructuring the education system was embarked upon immediately after the transfer of power, and following consultative processes legislation was promulgated and the state embarked on one of the most comprehensive 'modernizing' ventures imaginable. However, education transformation in South Africa, as Ozga (2005) postulates for 'travelling' policies, remains embedded in the legacy of the past, and the mediation of policy is localized according to the practices and cultures of different contexts and discourses. As the restructuring of the South African education system is a vast project that leaves little untouched, this background merely serves to sketch in the broad outlines of some of the tensions and concomitant challenges for leadership in schools.

The transformation of the South African education system during the 1990s can, according to Parker (2002, pp. 17–18), be seen as 'three distinct phases' – a fourth stage was initiated when during the course of 2000 '. . . a number of bodies became operational' in the implementation of the myriad of new legislation. In the first, or pre-1994, phase education was characterized by what he typifies as 'structural stasis and cultural malaise'. Although policy initiatives flourished, the nineteen separate departments for four racial groups (Blacks, Coloureds, Asians and Whites) and ten ethnic groups (four ex-'independent' states Ciskei, Venda, Bophuthatswana and Transkei and six ex-'self-governing' states Gazankulu, Kangwane, Kwazulu, Kwandebele, Qwaqwa and Lebowa) were stymied as their legitimacy and authority were shattered. This was followed by a second phase which 'saw the manifestation of policy in the emergence of new structures, roleplayers and authoritative bodies able to establish commissions and task teams with a legislative authority grounded in the interim Constitution' (Parker 2002, p. 18). A national, and nine provincial, departments of education were established as well as several prominent statutory bodies, such as the South African Qualifications Authority (SAQA), the

Education Labour Relations Council (ELRC) and the South African Council for Educators (SACE). Several White Papers and reports on higher education and the governance and funding of schools followed. The third phase 'was part of a more general reappraisal of policy within the context of the Growth, Development and Redistribution (GEAR) strategy and its far tighter fiscal framework'.

The fourth, or implementation, phase saw an increasing emphasis on accountability at all levels of the system and the establishment of *Umalusi* responsible for the assurance of the quality of general and further education and training; the Higher Education Quality Committee (HEQC); and several Sector Education and Training Authorities (SETAs). Some of the additional developments to precipitate this were the development of a 'Whole School Evaluation System', a new teacher appraisal system partly linked to performance rewards, a quality assurance system for continuous assessment in schools and a potentially compulsory national education programme for school principals. The growing concerns with regard to the delivery of policy, as well as the global engrossment with performance management, are increasingly influencing policy development in South Africa. State departments are required to develop performance-based management programmes – a national investigation into service delivery as well as the privatization of semi-state service delivery institutions can also be seen as a shift towards the modernization of the workforce.

Closer to the lives of teachers and schools was the impact of the implementation of an outcomes-based curriculum in 1996, *Curriculum 2005*, which has since been revised to become the National Revised Curriculum Statement. In the rush to transform the system the strategic and tactical complexity of the role of an outcomes-based curriculum was hugely underestimated and, as Jansen (n.d., pp. 46–51) argued, could be seen as merely symbolic – as it could be announced that the discriminating curriculum of apartheid was now something of the past. It was, however, a curriculum that not only changed the traditional conception of subjects to learning areas but also implied a new pedagogy and assessment practice. The concomitant absence of learning materials challenged most teachers' experience and courage. The initial implementation of the new curriculum was furthermore accompanied by the redeployment and rationalization of teachers to ensure the equal distribution of staff according to ratios of 1:35 in secondary and 1:40 in primary schools. Large numbers of teachers, mostly experienced, were retrenched and left the system. Schools located in privileged areas were able to charge school fees that enabled them to employ additional staff, whereas the traditional disadvantaged schools did not gain sufficient numbers of pupils to realize the expected relief. This policy change translated into a system embedded in diverse, historically patterned contexts that elicited diverse responses that often led to contradictory effects.

The vast national and provincial overhaul of the education system left the material manifestation at institutional level and the habitus–field relationships, to use Bourdieu's (1990) conceptionalization, largely intact. Apart from a few, so-called, ex-Model C schools (historically for White learners) that have become fully integrated, the geographic spread of schools linked to the historical racial segregation of residential areas remains the same. Although indicators, such as the 'teacher:learner ratio' and 'per capita expenditure', changed at the school level the same group of people pattern the habitus and field of particular schools, perpetuating existing inequities.

The wave upon wave of policy change and reform sorely challenged leadership in schools and 2004 saw large-scale investigations into the morale and workload of teachers.

Tensions shaping the democratization discourse and the challenges for education leadership

Democratizing education against the background of the legacy of apartheid posed major challenges to leadership in schools. Instead of the anticipated participatory democratic reconstruction of education, teachers enmeshed in the habitus of particular contexts are increasingly seen to be in need of remaking, or of being equipped with new skills, to enable the standardization of provision. While transformation aims at enabling the realization of a more desirable (equal) or democratized society, the education policy text represents the formal or textual restructuring of these interactive patterns. There are, however, more complex interactions and patterns than those defined in the already complicated policy texts that play out amongst various role-players in different fields of interaction, which often recreate and reshape policy intentions.

The habitus and interactive fields of the people at the various levels and spaces of the education system are decisive in interpreting and acting on the policy, including the curriculum. The actors, or groups of actors, at the different levels of the policy process should rather be regarded as filtering or mediating the process interactively within the discursively developed historical context, or as a matter of habit within a particular field (Lingard and Christie 2003). This implies that the functioning of the education system is based on what Bourdieu sees as habitual patterns of interaction embedded within fields that vary across the different local settings.

I want to follow Foucault who, when describing schools, does not focus on:

> the ideals of education or its hidden class functions but the detailed organization of the (monitorial) school as a purpose built pedagogical environment assembled from a mix of physical and moral elements; special architectures; devices for organizing space and time; body techniques; practices of surveillance and supervision; pedagogical relationships; procedures of administration and examination. (Hunter 1996, p. 147)

This speaks to Ball's (1990a) interest in educational sites as generators of a historically specific (modern) discourse, that is, as sites in which certain modern validations of, and exclusions from, the 'right to speak' are generated. Education sites are not only subject to discourse 'but (are) also centrally involved in the propagation and selective dissemination of discourses, the "social appropriation" of discourses' (p. 3). Educational institutions control the access of individuals to various kinds of discourse 'in its distribution, in what it permits and what it prevents, it follows the lines laid down by social differences, conflicts and struggles. Every educational system is a political means of maintaining or modifying the appropriateness of discourses with the knowledge and power they bring with them' (ibid.).

The initial expectations of participation that originated in the democratic discourse of the struggle contributed powerfully to the transformation process and the shaping of the institutions to deliver on policy promises. However, the discourse around education is changing. Participation is reduced to a formal consultation process with insufficient time to respond, whilst school governing bodies are gradually stripped of real powers and are increasingly functioning as part of a top-down chain of command – often being reduced to taking up additional administrative responsibility. I want to argue that leadership challenges in this transformation are embedded in the tensions between what can be seen as modernization and the historically developed plural school contexts in which teachers engage with learners. School contexts vary in South Africa not only in the variety of geographic spaces (rural and urban schools), language and ethnic difference (11 official languages are acknowledged), class difference and the legacy of racial separation that imbue most of the education discourses, but also with regard to the impact of globalization. Teachers, considered as the lynchpin in this transformation, are generally argued to lack capacity and to require 'remodelling'.

The implementation of the Schools Act 1996 (RSA 1996) (and its consequent amendments) can be seen as the major shaping force for the democratization of education in South Africa. Against the background of the racially (Whites, Blacks, Coloureds and Asians) and ethnically based differentiation in the education system, this Act had to ensure a uniform system for the organization, management and financing of schools and was 'motivated by the principles of inclusion, equity and redress' (Sayed and Soudien 2005, p. 115). The implementation of this act should, however, also be read against the background of an international tendency to decentralize or change the way schools work (Dyer and Rose 2005, p. 108). In South Africa it was furthermore shaped by the 'constructs put on these by the policies of inclusion and decentralization that were negotiated during the establishment of the new post-apartheid state' (ibid., p. 116). This meant that the introduction of a system of decentralization during the 1980s, for the White sub-system of education to increase parental participation based on the rhetoric of privatization and competition amongst schools, vied with notions of democratic participation and equal education for all. The so-called Model C schools, which were constituted on similar principles to the quasi-market related policies deployed in England during the same period, became the visible symbols of educational privilege and inequality. The notion of what has become known as ex-Model C schools has become a label that rhetorically shapes the discursive practice about access to schooling as well as the working environment of teachers. The Schools Act 1966 (RSA 1996) gave parents the responsibility for governing the schools their children attend through the establishment of school governing bodies (representing parents, teachers and learners, as well as members of the support staff). Apart from determining the school's language policy, maintaining the school's property, paying for services, purchasing textbooks and determining the school's extra-mural programme, the School Governing Body has the right to levy school fees, recommend teacher appointments and appoint those paid from school fees.

Ten years after its inception the deepening of the divide between the privileged schools and the rest has become increasingly visible. It has seen a commission of inquiry as well as amendments to the Act to gain back some of the powers accorded to schools. Decentralization is based on the redistribution of power and a shift of responsibilities and it has been argued that the benefits claimed only manifest in societies with strongly entrenched democratic values and a well-educated population. The expectations with regard to equal and uniform education for all have become imbued with notions idealizing the ex-Model C schools. Because of the ability of these schools to employ additional teachers, as well as provide better resources, their concept has become influential. Contrary to the modernization project in England, which is very much focused on the provision of additional support to alleviate the burden of teachers, inequalities in resource provision fundamentally drive the discourse of education transformation. Although the national and provincial structures provide for a major overhaul of the system, they have left the education institutions largely untouched – much as they did during the apartheid era. The geographic spread of schools is still linked to the designated living areas and embedded in local cultural patterns implying that although national indicators signify that state provision of education has radically changed, the same group of people pattern the same schools under the same conditions. One of the teachers in Smit's research (2000) put it thus:

> I actually believe that it widens the gap, because your better teachers, you know your superior teachers can have an absolute ball, which means your independent school teachers, your teachers that are better qualified, that have better experience, know about lateral thinking, . . . they know where to hold on to the syllabus.   (p. 77).

Apart from the additional resources for schools that remain the privilege of schools able to raise substantive school fees, ex-Model C schools have become constitutive of a discourse that scripts teachers' ability to cope with transformation. This creates a fundamental tension similar to that in England (see Chapter 1), which has 'sought to extend public funding of education and to enable inclusion and equity', and also 'to extend private (semi-private in South Africa) schools to keep the middle classes in the system provision of education, and so to enable differentiation and competition'.

Apart from the resource difference amongst schools, the duality of responsibility or accountability in the system is bound to influence teachers' working lives. To whom will they be held accountable – the governing body or the state? These relationships are strongly regulated on a national level where the Teaching and Learning Resource Committee (TLRC) and the unions act prominently, participating in education policymaking as well as issuing teachers' employment contracts. The decentralized power of school governing bodies does not include any powers with regard to the curriculum and assessment, which could be seen to be the core activities of schooling, but works by means of reward systems. District offices, which have taken shape in South Africa on the basis of delegated authority from the provincial education department, are seen predominantly in terms of the support they are supposed to accord schools. Narsee (2005) argues, however, that 'the support provided by districts to schools reflects that which is intended by government, rather than that experienced by schools' (p. 234). Her case study reveals the tensions between the agenda of the state and the needs of the school, which have implications for accountability as districts 'straddle the tensions between the policy, support and management roles expected of them' (p. 234). In the South African context the historical experience and contestation of state officials as 'inspectors' furthermore clouds the tension between management and support, with concomitant implications for accountability.

Parents whom teachers often criticize for being illiterate are accorded the right to participate in the governing of schools, creating another source of conflict. Contrary to this, teachers themselves are not given the same participatory opportunity, especially with regard to the development and implementation of Curriculum 2005 (cf. Smit 2000):

> The qualifications framework was already written in blood and we were told beforehand that we would have inputs into that . . . But the point was we had already been notified that these documents that we have been told we were going to be a part of, had already been written. So that was when I sort of backed off and did not become involved any more. . . .   (p. 73)

Carrim (2002) argues that teachers' different, often conflicting, roles have 'theoretical and ideological roots in the history of apartheid education' (p. 12). The irony is that whilst the intention is to reprofessionalize the teachers (or develop particular conceptions of professionalism), the effect is that 'teachers seem to be increasingly proletarianised, bureaucratically controlled and the multiplicity of their actual identities [is] misrecognised' (p. 309). Teachers are caught in the tensions and anxiety of transition – they want to work in new ways but are trapped by the legacy of the past. Lewin *et al*'s (2002, pp. 11–13) argument that teachers are strongly influenced by their own teacher experience and role models links this development closely with Bourdieu's notions of habitus and field. Teachers who continue to work in a particular environment, notwithstanding the transformation reflects historically developed power relations and systems patterns (i.e. timetable, classroom spaces and physical facilities), will continue working according to their deeply ingrained patterns of work.

School leadership in the decentralized context of South African education has become reduced to financial and conflict management, leaving teachers little time to become leaders of quality teaching and learning. Decentralization, it seems, 'worked most effectively, but not exclusively, in societies with strongly entrenched democratic values and well-educated populations' (Bray as cited by Dyer and Rose 2005, p. 108). This has the implication that although regulative audits and the concurrent paraphernalia are only now being deployed in the schooling system, the delivery of policy and the discursive practices are having a similar effect of creating a differentiated hierarchy in the education workforce (see Chapter 1).

Although education policy development in South Africa is basically driven from a democratic participatory model, Curriculum 2005 was generally experienced as a cascade top-down policy which went contrary to the expectations of both teachers and the public. Indeed, within the context of a funding policy based on equal teacher: student ratios (and the concomitant retrenchments and redeployments across all education sectors) the policy can only be seen to have contributed to the uncertainty, and even alienation, of teachers. An initially positive start made way for intransigence, unwillingness to cooperate, the entrenchment of long held beliefs, attitudes and fearfulness.

Outcomes-based education that underpins curriculum transformation in South Africa represents a shift in the equity debate to an education system that promises equal outcomes (outputs) and the absence of failures and dropouts. The main, and often the only, output measure featured in the education debate on the results of the education system remains the historically inherited 'matric exam' (colloquial for the Senior Certificate that follows the school-leaving examinations at the conclusion of 12 years of schooling). An annual outcry increasingly demands accountability from teachers with regard to matric results. The poor physical condition of many schools is acknowledged, but arguments still rage over the shocking quality of teacher education that threatens the pupils' future and that of the country. People look to teachers for reasons for the continuing failure of thousands of learners who sit for the Senior Certificate examination. Fuel for the fire is provided by reports of absenteeism, lost teaching hours, time spent away from learners and many other valid accusations that make the professional teacher the easy scapegoat for the failure of the education system to deliver equally to all learners.

The Senior Certificate examination, which in 2008 will be replaced by the new Further Education and Training Certificate (FETC), remains the dominant indicator and symbolic driver of discourses about the performance of schools. Although teachers had to implement the new outcomes-based curriculum, they have to revert to the existing curriculum for the last three grades of schooling (Grades 10–12). The need to ensure high pass rates based on training students to sit for the examination contrasts strongly with the tenets of the demands of the outcomes-based curriculum and continuous assessment. So although teachers are expected to be rescripted as transformative, as far as the school context is concerned, the old curriculum remains the most important power shaping both discourses and teacher actions.

Although the pre-1994 debate, as already mentioned, focused only on measurable input-indicators (e.g. teacher:learner ratio and per capita expenditure) which symbolized the failure of the education system, outcomes-based education shifted the focus of this debate to a promise of equal outputs. The achievement of equal outputs would be realized by transforming the education process itself, so that not only would the traditional 'irrelevant' subjects be left out, but the design and construction of learning opportunities themselves would fundamentally change. Teachers would be able to act in a more professional way and to plan, design and mediate locally relevant learning opportunities appropriate to the needs and learning pace of every learner – which would assure the attainment of equal outcomes by all. This called for the complete rescripting of teacher roles and actions in a context where few of the less visible, or implicit, structures changed. Reports on the training and workshops offered generally viewed them as inadequate. The words of one of the teachers in Smit's (2000) research sums it up:

> and then I must say that courses that I have attended where we were introduced to the outcomes based education situation, we just found that the people who conducted the courses, really it was of a very poor standard. . . .
>
> (p. 76)

Teachers' own sense of plausibility causes them to 'develop a strategic mimicry of the policy expectations which are counter-forces to the traditional conceptions of teaching, learning that teachers themselves believe in' (Mattson and Harley 2002, p. 284).

Notwithstanding the fact that the outcomes-based education approach represents the kind of fundamental transformation required in South African education, some serious practical and systems-related considerations have not yet been addressed. Some of the less obvious patterns and structures within education systems that are seldom analysed in terms of the tensions between the proposed ideal are:

- the tension between the formal structures for governance, as reflected in the formal distribution of authority, and the other less visible power relations embedded in local contexts or habitus and fields (e.g. traditional leadership, micro-politics);
- resource allocation patterns that are reinterpreted and reshaped in particular contexts to perpetuate patterns of dependency. The discursive practices surrounding ex-Model C Schools and their resources perpetuate notions relating quality education with resources;

- learner access and distribution patterns; where the intended freedom of choice and access in a context of poverty, illiteracy and unemployment is shaped by 'absence of coercion', rather than active 'freedom to' (cf. Olssen *et al* 2004, p. 184);
- the extent to which curriculum structures and patterns of attainment engage with different cultural, social and symbolic capitals;
- spatial (institutional geographic) patterns (facilities and learning/teaching material);
- discursive patterns/structures, such as the tension between the historically inherited matric exam and the new curriculum; and continuous assessment, with expectations of making failure something of the past, whilst incorporating the 'pass one, pass all' ideals of the struggle;
- habitus and field-bounded engagement with temporal and rhythmic patterns of schools, such as those imposed by timetables and progression in the curriculum (or what Lynch (1989) in her work on the hidden curriculum called 'processing in batches').

Against a background of increased attrition rates amongst teachers and the serious impact of HIV/Aids, research commissioned by the Education Labour Relations Council (Phurutse 2005; Hall *et al.* 2005) on factors affecting teaching and learning in schools and their impact on job satisfaction, morale, workload and HIV/Aids, reveals serious dissatisfaction and despondency amongst teachers. A major issue is that the waves of transformation never seem to settle.

Of particular interest is the focus on the increase in teachers' workload that is ascribed to the various policy changes in education, findings which point in the same direction as those revealed by research undertaken in England. Teachers in South Africa should, according to Hall *et al.* (2005), 'be released from administrative tasks and other activities that increase their workload and distract their attention from teaching' (p. 29). The past two years has in the meantime seen the introduction of a semi-performance-based system of appraisal in schools (integrated quality management system) whereby 1 per cent of teacher remuneration will be based on performance appraisal, pointing the school workforce in a similar direction to higher education.

Leadership: towards more deliberative democratic engagement with policy

Instead of a serious analysis of the structures or patterns of power in education systems and their relatedness to the different local contexts and discourses, education transformation in South Africa has become infused with 'apartheid's trope'. A trope's 'specific function is to compress and inscribe historically developed collective understandings in a very short space'; it therefore reduces the complexity and contentiousness of events in favour of 'what everyone knows'

(Townsley 2001, p. 99). It is high time for South Africa to move beyond what Kraak and Young (n.d.) call

> the political culture forged in struggle and opposition in South Africa prior to 1994 and the very different political culture that is needed to underpin a high-performance system of education and training in a democracy that can 'deliver' skills and knowledge needed by the majority of the population.
>
> (p. 9)

Thinking about leadership in education, I would like to argue for a move away from 'mainstream organization theory that assumes and takes for granted the existence of organizations as material entities "out there" in the world' (Westwood and Linstead 2001, p. 4). This has the implication of the *model* not representing the organization, but the *organization* as representation of the model: 'the construction of the object results from the application of a theory to the real world; the constructed object exists (has sense) only in relation to this theory' (Degot as cited in Westwood and Linstead 2001, p. 4). It furthermore entails that 'organization has no autonomous, stable or structural status outside of the text that constitutes it. The text of organization itself consists of a shifting network of signifiers in dynamic relations of difference' (ibid.). It is not a scientific argument about the more accurate, rigorous, clear, consistent or parsimonious representation of school as an organizational reality, but is part of what Chia and King (2001) see as a fundamental rethinking.

One of the predominant arguments in education policy discourse in South Africa focuses on what is uncritically described as 'the realities of' the legacy of apartheid, these 'realities' being expressed in terms of statistical indicators (per capita expenditure; student:teacher ratios and school-leaving examination results for the various racially provided sub-systems) that originated during the apartheid era from the contestation of education and the state's representation of education. This notion of 'realities', linked to the ex-Model C school symbol, permeates the critique of education transformation and shapes school leadership thinking and stories in a variety of contexts. This imposes constraints on the play of other signifiers in the 'text of organization' and freezes other meanings that could inscribe alternative order on the flow of events in schools.

Claims for effectiveness become discursively shaped by the underpinning notions of competitiveness and profitability, with schools attaining a sense of reality that is an equated progression towards the 'ideal school' – 100 per cent matric pass rate, excellent facilities (especially computers) and school governing bodies appointing 'good teachers' (trainers for the matric exam) – with no concern for social justice. In many less well-endowed schools this has the effect of them powerlessly awaiting the improvement of the physical facilities and the 'equipping (of) teachers with skills' necessary to make the school successful. The inappropriateness of this becomes clear when the 'reality of school' is questioned and seen merely as 'contingent assemblages put together under "blind" historical circumstances' (Hunter 1996, p. 147). When it is understood that schools do not have autonomous, stable or structured organizational status outside of the inter-active narratives and texts that constitute them, it becomes necessary to focus on the shaping discourses or 'the meta-language of organisation which deals with the ontological prior process of fixing, forming, framing and bounding rather than with the content or outcome of such processes' (Chia and King 2001, p. 326).

Rethinking schools as discursive constructions where meanings are emergent, deferred and dispersed (Westwood and Linstead 2001) opens up a critical creative space for school leaders – in the interest of social justice and transformation – to engage with competing discourses and narratives.

Conclusion

South African educational policy development is strongly inclined to follow the English example. This could be ascribed to the colonial tradition, but also to partnerships and research agreements across our national boundaries. South African policy development is also strongly influenced by English consultants and civil servants. In this regard 'modernization' is no exception. Whereas transformation in South Africa is still strongly based in democratic and empowerment rhetoric, the influence of new-liberalist thinking is absorbed without realizing the implications for democracy.

Similar to Gunter and Butt's argument in Chapter 1, freedom of choice became one of the leading values underpinning democratic transformation. Yet, the manner in which this plays out increasingly deepens the inequities amongst different groups. The supporting rhetoric of school improvement merely benefits those environments that can afford more resources, whether physical or human. High-achieving schools deliver on the promise of global competitiveness, but schools in disadvantaged areas remain captured. Efforts to improve schools by means of additional training of teachers merely result in deprofessionalizing teaching. Not only because the waves of reforms require the remaking of teachers, but also because it is assumed that this can be done through the provision of one-week workshops.

Modernization, where, on the one hand, power is increasingly centralized by the state (curriculum and assessment) and, on the other, decentralized through local management, recreates megalithic control bureaucracies while claiming the opposite. Progressively rolling out alternative manners of acting in schools very seldom takes cognizance of the complexities of human dispositions and historically established power relations. Instead of allowing for democratic spaces of engagement and the mediation of meaning in the best interest of learners, actors are controlled according to standardized checklists. In a context of individualized performance management, teachers' unions and professional organizations increasingly lose their collective bargaining power. As the new-liberalist discourse of competition and agency is internalized, teachers become scripted actors serving a global economy and its rhetoric of blame.

Chapter 12

Remodelling schools and schooling, teachers and teaching: a New Zealand perspective

Tanya Fitzgerald

Introduction

The educational reform agenda and the resultant restructuring of schools in New Zealand has proceeded with marked similarity to England (Thrupp 2001; Robertson and Dale 2002). Since 1989, schools have been subject to widespread and constant changes that are premised on fiscal efficiency and organizational effectiveness that has shifted responsibility and accountability for schooling from the state to schools; from centre to periphery. Since these reforms were initiated almost two decades ago, schools (as organizations) and teachers (as professionals) have, as this chapter will argue, incrementally been the focus of forms of managerialism that have sought to remodel their educational purposes and professional practices.

Although the reform of the school workforce has not proceeded with the same degree of 'efficiency' as in England, this is not to suggest that modernization and remodelling is absent from the New Zealand landscape. While at this point in time this explicit language is largely omitted from policy rhetoric, remodelling practices that have functioned to effect structural changes to schools and contractual changes to teachers' professional activities have implicitly produced an unambiguous level of workforce reform that has reformed schools and schooling, teachers and teaching. As a direct consequence, the focus by the state and its agencies on ways in which schools are organized, led and managed, the regulation of teaching and teachers' work as well as increased emphasis on pupil outcomes are central components of the remodelling agenda that seeks to ensure the insistent demands of the global marketplace and knowledge economy are simultaneously understood and met. In similar ways to practices in England, workforce reform has been underpinned by the modernization of schools and schooling and the consequent modernization of the teaching profession. In multiple ways therefore, New Zealand, at the geographical periphery, continues to transport and rework policies and practices from its ideological centre.

In the first phase of workforce reform, the rhetoric of self-management was co-opted to effect a number of structural changes that aligned schools with the demands of the market. This initial remodelling of the management and administration of New Zealand schools, under the aegis of educational reform, positioned schools as objects of the state agenda. The structural shift in relocating accountability and responsibility from the centre to the local school was a necessary prerequisite to the second phase of remodelling that shifted the focus of schooling and teachers' work from inputs and process to outcomes and product (Olssen *et al.* 2004). In this second phase, the introduction of regulation and performance management increasingly placed emphasis on public accountability of teachers via the creation of a managed profession (Codd 2005a). Once this reorganization was accomplished, attention turned to implementing strategies to align pupil and teacher performance to ensure their 'fit' with the global marketplace (Ozga 2000a and b; Blackmore and Thomson 2004). Accordingly, the radical transformation of ways in which New Zealand schools were managed, led and governed introduced new forms of control and accountability that increasingly adopted the tenets of commercialism (such as schools marketing their 'services') that repositioned parents and students as consumers of a product.

Distinctively evident across all stages of the reform process is the influence of managerialism that concentrated on systems, procedures, policies and practices that permeated the structural reorganization of schools (Fergusson 2000). Thus, the architecture of remodelling was founded on the re-formation of the purposes and structure of schools and schooling and the reprofessionalization of teachers. More recently, concerns about teacher recruitment and retention have stimulated the contractual remodelling of teachers' professional work and activities that has the worrying potential to effect irrevocable changes to the school workforce.

This chapter is a departure from previous accounts of educational reform and modernization that have adopted a historical-political approach. That is, these accounts have emphasized change in government or political ideology to examine the interface with shifting education policy (e.g. Codd 2005a; Thrupp 2005). While I do not disagree with previous analysis, my intention is to focus on two distinct phases that underpinned the remodelling agenda and proceeded in two unambiguous phases.

The first phase, 1989–95, I label the 'functional period', to denote the conversion of schools to efficient and effective functioning self-managing business units that competed in the marketplace for students and resources. In this period, managerialism was the vehicle for the introduction of the practices of new public management that redefined how schools were organized and operated (Boston *et al.* 1996) and modernization was directed at reform within schools and the intensification of the work of teachers and pupils. Thus, schools were located as the 'problem' to be remedied through reform, restructuring and regulation.

The second phase, 1996–present, I label the 'production period' in which the performance and outputs of teachers and students were restructured in order that schools and schooling made 'a bigger difference for all students' (Ministry of Education 2005). The unassailable rhetoric of modernization was co-opted to produce teachers (as current workers) and students (as future workers) with the necessary skills, knowledge and abilities to meet the demands of the global marketplace. In this second phase, teachers were constructed as the 'problem' and hence subjected to mechanisms such as performance agreements and performance management to control and regulate their professional work (Gunter 2001; Codd 2005b).

This chapter traces these two phases of modernization and argues that the external reform of school management, administration and organizational structure was a necessary precondition for the modernization of teaching and teachers' work. Across these two phases there is, as I will argue, a shift in attention from structures to standards that converge around a number of key issues that are fundamental to the remodelling agenda: the commodification and marketization of schools and schooling (Apple 2001); a focus on the efficient and effective performativity of teachers and students (Codd 2005b); the intensification of political control over curriculum; the assessment of learning and the teaching profession itself (Fiske and Ladd 2000); increasing demands for evidence-based policy and practice in a climate in which reform is rarely based on evidence; and the constant exclusion of the voices of teachers (Ball 2003; Whitty 2000) and students (Thomson and Gunter 2006) from policy.

Managerialism: the functional period

As in many other Western countries, educational administration in New Zealand was subject to widespread systemic reform in the late 1980s. Capper and Munro (1990) have argued that a major factor in the call for reform was the high level of public dissatisfaction with teachers and their professional work. Accordingly, 'the need for reform' (Government of New Zealand 1988, p. iv) to ensure 'our children . . . receive the education to which they are entitled' (ibid., p. iii) was articulated as the antidote for this discontent. Curiously, rather than being directly concerned with the 'problem' of teachers and teaching, the then Labour Government, acting on the direct advice of the Treasury (New Zealand Treasury 1987), proceeded to implement structural and organizational changes to schools and schooling. This initial period of educational reform (1989–95) was characterized by the introduction of the architecture of remodelling that radically transformed ways in which schools were led, managed and governed, the curriculum, skills and knowledge that were imparted, the work of teachers in classrooms and staffrooms and the relationship between schools and their community and schools and government. Schools were thus transformed to function and compete in the educational (and later global) marketplace that reconstituted communities as clients or consumers and education as a (private) product (Codd 2005a). Educational reform was predicated on an interventionist model whereby government actively and deliberately introduced a 'new system' (Government of New Zealand 1988, p. 1) that would 'result in more immediate delivery of resources to schools, more parental and community involvement and greater teacher responsibility' (Government of New Zealand 1988, p. iv). Accordingly, this 'new system' was designed to be 'a good mixture of responsiveness, flexibility and accountability [that] placed decision making as close as possible to the point of implementation' (ibid., p. iii). The rejection of the previous system was popularized via a discourse that suggested that the 'need for reform' was both justified and 'generally accepted' (ibid., p. iv). Change was inevitably presented and delivered as a commitment to unshackle the past and engage with the 'new' and an orientation to secure 'our future' (ibid., p. iii) through the introduction of devolution and delegation, standards and accountability, flexibility and choice, innovation and responsiveness.

This first phase of educational reform included the introduction of site-based management, increased responsibility and accountability of schools for pupil outcomes, fiscal efficiency, curriculum innovation particularly in the areas of literacy, numeracy and IT, increased marketing and marketization of schools to attract (and retain) local pupils, entrepreneurial activities to lessen the impact of reduced government spending, and devolution of school governance to the local community. With a similar mandate to OfSTED, the Education Review Office (ERO) inspected, audited and reported publicly on schools. These reforms delivered 'marked changes in structures and organization' (Government of New Zealand 1988, p. 39) that reconceptualized education as 'unavoidably part of the market economy' (New Zealand Treasury 1987, Vol. 1, p. 133) and as a market commodity subject (Smyth 1993; Thrupp 2001). Primarily, the relationship between the state and schools, teachers and parents, teachers and the state and school and community was irrevocably altered.

The shift in responsibility from centre (government) to periphery (schools) was accompanied by a contradictory discourse. On the one hand, site-based management relocated decisions about schools and schoolings from a national platform to the 'local' whereby the governance of schools was under the auspices of the community. Yet, on the other hand, by repositioning education as a private commodity for consumption, the 'national' and 'global' marketplace dominated and consequently the 'local' did not assume the same level of attention. In effect, education has become another product on the market dominated by consumer choice and consumption practices – in much the same way as DVDs, iPods, cars or cheese. Schools therefore were a function of the market, and consumers (parents) were afforded a level of choice regarding which school to send their children to. As has been commented elsewhere, those parents who did not have the necessary cultural and economic capital in the educational marketplace were not able to exercise their choice about which schools to enrol their children in (see, for example, Whitty *et al.* 1997; Apple 2001). The politics of choice were raced, classed and gendered whereby the privileged (Pakeha/white, middle class and male) could ostensibly gain a competitive advantage for their children via their school and schooling (Gewirtz *et al.* 1995; Robertson and Dale 2002).

From 1991 onwards, attention turned to restructuring and reforming curriculum and assessment in order that 'education would deliver the skills and attitudes required for New Zealand to compete in an increasingly competitive international economy' (Ministry of Education 1991, p. 2). The New Zealand Curriculum Framework (NZCF) that was introduced identified seven essential learning areas which contained specified achievement objectives that were measured against eight clearly defined levels for each of the predetermined strands of each subject level. Learning outcomes dictated what was to be achieved and assessments were directly related to standards that specified outcomes. In other words, the function of schools and schooling was not centred on the learning process but on outcomes; the product. The structure and content of the NZCF was linked with 'relevant' knowledge and skills (connected with employment) that also identified and labelled the characteristics of future citizens (Peters and Marshall 2004). Not only was curriculum and assessment standardized, so too was the work of teachers. The NZCF was non-negotiable, thereby future-proofing the curriculum (Ministry of Education 1993). Or, did the NZCF in fact teacher-proof the curriculum? Could teachers become more effective if told what to teach and what to assess? These changes provided impetus for the public scrutiny of teachers and their work that was one of the hallmarks of the modernization agenda.

Although *Tomorrow's Schools* (Government of New Zealand 1988) promised a level of local participation in decisions about curriculum, there were few, if any, opportunities for teachers to respond to the needs of their community. And while the intention may have been for education to produce students with the necessary skills, knowledge and abilities to contribute to the economy and global marketplace, in effect our schools and schooling became a marketable service. The production of new global citizens, global consumers and global workers stimulated the globalization of education; education was repositioned as a major export product. Hence, teachers in schools functioned to produce students with the necessary skills, knowledge and abilities for the global marketplace. Arguably, the function of schools to produce citizens able to participate in a democratic society (Apple 2001; Codd 2005b) had been subordinated by the market demand to produce global citizens able to function in a globalized world.

Codd (2005b) correctly asserts that the growth in export education was not one of the planned effects of the reform and restructuring of education. The consequent commercialization of schools and schooling in terms of the national and global marketplace should not have been unanticipated. The essence of educational reform was to locate schools as a function of the market and subject to consumer choice and demand (Smyth 1993). As a product, one of the direct consequences of this repositioning and marketization of schools and schooling is that this product has been projected onto the global arena (Fiske and Ladd 2000; Singh *et al.* 2005). Not only was education now a global product but so too were the skills required for production and distribution.

The life cycle of any marketable commodity is to serve the demands of both local (national) and international consumers. Education, as a product, operated no differently in a quasi-market. Reduced expenditure on education prompted schools to focus on entrepreneurship as a way of increasing their financial viability. This involved initiatives such as increasing voluntary parental contributions, corporate sponsorship and school rebranding (for example, Bairds Intermediate in South Auckland was renamed Bairds Mainfreight Intermediate after securing sponsorship from a haulage company), acceptance of curriculum materials that were designed, developed and printed by local commercial companies interested in securing the attention (and spending power) of students (for example, McDonald's), involvement with government contracts designed to secure change within schools, and the international marketing of schools to attract full fee-paying students. International students in New Zealand schools are a billion-dollar industry that has created up to 20,000 jobs (Deloitte New Zealand 2006) and these fees are used by schools for new buildings, resources (such as computers), more teachers and to supplement the operational funding provided by government. A recent report documented that there were 12,789 international students in New Zealand schools; of these 94 per cent were enrolled in secondary schools and 6 per cent in primary schools (Deloitte New Zealand 2006).[1] The recent reduction in numbers of international students (reported as 15,259 by the Education Review Office 2003) can only rebound to the financial detriment of schools.

Unsurprisingly, government now places a levy on each school according to the number of fee-paying student enrolments[2] (ibid.) and since 2002 has introduced regulatory control over schools and their provision of care for international students (Education Review Office 2003; Ministry of Education 2002a). This has created a paradoxical situation: on the one hand, schools have been forced to engage in entrepreneurial activities as a direct result of the educational reforms, and those schools that are 'successful' are therefore, on the other hand, required to pay levies to government.

There can be little doubt that the desire to relocate financial responsibility for schools and schooling was one of the driving motivations behind the reform agenda. Schools that competed for resources and students arguably maximized the investment of the state in education. In similar ways to businesses, schools were provided with a bulk-operating grant and were required to formulate strategic plans, exercise fiscal responsibility and engage in a range of entrepreneurial activities to alleviate any deficits. The financial costs, accountability and responsibility for governing, leading and managing schools were therefore shifted from government to the local level. Significantly, the demise of the bureaucracy of education (local education boards, inspectors and an unwieldy Department of Education) was a necessary prerequisite for the modernized school and, in the second phase, the modernized workforce.

The commodification of education and commercialization of the school (Eason 1999) characterized the functional period. Education was a commodity for consumption at both the local and global level. As a commercial product, the selling of educational services to international full-fee-paying students provided a means by which New Zealand schools could simultaneously engage in activities that were fiscally expedient and would attract international economic attention. Not only, then, was education subject to demands imposed by the global market, but the skills, knowledge and abilities of teachers and students as future world citizens and workers were commercialized. Changes to the structures of schools and schooling in this first phase were the legislative and ideological precedent for further reforms that significantly impacted on teachers and teaching.

Modernization: the production period

As I have outlined, the functional period delivered change to schools. The second phase of modernization (1996–present) induced changes *within* schools. More specifically, the professional autonomy of teachers was eroded, principally because they were located as an educational 'problem' to be remedied and regulated by the state (Fitzgerald *et al.* 2003; Codd 2005a). In line with the ideological stance that education was a product to be consumed, teachers were positioned as critical to the achievement of stated financial, strategic and entrepreneurial objectives. As a result, teachers were repositioned as producers of commodities (students' skills, knowledge and abilities) that could contribute to the national and global economy (Singh *et al.* 2005). These changes within schools were couched in the discourse of improving quality and standards that, in turn, produced a level of competitiveness (between schools and within the global education market) and responsiveness to the insistent demands of the market. The modern school and the modern marketplace share a symbiotic relationship. A modernized school, however, requires amongst other things a modernized workforce. There were several ways in which this proceeded.

Since 1996 the teaching profession in New Zealand has increasingly been subjected to policies and strategies of surveillance that have served to introduce a culture of managerialism and performativity (Ozga 2000b; Codd 2005a). Rhetoric suggests that these policies have been underpinned with the desire to create 'a positive framework for improving the quality of teaching and learning' (Ministry of Education 1997, p. 1). Yet there can be little doubt that policies such as the formal registration of teachers with a national body, the Teacher Registration Board (TRB) (1994), performance agreements and mandatory performance appraisal (Ministry of Education 1997), the introduction of the *Professional Standards* (Ministry of Education 1999) and procedures for salary attestation have served to deprofessionalize the work and status of teachers and the teaching profession (Codd 2005a). While public pressure for teachers to be accountable for their work has been cited as one of the motivating factors for the reform of schools and schooling (Capper and Munro 1990), this second phase of modernization has had the net effect of bureaucratizing teaching (Fitzgerald *et al.* 2003). Moreover, the silent message that has been relayed is that teachers cannot be trusted. Hence the systematic introduction of policies and procedures that are explicitly designed to control and regulate the profession (Ozga 2000b). More significantly, policies such as compulsory teacher registration, attestation and performance management now determine what 'counts' as a good teacher and good teaching, thus shifting control over the profession from teachers to government; from the profession to the periphery.

These changes have produced a new climate in which teachers work: teachers now experience increased hours, increased class sizes, increased administrative tasks, greater accountability and more complex mechanisms for reporting teacher and student outcomes (Fitzgerald *et al.* 2003). This has led to a sense of loss of professional autonomy and judgement (Ozga 2000b; Codd 2005a). In effect, government has continued to erode the profession through surveillance and control mechanisms such as the *Professional Standards* that standardize and prescribe what teachers ought to accomplish. Furthermore, this codification of teacher practices has introduced a skill hierarchy between teachers (classified as 'beginning', 'classroom' and 'experienced'), 'unit holders' (teachers with additional leadership and management responsibilities) and senior leaders (deputy principals and principals) (Ministry of Education 1999). In order for teachers to 'keep abreast of constant changes', they are required to undertake professional development each year (Secondary Teachers' Collective Agreement [STCA] 2004–07) and are monitored by other teachers as an integral part of the performance management process (Ball 2003; Fitzgerald *et al.* 2003). It is highly doubtful whether these systems, designed to produce more professional and autonomous teachers, will achieve these purposes when, in reality, these are new (seemingly modernized) methods of surveillance, control and conformity.

The emphasis on hierarchy and regulation has extended to the principalship/headship. Educational reform, while espousing that the principal/head was the professional leader of the school (Government of New Zealand 1988, p. 10), simultaneously positioned the principal/head as a worker of the managerial state with responsibility and accountability for teacher performance, levels of student achievement, fiscal and strategic management, school improvement initiatives, education policy and legislative compliance as well as overall school performance as determined by the ERO. Accordingly, the principalship has been reformed and additional training and qualifications have assisted with producing the modern leader; a leader that is inevitably gendered, raced and classed (Blackmore 1999; Fitzgerald 2006). Notwithstanding this point, principalship is subject to intense scrutiny and located as the solution to raising school, teacher and student performance. One of the policy remedies initiated has been the introduction of a principal induction programme based on the skills, knowledge and competencies identified by Hay McBer Group (2001). In similar ways to the capture of leadership preparation and development in England, the state has maintained an abiding interest in the programme in New Zealand (Brundrett *et al.* 2006). It is not unreasonable to suggest at this point that New Zealand may again borrow policy initiatives (Thrupp 2001; Robertson and Dale 2002) from England and introduce some form of licence or registration for leadership, thereby opening up the possibility of institutionalized leadership that is regulated by the state.

This second phase of modernization has been characterized by the production of highly regulated models of what constitutes a 'good' teacher and a 'good' leader. And as I have outlined in the previous section, these 'good' teachers and leaders contribute to the production of 'good' workers and global citizens. Since 1989, the nature of teachers' work and teaching has shifted considerably; from an emphasis on nation-building and citizenship (Codd 2005b) to a focus on the knowledge economy and the production of knowledge-based societies. Schooling has therefore mutated from a way of preparing young people for broader purposes (such as participation in a democratic society) to a mechanism of selection and preparation for the local and global labour market. To ensure that the needs of the economy and global marketplace are met, teachers' work has been reorganized 'in such a way as to facilitate the kind of outcome that is required by the State' (Smyth *et al.* 2000, p. 26). The curriculum, one of the key areas that was not devolved to local schools in 1989, not only prescribes what teachers ought to do but also determines what 'counts' as official knowledge (Apple 2001). In other words, 'good' students will learn 'good' knowledge from 'good' teachers and get 'good' jobs. For this to occur, the agency of teachers has been co-opted to engage in economic and identity work on behalf of the state. The control of teachers' work and ways in which they act (or react) is central to assure the state that 'good' students with 'good' knowledge are being produced. Smyth *et al.* (2000) suggest that there are five particular strategies that contribute to the engineering of compliance and consent from teachers that underpins my analysis here:

1. Regulated market control creates a situation whereby consumers (parents) exercise their economic choices in the school selected for their children. To be able to attract parents to the school, it becomes imperative that the organization and teachers act in ways that capture the market. The needs and wishes of consumers are therefore paramount and the school and its teachers are responsive to market demands and pressures. In New Zealand, the introduction of enrolment schemes (Government of New Zealand 1988, Section 5.3) for some schools that are deemed popular has arguably increased the demand for and desirability of these schools. This has subsequently affected residential real estate prices in the 'local' area and it is not unusual for properties on the market to advertise the school zone as one of the selling points.

2. Technical control is exerted through the specification of what is taught (curriculum), how this will be taught (pedagogy) and student outcomes (assessment). As pointed out earlier, the NZCF that was designed to future-proof (Ministry of Education 1993) the curriculum also ensured that curriculum was teacher-proof. Providing teachers with learning outcomes, curriculum materials, assessment activities and exemplars is a form of technical control of their skills, knowledge and practices. The focus on particular forms of professional development to support curriculum change further exerts a level of technical control over teachers' work.

3. Bureaucratic control and the bureaucratization of teaching and teachers' work (Fitzgerald *et al.* 2003) is imperative to the production of the kinds of outcomes required by the state. Systems such as teacher registration, standards, codes of conduct, attestation and performance appraisal are all forms of bureaucratic control that serve to inform the state and its agencies such as the ERO that teachers are performing in expected ways. The presence of senior teachers, middle leaders, senior leaders and principals/heads that are regulated by the ERO and NZQA confirms the bureaucratic nature of schools and the bureaucratization of teachers' work. Information about teachers' work and student outcomes is transferred from the classroom and school to the state via the intervention of the ERO and NZQA that report outcomes and adherence to standards. These agencies can be directed by the state to specify, change and control teachers' work.

4. Corporate control is a process whereby the governance, management and organization of schools are derived from the tenets of business management. The creation of Boards of Trustees as employers and governors, the renaming of the Principal as the Chief Executive Officer of the Board, the establishment of national education and administration guidelines and the introduction of charters and mission statements (Government of New Zealand 1988) replicate business management practices. These practices have created several layers of bureaucratic separation: between the state and schools, governors and managers, school and community and teachers, governors and managers. The principal acts as the professional auditor of teachers through the appraisal, attestation and registration process and Boards of Trustees act as auditors by way of the employment and appointments process.

5. Ideological control is a more subtle process that seeks to advance particular views about what counts as 'good' teaching and being a 'good' teacher. As Apple (2001) notes, the official curriculum and official knowledge imparts information that the state has deemed acceptable to its agenda. Provided that teachers accept this official knowledge, can produce 'good' students' with 'good' knowledge and collaborate in processes designed to monitor and judge the standard of their work, then ideological control can be asserted. More recently, ideological control has been further strengthened through the imposition of a rhetoric that suggests that New Zealand students do not perform as well as their peers in international league tables. This has resulted in constant references to 'a long tail of under achievement' (Ministry of Education 2003) and the linking of the policy and research agenda, particularly in the areas of literacy, numeracy and scientific knowledge, to data reported in the report *Learning for Tomorrow's World* (OECD 2003). This has, in turn, led to renewed attention to those students who are labelled 'under achieving' or 'at risk' (Ministry of Education 2003) as well as those with the potential to significantly improve New Zealand's position on international league tables. Teachers' work is therefore ideologically co-opted to assure the state that their professional practices will meet the needs of these students.

In effect, this second phase of remodelling schools and schooling, teachers and teaching[3] has been characterized by an ideological shift from the commodification of education to the commodification of teachers' skills, knowledge, abilities and professional practice.

The remodelling agenda

It is likely, given the policy borrowing that occurs between England and New Zealand (Thrupp 2001; Robertson and Dale 2002), that the school workforce will be further subject to remodelling practices along similar lines and underpinned by political concerns regarding the age of the school workforce and issues of teacher retention. A small-scale qualitative study commissioned by the Ministry of Education in 2002 (Ministry of Education 2002b) outlined the current recruitment and retention issues faced by secondary school teachers. These included:

- the profile of the teaching profession in the wider community;
- the amount and frequency of administrative tasks teachers were expected to undertake;
- the expectation that teachers participate in extra-curricular (frequently labelled co-curricular) activities such as sport and cultural activities;
- the teaching and administrative loads carried by those with extra responsibilities;
- changes in remuneration to align teaching with other professions;
- pupil behaviour that adversely affects classes;
- class size.

Neither these issues nor attempts to rectify these problems are unique to the New Zealand situation. Recent responses to these issues are aligned with similar remodelling strategies in England and forecast the possible transformation of schools and schooling.

In 2003, a Ministerial Taskforce on Secondary Teacher Remuneration was established that developed 'recommendations to ensure a supply of high quality, appropriately qualified secondary teachers who will improve the learning outcomes of all students' (STCA 2004–07, 2.1.1). These recommendations, documented in the recent STCA agreement, underpin the contractual agreement between the secondary teacher union and the state:

- increased remuneration of teachers;
- time release;
- the need for teachers to 'invest in and build their capacity' (STCA 2004–07, 2.1.2) through increased qualifications;
- development of professional practice through professional development;
- professional development to 'keep abreast of constant changes' (STCA 2004–07, 2.2.3a);

- paid sabbatical leave to increase qualifications;
- further research into teacher workload that investigates 'work practices, role definition, non-contact time and the use of specialist and ancillary support' (STCA 2004–07, 2.2.1a);
- non-contact time for ICT management and online teaching;
- introduction of Specialist Classroom Teacher for 'the professional development and guidance, mentoring and induction of other staff' (STCA 2004–07, 3.8A.3).

These recommendations form the basis of the reform agenda that will effect changes to contractual relationships, workload, teaching and administrative tasks, use of non-contact or release time, professional and career development, the deployment of ancillary (administrative) staff and the introduction of a more diverse workforce. Reading this reform agenda against the remodelling strategies outlined in Chapter 1, New Zealand has again transported and reworked education policy across transnational boundaries.

These changes are being worked through incrementally. Guaranteed non-contact time for secondary teachers and classroom release time (CRT) for primary teachers was implemented in 2005 and the Specialist Classroom Teacher model was introduced in 2006. While speculative at this point, it is likely that the recommendations listed above will prompt changes to the professional culture of teaching. It is highly probable that the rhetoric of remodelling will be deployed as the 'solution' to 'problems' that the profession faces and increase the scrutiny teachers face to meet demands of the global marketplace. The curious solution to issues of teacher recruitment and retention is organizational efficiency and effectiveness, terms that litter the STCA. These solutions, derived from the neo-liberal reforms of the 1980s and 1990s, are, I would suggest, not new.

What appears missing from the recommendations or any of the documents cited is coherent, robust and independent evidence that evaluates *why* such changes are required. Although there is evidence that teacher recruitment and retention is a problem, there is no evidence presented that suggests the above recommendations would work. New Zealand is ideally placed to assess the impact of remodelling in England prior to policy development and implementation. This involves a necessary divorce from the ideological centre.

More significantly, how have these recommendations that affect schools and schooling, teachers and teaching been discussed and debated with students? Or do students remain the objects of the reform agenda?

Conclusion

Remodelling schools and schooling, teachers and teaching has been systematically occurring in New Zealand since 1989. Although the reform of the school workforce along similar lines to England is on the horizon, the architecture of remodelling was founded on the re-formation of the purposes, structure and function of schools and schooling and the subsequent reprofessionalization of teachers and teaching. Remodelling has stimulated changes to schools and within schools that have altered relationships between schools and the state, schools and community, schools and principals/heads and between teachers and students.

Educational reform has proceeded at a significant pace that has radically transformed New Zealand schools. In the first phase, the initial remodelling of the management, administration and governance of schools positioned schools as the explicit object of reform. The shift in responsibility for schools and schooling from the state to schools was accompanied by demands for fiscal and organizational efficiency and the re-production of education as a commodity that was subject to the demands of local and global consumers. In the second phase, the control and regulation of teachers' work through performance management, registration, attestation and the introduction of standards relocated teachers as the objects of reform. More recently, changes to teachers' contracts have emphasized the increased level of contractual remodelling that is occurring in New Zealand schools.

I am left at this point with an intense disquiet. For almost two decades schools in New Zealand and England, although not exclusively or uniformly, have experienced the impact of managerialism and modernization that has served to change the nature of schools (as organizations) and teachers (as professionals). An antidote that is prescribed to remedy the 'problem' of the impact of widespread and systemic reform is located in the rhetoric of teacher leadership. That is, leadership by teachers is stipulated as the means to build capacity within teachers to sustain change and cope with increasing demands (Lambert 2000). My disquiet is related to a question that I would like to pose here – what if teacher leadership, or distributed leadership as it might be labelled, is the new form of managerialism? Have we been (or remain) seduced by the discourses of modernization?

And, finally, what appears to have been overlooked in the research and theorizing about educational reform and modernization is the effect on students in New Zealand schools. Although Ball (1997, p. 241) has argued that teachers are an 'increasingly absent presence' in reform, students have remained as objects of reform and are, accordingly, significantly absent voices in debates. To remedy this situation, serious questions should be asked about the nature and purposes of schools and schooling and those questions should be addressed to students who are, after all – to co-opt the language of neo-liberalism – the clients. One of the challenges of modernization I would argue, is for students to be actively included in debates and student voices to be used as evidence for informing policy. Until that occurs, remodelling does not, on the surface, appear to be modern at all.

Chapter 13

'Getting a Toyota factory': continuity and change in Ontario's elementary teacher education programmes

Elizabeth Smyth and Kathy Broad

Introduction

In an article with the headline 'WLU gets teachers' college', Ontario's Wilfrid Laurier University announced that it was establishing a Faculty of Education and, beginning in September 2007, it would offer a one-year teacher education programme to post-baccalaureate students. Its programme, focusing on elementary mathematics, science and special education, will be offered to 90 qualified applicants. Laurier's President remarked 'This is a very happy day . . . . If we were a municipality, this would be like getting a Toyota factory' (D'Amato 2006). Comparing the acquisition of a Faculty of Education to that of a multinational automotive plant is a telling comment on modernization and teacher education, and one that has both resonance and dissonance with current practice. Over the past decade, the provincial ministries that regulate teacher education (the Ministry of Education and the Ministry of Colleges and Universities) have encouraged diversity of providers of teacher education programmes. At the same time, the 'arm's-length' organization that regulates the profession, the Ontario College of Teachers, in collaboration with both the universities and the field, has implemented standards of practice that govern all stages in teacher preparation and development (from initial teacher education through career-long learning). In response to the public and professional criticism, and academic denouncement of minimalist and reductive credentialling, the Ministry of Education rescinded the legislated Ontario Teacher Qualification Test (Glassford 2005) for beginning teachers and replaced it with a new teacher induction programme that focuses on developing practice. Ontario teacher education is more focused on professional formation than technical teacher training, recognizing the moral purpose of teaching and connecting 'directly with emerging conceptualizations of teaching that attend to the relationships among the technical competencies of teaching, critical knowledge bases and contextual forces' (Rolheiser and Evans 2004, p. 129). This takes place within the context of the research-intensified university that struggles with the challenges of enhancing the civil society as it forms the next generation.

While Canadian teacher education has deep historical roots bedded in the English system, it has developed along a somewhat different trajectory – especially within the current era of reform. Professional formation of teachers occurs within a university environment, while integrated within partner school districts for the practicum experience (known in other countries as teaching practice) and the building of learning organizations through induction programmes and ongoing teacher professional development (Fullan 2001). Through a case study of the historical evolution of teacher education programmes for those seeking to teach at the provinces' elementary schools (Kindergarten to Grade 8), this chapter argues that the history of teacher education can provide another lens with which to view the modernization agenda. Ontario's institutions of teacher education were (and we would argue, still are) critical components in the educational reform agenda. They can be seen as agencies of modernization of the teaching workforce that regulate who enters the profession and establish benchmarks for career mobility (Heap *et al.* 2005). Yet, while they are sites of contested leadership as the university, the state and the professional organizations all strive for influence over policy directions, the image of the 'teacher as technician' is unfamiliar.

Young and Hall (2004) question if teacher education in Canada and England are literally and pedagogically oceans apart. A historical case study of the evolution of Ontario's teacher education can help to answer this question. This case documents how, through collaboration among the field, the profession and the university, teacher education programmes have moved from stand-alone government-administered institutions in which highly regulated programmes were delivered by civil servants, to their present (and largely unchallenged) location in university-based colleges and Faculties of Education where teacher candidates acquire the research-based knowledge and skills to emerge as Bransford *et al.*'s (2005) 'adaptive experts'. Unlike the current situation in England, there is no move to fragment knowledge and skills by teasing apart the complex job of teaching and assigning some duties to a para-professional. In fact, 'the underlying principle for our approach to teacher development is that teachers must at all times be respected as professionals, deserving the same respect as other professionals' (Ontario Ministry of Education 2004), with ongoing professional development focusing on teaching, not technical training (Fullan *et al.* 2006).

Educating Ontario's elementary school teachers

According to Section 93 of the British North America Act (1867), the Act that established Canada as a country, it is the provincial governments that hold power over virtually all elements of education – and that includes teacher education. The establishment of Laurier's Faculty of Education marks both continuity and change in the history of Ontario's teacher education. It continues a trend of publicly funded universities wanting to have a Faculty of Education on campus. It represents a change insofar as Laurier is an Ontario-based non-sectarian and pub-licly funded university. Within the past decade, both the Ministry of Colleges and Universities (the provincial bureau that approves all new academic programmes within Ontario universities) and the Ontario College of Teachers (OCT) (the agency that credentials teacher education programmes) have designated private, denominational and foreign universities as 'permitted institutions' for the design and delivery of teacher education within the province of Ontario. With the addi-tion of Laurier to the provincial roster, qualified teacher candidates can acquire their teaching credentials at 13 publicly funded Faculties of Education, where their tuition fees will be subsidized by the Government of Ontario. Should they elect to study at one of the private denominational universities, or on the Ontario campus of a foreign university, they are responsible for 100 per cent of the fees (see for example Charles Sturt University 2006). Admission to all Faculties of Education is highly competitive, with grade point average being a significant factor in the final admission decision. While there are attempts to attract candi-dates who represent the diversity of the Ontario population, indigenous peoples, differently-abled, culturally, socio-economically and linguistically diverse com-munities continue to be under-represented (Kosnick *et al.* 2003).

For most of the past two centuries, Ontario's elementary school teachers and their secondary counterparts were educated in different institutions and with strikingly different conditions for admission (Stamp 1982). Those seeking to teach at an elementary school had two options: to attend a model school and participate in an apprenticeship model or, after its establishment in 1847, to attend a provincial normal school, later called the teachers' college (although, as is evident in the headlines of the newspaper article quoted at the beginning of the chapter, this name persists in the vernacular – even until today). The model school path was terminated in the early twentieth century and atten-dance at the normal school became the accepted mode. For those preparing to teach in secondary schools, attendance at a university-based (or affiliated) pro-fessional school followed completion of a university degree.

Between 1847 and 1963, the vast majority of Ontario's elementary school teachers obtained their teacher education by attending one of thirteen, region-ally located normal schools (renamed teachers' colleges in the 1950s). Unlike England, where the teacher education institutes were usually residential and often segregated by gender and religion, and Quebec where denominationally segregated and religious-administered schools of pedagogy dominated the land-scape, Ontario's elementary teacher education institutions generally offered one-year co-educational programmes to 'day students' who attended these non-denominational government-administered and publicly funded schools free of charge.

Admission standards to the provincial normal schools fluctuated annually, driven by the projected demand for teachers. Throughout the early to mid-twentieth century, teacher candidates were admitted with four years or five years of high school (Grade 13), with successful completion of anywhere from five to eight subjects in their fifth year of high school. The length of the programme likewise varied, depending on the entrance requirements met and the demand for teachers, with the result that, depending on the year, beginning teachers were sent to their own classrooms, after completing programmes of various lengths. Some began their careers after a one-year course (for students out of Grade 13); a two-year course (for students out of Grade 12); a combination of pre-service and in-service course for students out of Grade 12 or 13 (one summer term followed by one year of teaching and then one full year at the teacher education institution). To receive a teaching licence, students had to sit examinations in the subjects they studied as well as successfully completing teaching practice. Students could only appeal failures on their subject papers if they had successfully completed all their practical experience. Graduation lists were submitted annually to the Ministry of Education, the agency that licensed the candidates to teach up to Grade 10. Most teachers' college graduates were young people, often only a couple of years older than some of their pupils.

The members of the instructional staff of the teachers' colleges were known as teaching masters – a title indicative both of rank and gender. Most masters began their careers as teachers, were subsequently promoted to principals and then joined the public service as school inspectors. Teaching masters were appointed by the Ministry of Education through a process that could be characterized as a coupling of promotion through the civil service ranks and a reputation as a good teacher, rather than transparency. While the majority had acquired an initial post-secondary degree, some possessed a Master's degree and a few had earned doctorates.

The masters were employed on a twelve-month contract. In addition to teaching the student teachers and supervising their practical experience, the teaching masters worked through the summer, delivering professional development courses to experienced teachers. They frequently relocated to teach these courses. Some masters engaged in textbook writing and research in the areas of child development, although scholarship, as defined by research and publication, was not part of their job description.

Thus, for most of the nineteenth and twentieth centuries, Ontario's teachers' colleges were owned, operated and financed by the Ministry of Education. They were regulated apart from the province's other institutions of post-secondary institutions by the Teacher Education Branch of the Ministry of Education. They were gendered environments wherein a predominantly male staff taught a predominately female study body. Where female staff were employed, they held the positions of Dean of Women, librarian or instructor in such female-dominated subjects as domestic science and women's physical education. Teacher education was ripe for reculturing in response to widespread public and professional critique.

Critiques of Ministry-controlled teacher education

For most of the twentieth century, the initial preparation of Ontario's teachers had been the subject of debate – even among those engaged in, and advocating for, reform in teacher education (Dyde 1904–5; Pakenham 1922). Discussions over the nature of programme, students, staff and governance ebbed and flowed throughout the first six decades of the twentieth century. Journalists, teachers' organizations, Royal Commissions, the public at large and the staff of the teachers' colleges themselves actively engaged in the debate. A key question was one of control: should teacher education be the exclusive domain of the Ministry of Education? Alternate modes of delivery, such as the provision of teacher education in free-standing institutions; the placement of teacher education within the universities and the education of elementary and secondary teacher candidates in the same institution schools were actively discussed (see for example Royal Commission on The University of Toronto 1906; Fleming 1971; Phillips 1977).

A persistent point of deliberation was the role of the universities in teacher education. Some contested that teacher education could best be delivered by the universities rather than by the Ministry of Education, pointing to examples of other provinces, like Alberta, which, since the 1940s, had placed all teacher education within the university sector (Bowers 1950). Others echoed the historical argument of the necessity for university imprimatur as a criterion for professionalization (Dyde 1904–5). While such rhetoric peppered the debates, no action was taken. Elementary teacher education remained firmly entrenched within the provincial normal schools.

In the early 1950s and 1960s, elementary school teacher education was closely scrutinized by a number of professional and political bodies (Royal Commission on Education (Bowers 1950); Ontario Conference on Education 1961). The flaws identified clustered around several themes. A one-year programme was too little preparation for freshly minted high school graduates to join the teaching profession. The Ministry of Education's tight control over curriculum stifled innovation. The process for appointments of teaching masters was anything but transparent. The programmes offered were too distant from the field. All of these factors contributed to a loss of status as 'the prestige of the Normal Schools has undergone erosion . . . instead of mingling with the main stream of educational thought and action in the province, [they] have become tranquil pools along its course' (Bowers 1950, p. 30). This assessment was particularly damning as it was written by those who knew provincial teacher education best – the teaching masters. Yet, from the Minister of Education down, change was resisted by teacher education's political masters. The short-lived experience of independent Faculties of Education at Queen's University and the University of Toronto were cited as examples for the need for central control (Phillips 1977; Smyth 2003). It was with the appointment of John Robarts (1959–62) as Minister of Education that long suppressed educational change and institutional restructuring commenced (Gidney 1999).

Underpinning the teacher-education debates were questions concerning how placing teacher candidates within a university setting could best prepare them for the elementary classroom. Within their studies, what should be the balance and integration of theory and practice? What might be the optimal structure for programme delivery? This movement was not merely restructuring; it was *recul-turing* both teacher education and the public perception of the teacher as a professional. As England moves to rethink the roles of the teacher and the teaching assistant, it might be useful to reflect on the Ontario debates of the 1960s and the words of Toronto journalist Bascom St John that found their way into Hansard:

> We wish . . . that something could be done to shake the Department of Education loose from the monolithic conviction that one year's training is ample for an elementary teacher of 1961. . . . There should be a plan to improve teacher qualifications . . . [we] should look to the objective of university standing for all elementary teachers.
>
> (Ontario Legislative Assembly 1961, p. 835)

From teachers' colleges to colleges of education

As part of the educational reform initiatives of the early 1960s, the Minister's Committee on the Training of Elementary School Teachers under the chair of C. R. MacLeod was struck on 28 September 1964 to examine and report on the preparation of elementary school teachers. During their two years of deliberations, the commissioners received briefs from 99 individuals and organizations that contained 'a remarkable unanimity' (Minister's Committee 1966, p. 2) which led them to conclude that 'inadequate academic education and insufficient maturity on the part of the student teachers' (ibid., p. 13) had resulted in the failure of elementary teachers to gain professional status. They wrote that there appeared to be a growing conviction among thoughtful parents and the public at large that most graduates from the teachers' colleges were too young, too immature and less well-prepared academically than they should be. With the pressures of supply – and not professional excellence – driving enrolment patterns, the committee warned that 'teaching has not properly challenged our ablest students, many of whom have chosen other careers in preference to elementary school teaching. Recruitment has therefore become increasingly difficult' (ibid., p. 12).

To enact its vision of a teacher as 'a scholar and an educated person' (ibid., p. 53), the committee recommended the relocation of teacher education to a university setting. The programme of study could be delivered in a number of modes including concurrently (education subjects taken alongside a degree in another academic discipline), consecutively (an education programme taken at the completion of a degree) or through an internship. As well, the committee recommended that both elementary and secondary teacher candidates be educated within the same environment and that, at the end of the programme of study, both a university degree and professional certification be granted.

The vision of elementary teacher education proposed by the MacLeod Report was clear. Teacher education would be university-based and would be of four years' duration. Beginning teachers would be three years older than those graduating from teachers' colleges. Admission would be based on grades and not on the previous 'places for all who applied' process. Fees would be charged. The programme would consist of four parts: academic/liberal education; foundations of education; curriculum and instruction; practice teaching. It would be delivered by both liberal arts professors and professors of education, who would be 'competent scholars and distinguished and successful teachers' (ibid., p. 56). The programme would be housed in a faculty, administered by a dean and governed by university regulations. However, education was not to be entirely severed from the Ministry of Education. The committee recommended that the Minister approve the appointment of the Dean and consult on the appointment of the instructional staff.

Minister of Education William Davis warmly welcomed the recommendations contained in the Minister's Committee Report. On 29 March 1966, Davis announced to the Ontario Legislature that he was 'in complete agreement with the programme suggested and it will be the policy of my department to implement the plans to this end as quickly as possible' (Ontario Legislative Assembly, 26 March 1966, p. 2009e). This began the most dramatic shift in teacher education in Ontario's history. The Minister charged the Deputy Minister of Education, J. L. McCarthy, and the Director of the Teacher Education Branch, G. L. Woodruff, to begin, on an individual basis, negotiations with the universities – a process which resulted in long and protracted work.

While the Ministry of Education may have been enthusiastic about this change, the universities were cautious. Speaking on behalf of the newly formed Teacher Education Committee of Presidents of Universities of Ontario, Carleton University's Dean D. M. L. Farr (1967) explained

> the importance of consultation with the academic senates of Ontario universities respecting the following aspects of the integration of teachers' colleges: admissions, curriculum, academic standards and staffing. The Council was unanimous in its conviction that in any modification of teacher education, the academic autonomy of the universities must be fully respected.   (p. 30)

Modern teacher education?

With the implementation of the Report of the Minister's Committee on the Training of Elementary School Teachers, Ontario's Teacher Education was launched on a challenging path. Significantly, there have been few studies of this period of teacher education. Hodgins (1971) and Thompson (1986) are two of the few exceptions. This epoch of transition in teacher education calls out for further investigation as both studies clearly identify the antecedents for modernization within their work. While histories of individual universities and Faculties of Education may comment on the background and implementation of this shift (McAuley 1990; Friedland 2002), no comprehensive or systematic comparative study has been undertaken.

One of the most fascinating elements in the movement to the universities was the transition in the nature of the work of the teacher educators. The historical record of the negotiations that took place between the government and one university – Lakehead University – provides some insight into the challenges that both sides faced. On 22 March 1969, a rare Saturday meeting of the Lakehead Senate was called to consider the proposed agreement between the Minister of Education and Lakehead University, regarding the matter of teacher education. In just under three hours, a wide-ranging discussion of the 19 clauses of the affiliation agreement took place. Much of the agreement detailed arrangements concerning the staff of the former Teachers' College and how they would be granted tenure. The wording is telling:

> To Civil Servants who are on the staff of Lakehead Teachers' College on June 30 1969, and transfer to Lakehead University, the University may grant tenure at any time, but where the University does not wish to offer tenure to any such member of the staff transferred to Lakehead University, the University shall give such member one year's notice of intention not to grant tenure, the separation to become effective June 30, 1973, provided that where tenure has not been offered by June 30, 1973, the Department of Education and the University will offer assistance to the person concerned in obtaining other employment and where no notice of intention not to grant tenure is given to any such member within these three years next following June 30, 1969, the University agrees to grant tenure to such member.
>
> (Lakehead University 1969, p. 7)

Financial enticements, such as study leave paid by the Ministry of Education, were set in place to encourage the 'civil servants' to obtain the necessary credentials for tenure. Analysis of the personnel lists of the calendars document that not all of the members of the former 'civil servants' made a successful transition to the university environment. For those who did, their lives were changed forever. However, as founding Dean Jim Angus (1970) observed:

> There has been no compulsion on Teachers' College Masters as there is on Professors in Faculties of Education in other jurisdictions to take advanced degrees, conduct research, publish, assume leadership in professional organizations, serve on academic committees, deliver scholarly activity on which promotion, tenure or merit increases in salary are normally based. This is not to suggest that some Teachers' College Masters have not done these things. Rather the point is being made that there has been no endemic need to do them.
>
> (p. 3)

He assessed that the 'lack of funds and facilities' and the fact that 'programmes and organizations . . . structured in the only model known to teacher educators, that is the elementary and secondary schools, have produced an artificial learning situation which demoralized staff and students alike contributing to a general feeling of futility' (ibid., p. 4). Was their new university-based situation any better? The relocation to the university campus has brought persistent questions concerning the nature of learning to practise as a teacher into sharper focus. As well, the growing dominance of the research culture within the university further complicates these questions. A University of Toronto (2003) planning document noted:

> Divided between a pre-service teacher education programme and a strong research mandate, Faculties of Education have often failed to achieve one or the other, or sometimes either, mandate well. . . . An argument can be made that a public research university has, as part of its public educational trust, the responsibility to conduct leading research and teaching in the field of education itself. (p. 57)

While some scholars have studied aspects of modernization and the work of teacher educators, there are many elements that remain unexplored. Studies of the impact of equity initiatives in teacher education (Coulter 1998; Kitchen *et al.* 2006) and analysis of the complexities of what it means to learn to teach (Britzman 2003) are promising beginnings, as are the studies of what reform means in preservice contexts (Cole 2000a; Fullan 2001).

Jim Angus (1970), the founding Dean of Education at Lakehead University, in Thunder Bay, Ontario, once described teacher education as 'a foster child in the Ontario educational family'. Within the twentieth century, he wrote, 'the foster child had become a pretty ragged Cinderella. A Prince Charming was needed to rescue it from the ashes of public neglect and intrinsic apathy. The question was where to find one' (p. 1). Was the implementation of the Minister's Committee on the Training of Elementary Teachers and the movement of all teacher education to the university campus the solution to the long-standing public and scholarly criticism of initial teacher education? The answer is both yes and no. One set of challenges was traded for another. The movement of teacher education onto university campuses did cause change in the teaching profession. Ontario teachers currently possess higher academic qualifications and a more thorough professional preparation than at any other time in their history. Yet their competence is still questioned, as evidenced by the comparison of provincial test scores in the press. This attention to student achievement viewed as a measurable teacher output and productivity evokes an image of the mechanistic. Others may view this public scrutiny as the logical fate of a feminized profession, where efficiency and effectiveness must be secured through external surveillance. Some scholars argue that as women have raised their professional ambitions, they have moved to fill 'productive spaces' created by the movement of men into other areas of employment (Weiner and Kallos 2000).

From the beginning of the twentieth century, questions were raised concerning the place of professional teacher education within a university that was increasingly shaped by the norms of science: the debates between the theory and practice of education, the interplay among the university that taught those wishing to become teachers, the provincial government who licensed them as practitioners and the local school boards who employed them as teachers would require constant negotiation. Almost 70 years later, J. R. McCarthy, the Deputy Minister of Education who oversaw the transition of all teacher education into the universities, further contextualized these challenges. Addressing an invitational conference on 'Teacher Education: A Search for New Relationships', McCarthy (1970) cautioned his audience of teacher educators:

> It will be the task of the Faculty of Education to justify its position in the total university context . . . they will attempt to win academic respectability within the university by attempting to meet the criteria of academicians who know little or nothing about professional education. If they succumb to such blandishments, they will eventually lose their reason for being: first because they will be a poor shadow of arts or science faculties; and second because they will be useless in terms of the school system.   (p. 7)

Conclusion

By examining a case study of the location, and hence purposes, of teacher formation in Ontario we can show the location of modernization trends and interventions in time and space. When the focus is predominantly on the future then the public can lose its collective memory as important debates and ideas are lost or become unspeakable. We need to ask why it is the case that the teacher in Ontario as 'a scholar and an educated person' was also accepted in England, and now seems to be regarded as 'unmodern' in the remodelling agenda. What seems to be happening in England is a rejection of the university as a site for professional preparation and development, combined with an impatience with arguments that teachers have a specialized form of knowledge that should be developed through the interplay between research and practice. Hence there is a return to a form of 'on-the-job' technical co-option of adults deployed into the classroom to discover ways of doing the job. As England unravels the professional formation of teachers through the acceleration, in both numbers and roles, of a non-teacher-trained teaching assistant workforce teaching, then our case serves as a useful reminder of the debates about university-based teacher training. This case demonstrates that, while the move from teachers' colleges to university faculties may seem like a quiet transformation, it was in fact a radical reorientation, as the status of elementary school teachers shifted from that of a sub-professional underclass to that of university graduate of a professional school. Thus, it offers a cautionary tale to those who undertake to reduce the complexity of teaching by segmenting out the skills required and thus underestimating the knowledge required to exercise those skills. Could this result in undervaluing or deprofessionalizing the workforce and, thus, changing its status?

We would argue that teacher educators and policymakers can take lessons from the past to inform current practice and decision-making. With their past histories of mergers and takeovers (Lang and Eastman 2002), Faculties of Education provide examples of both cosmetic and deep change. Based on this case study, we contend that it is necessary for Faculties of Education to assume multiple, interrelated and, at times, conflicting roles within the larger domain of teaching and learning. With their strong research orientation and continual mode of critical self-study, they can rise above the 'Toyota plant' analogy of the opening anecdote to serve as sites of necessary engagement with the policies and practices of current local, provincial and national governments. They create innovative pathways through which they can partner with government and professional agencies, who credential their programmes while maintaining a stance that is both critical and proactive. They stimulate public debate over the nature of civic engagement, literacy and numeracy in an age of globalization. They shift government policy and reculture themselves to move beyond the mechanistic accountability exercises associated with the 'publish or perish' syndrome (Cole 2000b) as they actively participate in an informed critique of the rise of the 'knowledge economy'.

Teaching is a complex task which requires multiple knowledge bases in order to make sound professional judgements in response to learner strengths and needs. Through wrestling teacher education from the domination of the technocrats within the Ministry of Education and placing it within the research community, ongoing debates concerning the nature and practice of teacher education are encouraged. Unquestionably, new challenges have emerged and continue to confront teacher educators: the need to balance the shifting demands of the field and the university context; the complex knowledge basis that beginning teachers must master; the tensions created by competition among the need for research and innovations set against increasing externally imposed standards and accountability measures; the demands of growth and change such as an increasingly diverse school and teacher education population and the challenge of integrating emerging technologies within teaching practice. These tensions encourage productive discourse to ensure that an educational system emerges that is not merely modernized, but transformed.

Chapter 14

Navigating 'global' modernization policies in education: responses from Australia

Lesley Vidovich

Introduction

The phenomenon of globalization provides the broader context for understanding modernization policies in education and links the focus of this chapter – Australia – to other chapters in this book. In an era of a 'global knowledge economy', education moves to centre stage in public policymaking as it produces the human capital, in the form of the knowledge, skills and attitudes of students entering the workforce, to enhance national positioning in the global marketplace. Thus, one might postulate a polemical position that international economic competition can become the *raison d'être* of education, or at least a key driving force behind government-initiated education policy development. I would argue that for teachers, the repositioning of education in a global knowledge economy has meant a reconstruction of their professional identity, with implications for the authentic quality of teaching and learning, to the extent that we should emphasize the need for modernization policies to carry a warning – 'handle with care!'. But more of this later in the chapter.

First, a closer examination of globalization is required. Globalization has been defined in a multitude of ways, but essentially it refers to the greater interconnectedness of the world. Bottery (2006) points out that there are many different forms of globalization, including economic, cultural, political and environmental, but he maintains that it is economic globalization which sets the framework; it 'captures the discourses' of the other forms of globalization. I suggest that it is important to differentiate two separate dimensions of globalization – technical and ideological. The former refers to the effect of compressing time and space such that communication across vast geographical distances becomes very fast, and the latter refers to a shift in the underlying system of values which circumscribe the development of public policy. I would argue that it is the coupling of the technical and ideological dimensions of globalization that has brought a significant shift in the nature of education policy in many parts of the globe. In particular, neo-liberalism with its market ideology featuring the organizing principle of competition has rapidly traversed national boundaries and reached near-hegemonic status in influencing education policy, including modernization agendas. Policy borrowing across national borders has been a long-established phenomenon, but arguably, it has been facilitated by globalization in both its technical and ideological dimensions. Henry *et al.* (2001, p. 36) suggest that one of the key factors involved in policy convergence is the growing presence of a 'global policy community' forged by international and supranational organizations such as the OECD in promulgating a new policy consensus around the knowledge, skills and attitudes for success in the global knowledge economy.

Globalization is often cast as an omnipotent, top-down pressure, forcing unwanted changes on passive nation-states. However, this conceptualization is too simplistic, and increasingly more sophisticated and finely nuanced understandings of globalization are being offered. For example, Marginson and Rhoades (2002) offer a 'glo-na-cal agency heuristic' which emphasizes that organizations and individuals actively engage with globalization at many levels from the global to the national to the local (regional levels such as the European Union and the Asia-Pacific region are also becoming significant). Their approach is to contest the conceptualization of globalization as a one-way top-down process and to emphasize the active construction of localized variations to 'global' policy trends; that is they focus on differential mediation of global trends under different localized circumstances. This is consistent with the approach taken in this book where the differential enactment of modernization policies in different national and local settings is highlighted, although notwithstanding that there is a strong ideological consistency in parallel policy developments in the different countries. In this chapter, I will focus on Australian 'incarnations' of the modernization agenda as a basis for critically reflective comparisons with England.

Remodelling the teaching workforce in an Australian context

Historically, education policy in Australia has been strongly influenced by that in England and the USA, and also, to a lesser extent, New Zealand and Canada. Although there is only limited use of the term 'modernization' in Australian education. With an emerging global knowledge economy, parallel discourses of restructuring and reculturing to achieve enhanced efficiency and effectiveness of education to serve the national interest have saturated Australian education policies over the last two decades. As part of the modernization agenda, teachers have been identified as a significant policy 'problem' in the drive to improve student learning outcomes. However, before turning to details of policies on teacher quality and standards, it is important to first understand the 'bigger picture' of modernization in the context of Australian education, particularly in relation to changing ideologies and power relationships.

Ideological shift: changing power relations

In Australia, 1987 marked a significant shift in the ideology underlying education policy. At the national level, the third Hawke Labor Government was elected. The economy was in crisis with Treasurer Keating famously referring to Australia as a 'Banana Republic' based on the size of the budget deficit. Economics quickly came to dominate public policy, including education, and when Dawkins was appointed Education Minister he wasted no time in restructuring his bureaucracy to create the Department of Employment, Education and Training (DEET)[1]. Many commentators noted the symbolism of the restructuring in that employment would now drive education policy (e.g. Dudley and Vidovich 1995). Education had lost its 'stand alone' status, and independent education commissions, with strong teacher representation, were replaced by a National Board where employers dominated, and decision-making was brought more tightly under the control of the minister. Minister Dawkins was strongly influenced by the OECD's human capital approach, linking education more directly to the economy. Dawkins chaired the OECD intergovernmental conference 'Education and the Economy in a Changing Society' in 1989, signalling a more global orientation for Australian education policy.

The ideological shift in education policy from the late 1980s, occurring at the same time as the ascendancy of 'talk' about globalization and global markets, was manifest in twin policy strategies of privatization (the transfer of public assets and functions to private companies) and corporatization (the restructuring and reculturing of the public sector to mirror private corporations). Arguably, given that a Labor government was in power nationally, corporatization was more politically acceptable, although privatization also accelerated. Corporatization in education, in theory, involves devolution of power from central authorities to 'self-managing schools' to facilitate rapid decision-making in response to changing external environments. However, the flip side of policies on devolution is policies to enhance the accountability of local sites to central authorities in demonstrating achievement of prescribed outcomes. With the combination of corporatization and privatization, market ideologies came to prevail.

Australia's federal political structure has been highly significant in the way education policy plays out across Commonwealth and State jurisdictions. Education is legally controlled by the States, but the Commonwealth has increasingly gained strong policy steerage through funding levers over the last 30 years. Traditionally in Australia, Coalition (conservative) governments have favoured States' rights and it has been Labor governments which have forged centralization of public policy (including education). However, with the ascent of a global knowledge economy, the 'national interest' has become a powerful discourse in justifying augmenting Commonwealth control for both major parties, regardless of long-standing political ideology. Of particular note is the increasing power of ministers of education at both State and Commonwealth levels. In addition to operating in their own domains, ministers have formed a powerful Ministerial Council for Employment, Education, Training and Youth Affairs (MCEETYA),[2] enabling them to become very policy proactive. However, the effectiveness of MCEETYA varies with the changing profile of political parties in government at Commonwealth and State levels. For example, when Labor was in power in all States as well as the Commonwealth in the early 1990s, rapid and incisive policy change occurred, and in particular a clear momentum towards a national curriculum was established (with England being a significant source of policy borrowing). However, by the mid-1990s an increasing number of Coalition governments caused the national curriculum to stall, and then each State moved on to develop its own version of an outcomes-based curriculum framework at different rates. In 2006, with a national coalition government in power this time, Commonwealth Minister Bishop announced a presage towards a national exam and national certificate at Year 12 level (school exit), but almost immediately the ministers from Labor States (a majority) rejected this move. Thus, the agenda for national coordination of curriculum in Australia has very much fallen victim to the dynamics of federalism. However, despite the difficulties of coordinated policy directions with such a federal system, the 'checks and balances' offered by a federal structure are frequently cited as an advantage because policy monopoly by any one level of government is effectively undermined.

In addition to the federal structure, another significant feature in Australia relevant to prevailing ideologies and changing power relationships is the relatively high proportion of private (non-government) schools. One-third of Australian schoolchildren attend private schools, and the percentage is rapidly growing, with active support and funding by the Commonwealth government (although it is the State governments which provide the bulk of funds to government schools). This form of privatization has accelerated in the decade since 1996 when the (conservative) Howard Coalition Government came to power. Support for private schools is consistent with Coalition ideology, and the 'drift' in enrolments away from government schools has become more like an avalanche. Given that the Commonwealth and the States are directing most of their funds for schooling to private (non-government) and public (government) sectors respectively, private/public divides in Australian schooling strongly intersect with the issue of Commonwealth–State power relations.

Therefore, with the development of modernization policies, including corporatization and privatization in Australia since the late 1980s, the new powerhouses in education are governments, especially education ministers. Governments have also co-opted employers into educational decision-making, reinforcing the primacy of economics. The role of industrial unions has waxed and waned and, as would be expected, their influence has been strongest when Labor governments are in power. However, unions have not been invited to the policy 'table' at the national level since the Howard Coalition Government was elected in 1996. Further, this government has enacted new and highly controversial Industrial Relations (IR) legislation in 2006 to severely limit union power such that individual Australian Workplace Agreements will prevail over any collective agreement. The unions and State Labor governments are together challenging these new IR laws in the High Court. In contrast to the augmenting power of governments and employers, teachers have lost power. As with industrial unions, the influence of teacher unions has also varied over time with the political party in power, although teacher unions have a relatively strong history in Australia, with structures mirroring the federal political structure so that they can exert influence at different levels. Teacher unions in the private sector have become more visible as the size of that sector has grown. Teachers, as a policy 'problem' in Australia, are the focus of the next section.

Teacher quality and standards

At the cusp of the new millennium, attention had turned, in earnest, towards teachers as the key ingredient in enhancing student learning outcomes, although a decade earlier Commonwealth Minister Dawkins had foreshadowed this priority in his White Paper on 'Strengthening Australia's Schools' (1998): 'the quality of teaching is central to the quality of our schools' (p. 5). Leadership in schools was also targeted as 'research suggests that leadership effects are second only to teacher effects in their impact on student learning' (Watson 2005).

In part, the impetus towards teacher quality and standards in Australia has been explained in terms of the need to solve problems of teacher shortages (Martinez 2004) and concerns about the low status of the teaching profession (Rice 2005). However, these explanations are not entirely satisfactory by themselves. Forecasts of impending and dire teacher shortages have been appearing for over a decade but they are still not evident to the extent predicted. However, there is widespread acknowledgement of the 'greying' of the profession and the possibility of unmet demands once the 'baby boom' generation of teachers retire. Teacher supply is uneven and there are some shortages in the areas of science, maths and ICT, as well as in difficult-to-staff schools in low socio-economic, rural and isolated locations. With regard to the policy 'problem' of the low status of teachers in society, a consultant evaluation of the national Quality Teacher Programme (1999–2004) which was designed, in part, to enhance the status of teachers, pointed out that there is a 'complex suite of understandings now emerging around the concept of teacher professional status' (DEST 2005, p. vii), suggesting that causes and effects of perceived low teacher status are difficult to determine.

It might be argued that the focus on teacher quality and standards in Australia has been less about shortages and status problems than about increasing teacher accountability to central authorities (often presented as a need to enhance accountability to the tax-paying public). The Australian College of Educators (White *et al.* 2003), amongst others, also take this view about the centrality of accountability in policies directed at teachers. Significant in the policy push to increase the external accountability of teachers has been a plethora of reports and forums at both State and Commonwealth levels pointing to the need for a 'new professionalism' (DEST 2003) amongst teachers. Here I will focus on just a few key turning points at the Commonwealth level to provide a 'taste' of the scene in Australia.

In 2000, the Commonwealth Department released the policy statement *Teachers for the Twenty-First Century* (DEETYA 2000). In the Introduction, Minister Kemp pointed out that although the Commonwealth does not employ teachers, its policy push on teacher quality is justified in terms of its financial investment in schooling (both government and non-government sectors) and its need to direct national priorities in priority areas such as literacy, numeracy, civics and citizenship, enterprise and vocational education in schools, indigenous education and drug education. In this policy, Minister Kemp made the link explicit between quality teachers and enhanced student learning outcomes: 'Highly effective schools and improved student outcomes are key objectives of the Commonwealth Government. Education of the highest quality is the foundation for all our futures. . . . Education of the highest quality requires teachers of the highest quality' (ibid., p. 3). The policy would inject targeted funds into four programmes over the subsequent three years: 'Quality Teachers', 'Quality Leaders', 'Quality School Management' and 'Recognition of Quality' (innovation and excellence awards), with the 'Quality Teachers' Programme receiving the bulk of the funds to 'lift teacher skills in priority areas' (ibid., p. 6). This was an agenda-setting document signalling increased Commonwealth steerage in policy about teachers, but at the same time taking a 'soft' approach, exemplified by expressions such as 'stimulate discussion about standards of professional practice' (ibid.), rather than announcing policy detail as a *fait accompli* so as not to alienate other stakeholders (especially States) and to bring them along with the Commonwealth's agenda.

Another major turning point in the Commonwealth's accelerating attention to teachers was the establishment of the National Institute for Quality Teaching and School Leadership (NIQTSL) (now with the added badge of *Teaching Australia*) in 2004 from recommendations of the report *Australia's Teachers, Australia's Future* (DEST 2003). NIQTSL is an independent body allocated initial Commonwealth funding of $10million to support and advance the quality of teaching, quality of school leadership and the status of the teaching profession (www.dest.gov.au 2006). NIQTSL is designed as an umbrella organization to bring together the entire profession of a quarter of a million teachers across the country. When Minister Nelson announced the establishment of NIQTSL, he emphasized it would be 'managed by the profession for the profession' (White *et al.* 2003). The Board includes representatives of four main constituencies – teacher professional associations, teacher unions, universities and parent groups. The roles of NIQTSL were envisaged as ultimately revolving around setting, assessing and validating advanced standards for teachers; accrediting pre-service teacher training institutions; research; and professional development and leadership training. Thus, at the national level, NIQTSL was 'marking its territory' in areas that were not directly impinging on the States. All Australian States/Territories had registration boards or teaching institutes in place or in progress in 2006. These bodies control initial teacher registration and States would inevitably resist Commonwealth intrusion into their control over supply of teachers in their jurisdiction. Given that the Commonwealth

Government has funded universities (the sites for teacher training) and used financial levers to control higher education policy for more than 30 years, obstacles to steering policy on teacher education would be relatively limited. The Chief Executive of NIQTSL, in recognizing the potential tensions between a national body and State institutes of teachers, emphasized 'we [NIQTSL] need to add value, not duplicate. We don't want to reinvent wheels or divide' (Buckingham 2005).

With regard to NIQTSL's development of a teacher standards framework, although the NIQTSL Chief Executive did not anticipate direct policy borrowing from any particular jurisdiction, Ingvarson (who sits on the NIQTSL advisory council and is Director of Research on teaching and learning for the Australian Council for Educational Research) believes a framework similar to that in the USA is possible for Australia (ibid.). In the USA, the National Board of Professional Teaching Standards (established in 1987) has overseen a comprehensive set of standards and has worked closely with professional associations and teacher unions in the process. In 2006, it was not yet clear whether NIQTSL teacher standards would be more generic or more subject-specific in nature, although early deliberations were being informed by the work of three major subject associations (mathematics, English, science). However, the task of setting, assessing and validating standards for every learning area and every age group would be very time-consuming and expensive. In 2006, there was silence on whether teacher standards would be attached to differential pay levels. Performance-related pay is very limited in Australia, although a few States have recently created a higher classification for classroom teachers to achieve a higher pay level (and remain in the classroom) based on an extensive application, portfolio and interview process (for example, Level 3 teachers in Western Australia). One might postulate that NIQTSL's moves to specify advanced standards may be a foundation for more extensive performance-related pay arrangements across the country, although it will inevitably need to be a more indirect relationship given that States are the employers of teachers – not the Commonwealth. The model from the National Board for Professional Teacher Standards in the USA might be a possible source of policy borrowing here. In the USA, teachers may choose to be assessed against the national standards (for a fee) on the expectation that employers are willing to pay higher salaries for those who have achieved the higher standards. However, it should be noted that only a small proportion (less than 1 per cent) of the approximately four million teachers in the USA have applied for standards assessment through the National Board (ibid.). Time will tell how this plays out in Australia.

Development of Australian policy about teachers since the millennium has witnessed an elision in the discourses between 'quality' and 'standards'. Arguably, the concept of standards as 'what teachers are expected to know and do' is more precise and readily measurable than the chameleon character of 'quality' (Vidovich 2001) which can mean 'all things to all people'. Standards are becoming rapidly entrenched as a central plank in the reconstruction of teacher professionalism and identity in Australia at both State and Commonwealth levels.

However, this policy agenda has been contested. The main issues revolve around the extent of ownership by the profession; that is, 'Who speaks for teachers?'.

Reviewing the first wave of teaching standards in Australia, Louden (2000) contrasted the approach taken in Australia where early attempts at specifying standards were closely aligned with the needs of State government bureaucracies (employers of teachers) with that in the USA where professional associations had taken a key role in driving the process. He noted that compared to teacher standards in the USA, in Australia they were developed more quickly and cheaply. He argued that in a second wave of development, Australian teacher standards should be more transparent, briefer, specialized, contextualized, focused on teaching and learning and matched by strong assessments, although he acknowledged that the latter is the more controversial part of the standards/assessments conceptual pair. Overall, he argued for greater professional ownership of standards. White *et al.* (2003), for the Australian College of Teachers, have pointed out that identifying 'Who speaks for teachers?' is a complex and contested issue. For example, they maintain that many classroom teachers do not consider unions, academics, education bureaucrats or even principals to represent them because they are all located outside the classroom. Further, they point to subcultures within teaching around subjects and the age of children taught, and therefore it is difficult to gain consensus on standards. Thomas (2005) maintains that a number of policies about teacher quality and standards across Australia have constructed deficit discourses on teachers, 'discourses that worked to marginalise teachers from policy-making processes, to take teachers "out of the equation" ' (p. 48).

The commentators referred to above have all critiqued *Australian* policy on teacher quality and standards. Taking a more 'global' view by comparing Australia, England, Canada and the USA, Larsen (2005) maintains that although various forms of teacher evaluation may provide some enhanced public accountability, this may come at the price of teacher anxiety, stress, mistrust and constraints to flexibility and creativity. If these negative consequences are pointers to possible effects of modernization policies, the irony is that reforms may be adding to the very problems they were originally charged with overcoming. In the next section some comparative reflections on English and Australian modernization policies are offered.

Some critical reflections on English–Australian comparisons

When the Blair Labour Government took office in 1997 on a platform of 'Education, Education, Education', in Australia we heard the echoes and many hoped there would be some significant policy borrowing, especially in my State of Western Australia given that the Labor Premier in the early 2000s, Geoff Gallop, was at university in England with Tony Blair and they remain close personal friends – a potentially direct mechanism for policy transfer. However, as the Blair Government's New Labour education policies evolved, some of us were not quite so enthusiastic about the prospects of policy borrowing from England. There are both similarities and differences in English and Australian policies for the modernization/remodelling of education and the teaching workforce. Although the differences are perhaps more a matter of degree and detail in accommodating different contexts, as they say 'the devil is in the detail'. The focus in the three subsections below is on gross patterns of similarities and differences.

Political ideologies and structures

There are recognizable parallel ideological framings for modernization/ remodelling policies in England and Australia, at least in part stemming from the overarching phenomenon of globalization and its neo-liberal, market orientation. This is despite the fact that for the best part of the nineties political parties of different ideological traditions have been in power at the national level in each country (Labour in England and conservative Coalition in Australia). In both countries, governments are not 'rolling back', but actively steering education policy (albeit 'at a distance'). The concept of government as 'market manager' is insightful here; that is, centralized control of market mechanisms featuring competition. For teachers, this has meant being targeted as a policy 'problem' in the drive to achieve a world-class education service.

At first glance, Blairite 'third way' politics (moving beyond dichotomies between left and right) which aim to bring together social democracy and the individualism of neo-liberalism, appear to be a potentially workable compromise for a Labour government rebuilding policy priorities after Thatcherism. Such an ideological coupling has been presented as the 'best of both worlds'. However, this hybrid ideology also contains some inherent contradictions. It has become apparent that differential power between the two sets of discourses is such that neo-liberalism provides the dominant framework within which social democracy must now operate.

Australia has not seen this 'third way' coupling of left and right driving policy development in the same way as in England. Arguably, at the national level there has been more unadulterated economic rationalism (a common term used for neo-liberalism in Australia) as the country has just 'celebrated' a decade of a Coalition (conservative) government under John Howard, and discourses of social justice have been rendered relatively silent. However, given Australia's federal political structure, there is a different set of ideological compromises required as it is rare to have the Commonwealth and all States with the same political party in power simultaneously, and further, the situation is in a continual state of flux as elections occur at different times. Perhaps if Labor is returned to power nationally in Australia, 'third way' politics and ensuing policy ensembles may be championed. In both countries, arguably, social justice might be seen as reconstructed in terms of the need for *all* individuals to perform to maximize human capital and thereby optimize national competitiveness in the global economy, rather than in terms of the needs of disadvantaged groups in society.

In Australia, notwithstanding the recent stronger centralist push in the 'national interest', education policy is less unified and coherent across the whole country than in England due to the federal political structure. Issues of centralized control also play out differently in Australia with more than one-third of children attending private (non-government) schools (and growing). Although the Commonwealth Government provides significant subsidy to these schools and it can use financial levers to steer policy, the sheer size and diversity of this sector tends to fragment efforts to achieve centralized control. Arguably, the Australian scenario has necessitated a 'softer touch' to education policy from the national government than in England in order to entice all stakeholders into line with the Commonwealth, as it does not have the legal basis for power in education. In England centralized control is stronger, and for some in Australia this is a 'benchmark' to be avoided with, for example, strong government steerage through OfSTED, a centrally prescribed national curriculum and the Training and Development Agency (TDA). Arguably, as centralized control increases so do the challenges to traditional notions of teacher professionalism.

Teacher shortages and the need for 'compensatory' policy

In Chapter 1 of this book, the primary reasons behind the most recent modernization/remodelling policies in England are identified as teacher shortages (due to problems of recruitment, retention and low motivation/morale) as well as the government's intention to transform school culture. These policy 'problems' are viewed by government as a serious impediment to improving standards, and thus a major thrust of the National Agreement (DfES 2003a) is to reduce teacher workload.

One might venture to suggest, provocatively, that there is less of a need for such a policy to remodel the teaching workforce in Australia because there is not the same degree of negative backlash from earlier policies which have pushed the conceptualization of teacher professionalism towards the limits. This recent English National Agreement might be seen as a strategy to 'compensate' for earlier damaging policy effects. Arguably, a culture of performativity or, as Stephen Ball would describe it, the 'terrors of performativity' (Ball 2003) has been more embedded in England, with strong centralized control and accelerating accountability requirements in education over a longer time period. In Australia in the early 2000s, teacher shortages are nowhere near as acute as in England. Arguably, the relatively softer approach of Australian governments to modernization policies (in large part necessitated by contextual circumstances) might be described as less 'high stakes' and less punitive for teachers compared to England. This is certainly *not* to say that Australian teachers have not suffered both policy overload and challenges to their professionalism. Their work has intensified and their voices have been marginalized, but perhaps to a lesser extent than in England.

In England, even performance-related pay, introduced for teachers through Threshold Applications from 2000, which was designed to motivate teachers and improve standards, appears to have had a less than desirable effect. Farrell and Morris (2004) presented findings of a large-scale survey indicating that performance-related pay has been met with strong antipathy by teachers who reported that it achieved little in alleviating morale problems, was divisive and was difficult to implement, especially in terms of isolating individual performance when teamwork was being emphasized. Arguably, when differential pay is attached to performance management, a culture of performativity is driven more deeply into educational institutions and classrooms, adding to teachers' sense of surveillance, and according to Gleeson and Husbands (2003) the primary effect is deprofessionalizing. There have been very recent pressures from the Commonwealth Minister for Education to institute performance-related pay for Australian teachers, and with this a culture of performativity is likely to be further entrenched in Australian schools as well.

Teachers' voices

In England, the National Agreement (DfES 2003a) which formed the foundation for remodelling the school workforce was signed by government, employers and unions. The National Union of Teachers did not sign, and it was particularly concerned about the increasing role of unqualified teachers (teaching assistants) in traditional teacher roles. Lack of NUT endorsement ought to have signalled a level of concern amongst the policy elite if they were genuine about working with the profession in a consultative process to address issues in the nature of teachers' work. It appears it didn't. Further, to a distant observer like myself, the use of PricewaterhouseCoopers to conduct a study on teachers' work for DfES which formed a basis of the policy direction leads one to question whether an accounting firm has a sufficiently broad conceptualization of teaching professional practice to analyse the finer nuances of teachers' work. Likewise, the choice of OfSTED for conducting an official evaluation of the policy implementation (2004) was interesting, given the negative 'baggage' that OfSTED carries for many teachers, especially with its very public 'naming and shaming' strategy, which is likely to undermine the discourse of the remodeling policy which purports to enhance support for teachers. Academic research related to this policy has also apparently been marginalized, and the fact that government policy on remodelling was agreed and introduced before the pilot TSW Project evaluation by a group of academics commissioned by DfES was completed suggests a predetermined policy agenda. Although teacher practitioners were represented in the Implementation Review Unit, arguably implementation review is far removed from being empowered to participate in setting the policy directions in the first instance. Teachers have become the objects of policy rather than active participants in the process.

In Australia, too, teachers' voices have been increasingly muted in modernization policy processes since 1990. However, there are some recent pointers to a potential upswing with, for example, greater inclusion of teachers in the development of teacher standards frameworks. Policy borrowing from the USA as well as Commonwealth–State power struggles, which may have left open some spaces into which teachers' voices can insert themselves, may have been significant here.

Overall, based on the gross patterns of similarities and differences between England and Australia sketched above, there is evidence of important localized mediations of global modernization policy trends. However, I would not want to overemphasize the differences as there are also many similarities, especially in terms of the underlying ideology. Although policy specifics vary, one major overarching theme is the changing nature of accountability and professional identity for teachers which accompanies modernization/remodelling policies. Arguably, accountability is one of the meta-discourses in policies aimed at modernizing/remodelling education (White *et al.* 2003; Smyth 2005; Watson 2005). The repeated themes percolating throughout this chapter – especially quality and standards – are essentially about the increasing, and changing nature of, accountability of teachers. However, far from being 'simple' (DfES 2004b, p. 4), accountability is increasingly complex with multiple accountabilities pulling in different directions, especially in an era of globalization. Managerial and market accountabilities have been foregrounded to achieve a competitive edge in the global marketplace, but these newer accountabilities have not replaced more historically entrenched professional and democratic forms. New accountabilities, which focus more on proving quality and standards to external stakeholders, have been layered on top of older forms, and this complexity needs to be acknowledged, in my view.

Mechanisms which emphasize the 'prove' (externally oriented) side of accountability over the 'improve' (internally oriented) side have implications for teacher professional autonomy and identity. In particular, the concept of 'managed markets', which have come to prevail with globalization, where a confluence of government managerial and market accountabilities operate, has a strong potential to shift control away from teachers and authentic learning and teaching. When the locus of policy control is beyond the reach of teachers, this must have a deprofessionalizing effect. Without access to policy power, teachers are reconstructed more as 'technicians' or 'puppets' of governments and/or markets. There is a need to reinvigorate the teaching profession, and arguably this could contribute to overcoming the recruitment, retention and motivation/morale problems which purportedly triggered the latest remodelling policy initiatives in England, and to a lesser extent in Australia.

Conclusion

Modernization policies which feature both increasing and new types of accountability as core concepts should carry a warning – 'handle with care!' However, I am not questioning the need for accountability *per se*, as complex and multiple accountabilities are appropriate in these globalizing new times. Instead, I believe there is a need to actively negotiate a 'hybrid' form of accountability which renders different types of accountability relationships more transparent, and also better balances newer managerial and market forms with more traditional professional and democratic forms. Ranson (2003) proposes a model of 'democratic public accountability', which is negotiated in the public sphere, and which involves collective deliberation, contestation, a strong sense of public good, shared understanding and dialogues about accountability to create a 'community of practice'. Trust is central in such a community of practice (see also Olssen *et al.* 2004; Bottery 2006).

Throughout this chapter the marginalization of teacher voice in modernization policies has been a recurrent theme. Thomas (2005) argues that an alternative is to reconstruct teachers as authoritative voices in policymaking, to allow them more autonomy, but also to make explicit the norms of professional practice which provides accountability to the public. Sachs' (2003) notion of an 'activist teaching profession' is useful here. She argues for a democratic professionalism in which an activist teacher identity is based on democratic principles, negotiated, collaborative, socially critical, future-oriented, strategic and tactical. This activist teacher identity contrasts with an entrepreneurial teacher identity which Sachs associates with current prevailing managerial (economic) discourses which promote an individualistic, competitive, controlling, regulative, externally defined, and standards-led identity. Thus, the emphasis for the 'new professionalism' of teachers *ought* to be critical and active engagement with policy. 'Policy is contested terrain' (Ozga 2000a, p. 1) and modernization/ remodelling policies *ought* to be more contested and subject to greater critical review by *all* stakeholders than is evident in recent reforms. Teachers are positioned at the heart of authentic teaching and learning, and in the interests of our children their voices *ought* to be heard loudly and clearly as modernization policies and practices are negotiated in the public domain.

I draw to a conclusion by returning to the phenomenon of globalization with which I began. Arguably this is the common antecedent to modernization policies across many countries. Globalization has contributed to the ideological consistency of such policies at different sites. However, in my view, there is a need to uncouple the ideological dimension of globalization from the technical dimension to open spaces for other (non-market) responses to new times, and this includes distinguishing between a 'global knowledge *society*' and a 'global knowledge *economy*' because society is a much broader construct in which all manner of 'rich' non-economic activities occur.

While there have been strong ideological parallels between modernization policies in England and Australia, there are also significant differences in the detailed nature and timing of policies in each country. This reflects Green's (1999) argument that global education policy convergence has been evidenced more in policy goals and discourses than in the detailed structures and processes adopted in different countries. We must examine closely the similarities and differences in purported 'global' trends, analysing the dialectic between 'the global' and 'the local' (Marginson and Rhoades 2002) to highlight the 'agency' that organizations and individuals can exert in actively negotiating policies and practices appropriate to different contexts. As we reflect on a variety of national approaches to modernization policies, we have an opportunity for critical and active policy *learning* rather than uncritical and passive policy *borrowing*.

On the one hand, modernization policies have reached 'epidemic' (Levin 1998) proportions – even 'pandemic' status (to continue the analogy) – but on the other hand, in the interests of preserving 'healthy' diversity (an essential for species survival in the biological world) the sort of standardization and homogenization which is promoted by discourses of 'world class' and 'best practice' as well as uncritical policy borrowing must be dislodged.

Chapter 15

The globalization of education and the modernization of schools: a comparative study of French and English educational policies

Régis Malet

Introduction

In France and England, two countries of solid traditions and strong national identities, systems of schooling have been built on distinctive values, principles and myths. These were established within cultural environments where the task of educating, creating social links and instilling the concepts of citizenship took on distinctive characteristics. Although all European countries are linked by philosophical and cultural traditions in education (and furthermore there is a general trend of gradual homogenization of education systems), the weight of each education system's history has consequently influenced its conceptions of educational action and the role of its schools and teachers.

Increasingly it seems to be accepted (Appadurai 1996) that if globalization 'alters the principles and perspectives of national education systems' (Green 2002, p. 14), under the influence of transnational political agendas that lead to the incontestable phenomena of convergence of public policies (van Haecht 1998), then the local conceptions and practices – marked by both political and cultural traditions – maintain a significant role in mediating and reconfiguring global political contexts into terms that are distinctive to themselves.

Globalization does not designate a single process of technical rationalization of school systems, or subject them to criteria of efficiency and profitability. Furthermore globalization goes hand in hand with a renewal of forms of individualization and subjectivization, as well as transforming schools' methods of regulation and administration. This is echoed, through local implementation, in new forms of social administration (Popkewitz 1993), or indeed through the 'governing of souls' (Novoa 2002).

The phenomena linked with globalization do not stimulate either apathy or inertia in the national education systems. On the contrary they highlight deep transformations that locally generate, in rich social contexts, the transposition of a distinctive culture and tradition of models of policy regulation (more or less prescribed), and of external injunctions to change. Within the context of education, most education reforms carried out in European countries have progressively promoted forms of regulation of educational action within converging academic spheres – even though these processes have developed at different rates of intensity and according to different political agendas, depending on the country. This implies a valorization of the academic establishment – which has become a pertinent organizational reference point on educational action – and a more ample conceptualization of educational work, now assumed by a larger educative community. It has also encouraged a more concentrated and participative approach to forms of work, and finally a less linear design of teaching professionals' careers.

At stake, within the context of converging educational policies in Europe, is the peer review of transformations in administrative models and schoolwork, viewed 'as social activities mobilizing (and mobilized by) at the same time socially localized and macro-social interactions' (Mabilon-Bonfils and Saadoun 2001, p. 188). Such transformations are culturally rooted and socially built. I shall base my analysis on two countries – France and England – which have both seen, over the past two decades, great changes in their schools' administrative policies, their forms of organizing schoolwork and the educational models they use.

School: a generic, but rather restricting, concept

Both the English and French language use the same word for the institution that delivers teaching: school and *école*. They have a common Greek origin: *skholê* (leisure, then study). Although in French the generic meaning, and its adjectival derivation, *scolaire*, are used to refer to all levels of education from primary school to *lycée* (the French equivalent to sixth form), the term *école* is nevertheless more restricted in France than in England. The French *école* refers only to primary educational institutions: primary schools. It is interesting to note the two distinct uses of the term in the two contexts. Secondary schools have, since their creation, displayed a distinctive identity in France due to the fact that they were created before primary schools (1805 for secondary schools, with the creation of the *Université Impériale*; 1833 for primary schools, with the *Loi Guizot*). Equally, following on from this, there is a concern to distinguish between schools for the masses and schools for the bourgeoisie. For this reason, under the Third Republic, the term *petites classes* (small classes) was used for secondary schools and the term *école* was reserved for primary school teaching.

Although the same educational division existed in England until halfway through the twentieth century, the term 'school' was not subjected to the same socio-semantic narrowing. It is still used to refer to both grammar schools, which have for a long time selected pupils by ability, and comprehensive schools (the British equivalent of French *collèges* and *lycées*). The grammar schools teach pupils who pass the 11+ examination, where it is available. This perhaps favours the middle classes, but working-class children are still able to access a grammar school education. The notion of educational differentiation was even widened to encompass Higher Education (School of Arts, Education, Economics, etc.), whereas in France, remarkably, the notion refers to non-university Higher

Education establishments, often of a prestigious nature (Ecole d'architecture, Ecole supérieur, Grandes écoles, etc.).

'School' is, essentially, a portmanteau word – but its use is greatly influenced by the culture and historical evolution of each particular education system. Indeed, I consider that in order to understand forms of administration amongst schools and teachers in contemporary times, it is necessary to place this study in context by considering the principles that previously presided over the development of schooling and teaching in the two countries. Here we find principles that we assume are still in use today, despite phenomena of transnational convergences that lead to a hybridization of form.

The English and French education systems were based on common democratic principles: free education, extension of the mandatory school age, abandonment of an elitist system and the end of the educational division within the primary–secondary school continuum. Nevertheless, the education systems' agendas of democratization were not identical; neither were the policy or curriculum reshuffles that they gave way to. Therefore, in accordance with the specific links between the individual and their community, we find very specific historical forms of construction of the idea of citizenship. These have had, and continue to have, major consequences on the conceptions of teaching and on the status of both teacher and pupil.

National conceptions of the social function of school and its administration

The French conception of citizenship, both political and individual, promotes an abstract idea of citizenship created by the French Revolution. This reflects the actions of an inclusive state (the centralized and unifying 'French model') built on the intersection of intermediate forms of belonging. This unitary conception fuels the dichotomy between the universal and the individual (Schnapper 2000). More than others, the French model accentuated censorship between public and private spheres and rejected from the concept of citizenship the sphere of individual interests or membership, other than towards the national (Gagnon *et al.* 1996; Starkey 2000). The French republican school system was built on values of integration and national cohesion. The criterion of universalism, of uniformity of curriculum, of supply and education – as well as the recruitment of teachers – are all indications of this concept of citizenship. This descending pyramidal model is echoed in the content of the curriculum and the pedagogic forms implemented in schools, especially in the secondary sector. The French 'encyclopaedic' nature of education is therefore based on rationalism, intellectualism (not concerned with the practical use of knowledge), egalitarianism and secularism, which leads to the particularity of leaving the child's moral upbringing to the family.

The French model, traditionally centralized, remains marked by the importance of assessment at each stage of the student's academic career and by a strong reference to a scholarly norm. For this reason, the French model favours a compensatory treatment of the student's scholarly difficulties, which is reinforced by the theory of socio-cultural disability. This compensatory pedagogy has constituted the organizing principle behind educational policies since the beginning of the 1980s; the ZEPs (*Zones d'education prioritaire*: Education Action Zones) incarnated this institutional treatment of academic failure at a national level. Yet it shifts the question of egalitarian policies of educational supply towards policies more marked by a concern for equity than equality. Beyond the tendency to decentralize the system – which gives a new emphasis to the local level – there is (in this model of the academic tradition) a form of institutionalization and a distributive conception of the management of social, cultural and educational heterogeneity.

The Anglo-Saxon conception of citizenship is, on the contrary, based around the community. It refers less to the idea of national, or state, integration and more to the active participation of citizens within their community. This promotes a less abstract and exclusive, more local and pluralist, concept of citizenship. This model emerged against the absolutism of the state and in favour of an affirmation of individual rights and local liberties. In the Anglo-Saxon model, 'you are a citizen by belonging to a certain community' (Schnapper 2000, p. 42) – therefore there is less of a gap in England between the public and private spheres. Intermediate membership is not *a priori* excluded from the much more pragmatic concept of life. When it comes to teaching, one finds a humanist conception of education based on individualism, pragmatism and a strong moral dimension, conceiving of the scholarly institution as a living community closely linked with its environment while still enjoying a strong autonomy.

Therefore, if the French idea of egalitarianism led to a uniform and national concept of school content, the English system has for a long time adopted an opposing model to define the curriculum – imparting upon the schools themselves, after validation from local authorities, responsibility for the curriculum and the disciplines on offer. As highlighted by Baluteau (1996), in England 'the legitimacy of the curriculum was not principally based on legalist actions but took its meaning from local rationality. . . . The prescription of knowledge resulted from the social and economic reality of the "region", more precisely, it ensued from the work of local actors around and at the heart of local authorities (parents, company directors, teachers. . .)'.

In accordance with these principles of promoting local liberties, it was this level that the management of educational affairs was long entrusted: English schools, in the widest sense of the term, are therefore traditionally the responsibility of intermediate administrative units (local education authorities, and education committees), before being the responsibility of the state. However, as we shall see, recent times have counterbalanced these founding principles. There is no single *British* education system, rather four 'home nation' systems, of which the English system is one. In England the system is characterized by a liberal quasi-entrepreneurial conception of education, which places schools in competition with each other. This, therefore, openly reinforces the family's as well as the school's status as consumer – which may benefit from private funding (in the case of city technology colleges, or more recently academies, maintained by private funds).

At the same time, the English model promotes a strong moral dimension (in no way exclusive of, or contradictory to, the liberal conception), with a concern to begin the educational process with the individual and his/her own potential (referred to as 'child-centred education'). A trend to uniform curricula is thereby less favoured. This moral dimension of education originates in grammar schools and public schools (Calvert 2000). Comprehensive schools, created from the late 1950s, took on this heritage by institutionalizing the moral dimension of education by promoting pastoral care – which in England defines the social and moral role of teachers. This social function was reinforced by the Education Reform Act of 1988 which promoted schools' responsibility in developing the 'moral, spiritual, social and cultural development' of pupils.

France has seen growing similarities developing between the worlds of education and business, in particular with the creation of technology colleges and professional *lycées*. These attest to considerations of economic rationality and a retreat of disinterested knowledge (Baluteau 1996). Nevertheless, it seems that by favouring a less concentrated model of educational power, this has led to a certain autonomization of schools. France has consequently maintained a consecutive approach towards education–qualification–employment in accordance with French centralism and the state's distributive function in terms of employment. This also partly explains the tightness around diplomas and school hierarchies – which educational systems that are more liberal and less centralized in their conception, like those in England, have little appreciation of. From this point of view, standardization – efforts to render a more uniform supply of education – as well as the organization of education into generic branches, would favour a consecutive conception of relations between education and employment. On the other hand, more integrative relations between training and employment would characterize narrower and localized training structures linked with the structure of employment.

Finally, the evolution of teacher training sheds light on these recent changes. The statutory distinction between *instituteurs* (primary school teachers) and *professeurs* (secondary school teachers), which the creation in France in 1991 of the IUFM (*Instituts Universitaires de Formation des Maîtres*: University institutes for teacher training) recently put an end to, has not existed in England since Butler's 1944 Education Act. Half a century before France, England influenced teachers' recruitment and conditions of service by creating education degrees for a proportion of trainee teachers (which only really came into effect with the creation of comprehensive schools). Until then the system had been fragmented by the criterion of birth, based on the same model as that within France. A concern for coherence in teacher training, which was delayed in France, and the equalization of the status and treatment of all teachers were adopted in England as soon as secondary schools became the natural progression from primary schools. The cultural gap between primary and secondary teaching, stemming from the social history of both groups of teachers, nevertheless existed in the same vein as in France. But if the same tensions around identity as those observed in France were at work in the English teaching system (Brisard and Malet 2004), the scars of statutory parity were further afield and consequently better dealt with in England than in France.

Paradoxical evolutions in the forms of school administration?

Opposite tendencies in the role of the state: decentralization versus state control

The current era testifies that the principles governing the development and administration of schools in France and England are far from being long-lasting. Indeed, the two countries have gradually adopted forms of school management which are a radical departure from the models that were in place early in the last century. In England, the state gradually expanded its power in schools and took on the function of prescribing and even enjoining change. Although this centralizing process has accelerated since the mid-nineties, it is in actual fact older. Apart from the creation of the Ministry of Education – which in France has existed since the nineteenth century, first as the Ministry of Public Instruction and then as the Ministry of Education – the Butler Act, in 1944, also saw a reduction in the number of local education authorities that were, until then, under the direct control of the Ministry. But it was with the Education Reform Act of 1988 that the state's control over schools accelerated, with the creation of a National Curriculum and an arsenal of assessments for each stage of the pupil's educational career (Key Stages). This trend was recently expanded to include teacher training, which has been based on standardized training programmes since 1998 for some disciplines, but which encompassed all subjects and education levels by the beginning of the 2005 academic year.

The English model of teacher management contrasted with the French system in that its organization was, until recently, horizontal – with local education authorities and schools largely 'equal'. LEAs were in charge of defining programmes, services and credits allocated to schools, whilst the schools themselves were responsible for recruitment, management and promotion of their personnel. The state, in this context, only exerted its role as motivator and supervisor. Aiming to raise accountability and correct performances deemed unsatisfactory in the English education system, the Education Reform Act of 1988 considerably reduced local education authorities' power and gave the state many new prerogatives to define programmes and to directly finance schools. The recentralization of executive power, initiated during Thatcher's era when the government reinforced the state's power over local authorities and extended its remit to encompass the control of teacher training, occurred through the standardization in the 1990s of teachers' competencies and a distinct shift in professional training from universities to schools.

In France, the process that saw the promotion of school establishments through the 1980s followed a different logic. A redeployment of administrative powers in school came about because of a noted lack of power in the uniform model – based on the egalitarian ideal of struggling against social inequalities that schools were faced with and, on the other hand, the need to adapt an education system in retreat from economic drivers. During the 1980s this led to a call for the increased accountability of local authorities and the administrative units within secondary schools. Transformations in the education system's manners of guidance therefore answered a double demand for profitability and equity (Lessard 2000). The 'collège unique' (one school for Years 7 through 11), established in 1975 by the Haby Reform, quickly encountered great problems and found it difficult to maintain its triple functionality: transmitting basic knowledge, socializing and orienting pupils. It already suffered from the traditional French encyclopaedic nature of teaching in secondary schools. Moreover, the persistence and evolution of disciplines maintained the cultural crucible between teaching, academic culture and pupils.

Additionally, the French system – based on uniformity of programmes and methods of assessment – has for a long time operated to reveal scholarly failure and the distance between the preference of certain pupils and the school's norm. The extension of schooling also impacted on pupils from different backgrounds, because it favoured social heterogeneity of classes. It was principally the increasing coeducation of pupils and the difficulties of managing heterogeneity that encouraged the gradual recasting of *collèges* in the 1980s, and of *lycées* from the beginning of the 1990s.

The policy of decentralizing decision-making in favour of education offices was accompanied by the granting of greater autonomy to schools. The laws of decentralization in 1982–3 allowed the state and the local authorities to share tasks and competencies and furthermore granted more power locally. In 1985 *collèges* and *lycées* became 'local public teaching establishments' (referred to as EPLEs in France), which had educational, administrative and pedagogic autonomy. The responsibilities of investment in education and of functionality credits were now entrusted to the region for *lycées*, and to the county for *collèges*. Each town maintained its responsibility for primary and nursery schools in accordance with the constitutional modes of primary and secondary stages.

From that moment the system consented to support local needs, initiatives and dynamics. The premise is simple: by decentralizing the national education 'machine', through the local regulation of education, it was hoped that management would be adapted to the needs of teachers and other stakeholders.

Common stakes: redeployment of the levels of decision-making and 'controlled autonomization' of establishments

There exist in France, as in England, three levels of decision-making within education: the state, the 'local authority/intermediate level' and the school itself. The intermediate level is represented in France by the *académie*, the region, the county and the town (regional, general and municipal councils for local authorities) and in England by the local education authority. According to a study by Thélot (1993), the structure of decision-making at primary and secondary levels is equally split: one-third for each level (school/intermediate/ state level). It is interesting to compare these figures with other countries: in the US, 80 per cent of decisions are taken by individual states; the school takes only 20 per cent. The situation in England corresponded for a long time to this model, conferring an important administrative power on local education authorities. In recent times, contrary to what has happened in France, there has been a radical shift in this tendency, which has led to a considerable weakening of the intermediate level to the benefit of macro-educative administrative units (the state) and micro-educative ones (the schools).

Since 1990, both countries have been subjected to huge modifications in their forms of guidance to schools. Despite strategies that are evidently distinctive from forms of deregulation of school administration, we consider that in the two cases – decentralization (France) versus state control (England) – there are common goals at stake. At the same time these transformations were governed by a shared agenda linked to the generalization of Europe's education systems through the 1960s and 1970s, which revealed an increasing concern with the economic performance of schools. Therefore, one can interpret the parallels through the 1980s of the emergence of forms of guidance that balanced (and even contradicted) national educational traditions, as clues to a globalization of scholarly stakes. These gave way to area-specific answers and modes of interpretation that remained symptomatic of a particular political and scholarly culture, which might prolong or upturn traditional policies of school management.

The French strategy therefore consisted of removing some of the state's power, to the advantage of local authorities and schools. But the strategy did not result in a complete loss of the state's initiative to manage scholarly matters – the recruitment of personnel and the definition of the contents of lessons remained national, for example. The state favoured reconciliation between schools and their local environments, in response to demands that the school system should adapt, in line with the spirit of realism and economic rationality (which we have seen was lacking in an education system marked by an encyclopaedic and disinterested tradition of teaching). The state also favoured a more standardized supply of training, within an education system marked by egalitarianism and standardization. These evolutions in the system were also accompanied by appropriate changes to the curriculum.

In England, successive governments attempted to take back control from schools. This was not an attempt to 'weigh down' the education system or to cripple its management, but rather to place schools back under the control of the state, while still promoting the school itself. This was done by shifting powers granted to the LEAs towards the governing bodies of individual schools. The state could, therefore, through the terms of this process, take advantage of adopting not only a motivational role but also a prescriptive role at minimal cost. The founding principles behind English schooling, which promoted each local government's prerogatives, had previously prevented this.

Encouraged by a normative state that gradually liberated schools from local administration – but which compensated this process with more direct central control of schools – the schools' ability to govern themselves led to an emergence of forms of school administration that promoted new managerial notions. These were often marked, conforming to New Labour's preoccupations and principles (linking economic realism and a concern for efficiency and social justice), by ethical preoccupations, revealed through aspects of school improvement, school effectiveness (Gray *et. al.* 1996; Stoll and Myers 1998) educational leadership and management (Mortimore and Whitty 1997).

Due to this, in the context of a state that assumed (or, if need be, preserved) a motivational and regulatory power, schools enjoyed some control over initiatives. Because of the dynamic element of transformations that were propelled by a concern for efficiency and profitability, schools became more autonomized. From this point of view the decentralization/centralization dichotomy is not effective, because these transformations come within the framework of a redefining of the legitimacy of the state's authority in scholarly matters (Novoa and Popkewitz 2001).

This process therefore came within the framework of a common agenda, which was the *promotion of micro-level administrations* (schools) that are given more responsibilities, yet are also subjected to more control and evaluation. Thus, both state control and the state's disengagement from scholarly matters appear relative in this light, because despite their context they are plagued by a common tension between control and autonomization. What clearly happened is that when the state wished to exercise increasing power over the administration of schools, the decentralized tradition of the English system favoured the brutal promotion of an evaluative state. This occurred because the power traditionally allotted to local governments was reduced, in part, in order to ensure central control (Broadfoot 2000).

Even if this convergence did not overshadow the particular forms that these evolutions resulted in, one notes that in France (as in England) a new form of organizing scholarly work developed. This promoted professional modes of education which were better devised and more participative, and which valued the teaching collective and the school community. At the same time, we note in France a retreat from the institutional model of work in school (Dubet 2002), to the benefit of a learned organization which is more autonomous and closer to its social and economic background yet subjected, in return, to demands of efficiency and assessment of its results.

Therefore, remarkably, in England, a country based on a tradition of community where organizational culture entered the world of education long before it did in France (Hargreaves 1994), one notes developments in the forms of regulation of hybrid schoolwork. This regulation was marked by a liberal model, which traditionally conferred on schools an important margin of autonomy when it came to recruiting staff, to developing their careers and to the schools' links with their social and economic community. It was also marked by a bureaucratic and standardizing model whereby the state accorded itself reinforced control over schools and the personnel who work there (Broadfoot 2000). In France, where work carried out by teachers is traditionally marked by an academic model and determined by the relationship with pupils (Obin 2002), this 'organizational turning point' was initiated over recent years but without using (for the moment) the same evaluative arsenal as in England.

The evolution of teachers' work in France: the difficult penetration of collaboration into culture

In England, the culture of organization entered the world of education long before it did in France. The community-based conception of the school, which exists linked to an ethic developed by the teaching profession in England, favours active participation of teachers in the wider educational community. This conception of the teachers' role, which traditionally goes hand in hand with professional corporatism, is anchored in a more collective conception of professional work as 'belonging to a particular community' (Schnapper 2000, p. 42). This conception is present in the political and educational thinking of Anglo-Saxons and is echoed in the traditional concepts of professionalism in teaching. More recently, as we have already seen, regulation has been extended within the work of schools. Schools were marked by both a liberal model, which gave individual schools significant autonomy when recruiting and within the careers of their personnel, as well as a centralized model, where the state granted itself reinforced control of establishments and personnel.

In France, where teachers' work in *collèges* and *lycées* is greatly affected by an academic model and determined by the teachers' relationship with pupils (Obin 2002), an 'organizational turning point' was set in motion using the same evaluative arsenal as in England. The process that saw the promotion of the individual school responded, as we have seen to a different logic, leading to a decentralized and territorial model of regulation of educational supply. Teachers' collective conceptions of work have, since the 1989 *Loi d'Orientation*, ceased to be encouraged through dispositions concerning the reform of *lycées* and the alteration of *collèges*. The room given for initiative has granted to schools the space to widen teachers' traditional missions. It has also increased the role of heads of school, who now fulfil the decisive function of mediators between institutional recommendations, teachers and the different agents and stakeholders within the larger school community. Increasingly subjected to a competitive academic world, their aims have gradually evolved from the administrative to the managerial. This evolution has been in relation to the weakening of the school's 'legitimacy in value' in favour of a 'rational legitimacy', based on the efficiency of the school's organization (Dubet 2002, p. 142).

Nevertheless, despite this evolution in the management of schools, the classroom has remained for French teachers the natural setting for their work and the environment in which to express their pedagogic autonomy. Decentralization seems to have had more influence on the administrative than on either the educational or the pedagogical domain. The 1997 Bill on teachers' aims integrated collegial dimensions, and broadened the teacher's role to involve greater team working and partnerships. It also called on teachers to became more reflexive and flexible. The Obin Report (2002) also pleaded for a collective professionalism amongst teachers, strongly underlining the need to promote both the school and collective notions of work in the everyday life of teachers: 'making teachers work in teams, leading them to collectively assume their educational responsibility, to transcend the barriers between disciplines depending on pupils' needs, to innovate within their pedagogy' (Obin 2002, p. 130).

The Thélot Report (2004) follows the same direction, and even goes further, by recommending a transformation of teachers' 'modalities of service', allowing the presence of teachers in schools beyond their teaching duty. By advocating an increased autonomy for schools – and the development of new settings for social contracts between heads of schools and teachers, with the aim of encouraging collective work – one can see, at least in intention if not in practice, a certain reconciliation with 'the learned professional organization', similar to that which has unfolded in England since the mid-nineties. Inspired by the Thélot Report, the Education Orientation Law, known as the Fillon Law, scheduled the creation, from the beginning of the 2006 academic year, of a 'pedagogic council' for each educational establishment. This council aimed to reinforce cooperative work amongst teachers, disciplinary coordinators and the management team. By commissioning the head of the school to appoint the members of this council from within the teaching body, this plan introduced heads into the pedagogic field and gave them the task of 'distinguishing' between teachers, by associating them with a council distinct from the school's administrative council.

This new plan – disparaged by teaching unions who saw it as an attack orchestrated by heads on pedagogic freedom and professional solidarity – was not in fact based on elective principles, but distinctive ones. This translated a political agenda (similar to the English model) which was to submit the changes to forms of social administration – in other words to make the schools *themselves* the driving factor behind the expected changes.

Nevertheless, these prescriptions and evolutions seem for the moment to have come up against a wall, and now generate more resistance than mobilization. Thus, in 2001, the weekly average time dedicated by teachers to teamwork, including school board meetings, was one hour and twenty minutes (Obin 2002). A study carried out by the DPD (Braxmeyer *et al.* 2002) reveals that only six out of ten teachers declare having had 'the chance to work in teams over the past three years'. The practices amongst teachers therefore seem to show a certain reticence about complying with official recommendations.

The Obin Report (2002) evokes the desirable development of a culture of collaboration in teachers' work, by inscribing it within a positive vision of the evolution of school organization: 'collective work, in schools, is deemed increasingly necessary and appreciated' (Obin 2002, p. 70). However, professional satisfaction amongst French teachers about the notion of cooperation does not mean one can ignore the particular tonality of their resistance to the idea of institutionalization.

In fact, collective work in France does not enter into the teachers' workload, which is limited to the hours that they *teach* (although time for lesson planning is also considered in relation to their workload). The intrusive nature of collective work is, besides, less the consequence of an authoritarian injunction to collective work, and more a professional norm in use in secondary schools in France. All that relates to educational practices within teaching is essentially considered by teachers to be a personal matter. They enjoy professional autonomy as to whether they choose to use other professional support – either within pedagogic practice or to deal with disciplinary problems.

In France, the injunction towards undertaking more collective work is principally moral. It calls for 'common sense', yet does not rely on procedures or guidance tools, and is both centred on methods and plagued by federative objectives. Where these procedures exist – for example, by means of projects – the institutionalization of the approach tends to place more emphasis on the formalization of plans and their evaluation, than on action. In the eyes of teachers, this reinforces the weakness of such plans. Furthermore, in a profession where professional autonomy is defined in relation to discipline and pedagogic relations, these plans create a sentiment of subordination to a prescribed exercise that does not engage the teacher in that which constitutes the essence of his/her activity (Malet and Brisard 2005a and b).

The efforts to construct teaching corporatism without integrating a policy that would award the collective a supportive function towards the pedagogic activity itself remain insignificant for teachers. Due to this, one does not reach, in France, the heart of the activity due to the firmness of professional norms and the division of pedagogic and administrative work. This division is much stronger than in England.

However, injunctions do exist: heads of schools are the primary recipients, in as much as they are the interface between administration and teaching. But the legitimacy, as well as the framework and the tools to endorse these orientations, is lacking. In what Olsen (2002) calls the 'old public administration', heads of schools were 'administrators, inspired by the regulatory logic, who applied and maintained with integrity juridical norms in a neutral manner and with the public's best interests in mind. This approach favours reliability, predictability and transparency' (p. 4). Aware of this 'slackness' within the system, teachers remain relatively calm about the effects that this might have on their own practice. Legitimized by disciplinary expertise, submitting themselves at their will to attend meetings, they do not have the feeling that the structure of their activity is at risk: 'we do feel trends that are beginning to emerge', testifies one teacher, 'they want to make us work more as a team but it's difficult to really incite people to do it, it depends on each individual, so on that aspect I'm not really worried' (Olsen 2002, p. 15). The link supported by the school's hierarchy is very significant in revealing teachers' confidence in a status that protects them for the time being from vague attempts to deeply transform their jobs.

The head of school's authority is weak. The rituals of administrative responsibilities are part of the hierarchic folklore to which teachers attach little importance. When it comes to intermediate levels of management, their diffused and not fully institutionalized nature favours dispersion and a weak mobilizing value from the work collective. This tendency is, for that matter, viewed by many as being artificial: ignorant of real forms of teachers' work it soon complies with a conservative and individualist rhetoric amongst the education workforce.

The collective exists on the periphery of administration in spaces set aside by teachers from their work with pupils. The partiality and gratuitousness particular to this investment of teachers' time easily renders it incompatible with an administrative framework.

Yet the division of work in France does not only apply to educational and administrative levels. Increasing heterogeneity amongst pupils, on both social and academic levels, and difficulties linked with the preservation of academic order call for the deployment of academic and social mediation. Here, again, to remain outside of the realm of teachers' prerogatives, the division of duties operates areas of mediation taken on by peripheral personnel, from both inside and outside the school (pedagogic counsellors, psychological career advisers, school psychologists, nurses, etc.), whose links with teachers are currently almost non-existent. Therefore each respective mission remains almost unrecognized. Teachers only barely assume a participative role with respect to their pupils' orientation, a duty that is incidentally inscribed in the secondary school teachers' status.

Conclusion

In France and England, the transformations of administering teachers and schools attests to common ambitions, if not methods. This seems to at least ensure, or maintain, the effective authority of the macro-political regime within a strong state, as well as to accord managerial and functional autonomy to the micro-political authorities that are schools. This has led, in England, to a weakening of the local education authority's powers and in France to a shift of accountability towards the local authority level, with a concomitant impact on the realignment of the state's educational budget.

The promotion of scholarly organization at the local level since 1990 has found means, with the introduction of new forms of social management within schools, to arm education reforms with neo-liberal inspirations using an arsenal of 'techniques of accountability' (Novoa 2002). These have ensured local implementation, supported by supervisory staff whose managerial roles have greatly increased since the millennium, especially in England, but also increasingly in France. In some ways, this has created a continuity between the evolution of forms of *scholarly administration* and *social administration* (Popkewitz 1998) of professional behaviour.

Contemporary reforms in schools have, according to some, been inscribed within the political project of reforming liberalism (Welch 1998). The modern state, both liberal and interventionist, would have evolved from indirect control (Lawn 1996, p. 21) to direct control over schools and teachers due to a concern for efficiency, predictability, reactivity and command, yet wrapped it up in a rhetoric of accountability and autonomization. This makes a programmed shift of control 'from body to soul' (Robertson 2000, p. 119) or an attempt to move towards a 'governing of souls' (according to Antonio Novoa's 2002 formula) more opaque. Based on a rhetoric of organizational autonomization and individual accountability, the political principles that animate it would be marked by a recurring concern for the cheapest guidance and control.

Based on the evolution expected within French teachers' work, the injunction to develop a collaborative professional culture clashes with a heritage as much cultural as structural which defines its specific form: the division of pedagogic and educational tasks is clearly established between, on one side, representatives of school life and, on the other, teachers. Here teaching is marked by pedagogic autonomy and centred around work in the classroom. The collective is in the background. The place of work for French teachers is, above all, classroom-based. The school remains an important place for conviviality and professional solidarity, but not strictly speaking *work*. It is therefore a momentous challenge for school administrators in France to develop these radical conceptions about teachers' forms of work.

Chapter 16

Conclusion: whither modernization?

Helen Gunter and Graham Butt

Taking stock

Our intention in this final chapter is to conclude the book, but not to assume any final settlement of the issues raised. What we can reasonably do is to provide an account of what is currently known, what this might mean and how things seem to be developing. In doing so we should like to acknowledge the evidence and analysis of our co-authors. The data we have used from the New Labour projects (Appendices 1 and 2) remain vital and interesting – not only because they show the intent and intensity of reform, but also because they illustrate what can be achieved in resolving issues of labour supply in schools. These data will remain a reference point because they capture a moment in time when investment was made in schools, combined with a desire to know what was working and why. We do not subscribe to a 'fast food' approach to understanding modernization – where all that matters is knowing what is happening now, or until we think that such knowledge is out of date, or until we lose interest in it and pass on to something else.

Much of what schools have achieved during New Labour's reforms is directly related to site-based management from 1988. Many of the schools involved in the Transforming the School Workforce Project realized this, adopting techniques and strategies learned since the late 1980s to further their development. Other schools had not gained as much from the 1988 reforms, or had been limited by the performance regime of the 1990s – therefore the Project gave them the necessary resources and permission to recapture the opportunities afforded by site-based management. In essence what we need to consider is whether remodelling is the means by which education can actually make valuable changes for the benefit of learners and learning, or whether it is about clearing up the mess caused by lack of investment in the late 1980s and the rapid and often contradictory reforms in the 1990s. It seems to us that we need to understand remodelling as another example of a reform that denied professional participation, but which made the profession responsible and accountable for its delivery.

There is a body of evidence that shows some visible and measurable outcomes for schools in doing remodelling:

- Government statistics show an increase in the number of teachers in January 2006 (up by 3,700 to a total of 435,600) and a decrease in the number of vacancies (down by 250 to 2,230); the number of support staff is up by 22,700 to 287,500, including an increase of 6,100 teaching assistants to reach a total of 153,100. While many schools now aim to employ more teaching assistants and support staff, this stage has not yet been reached according to the aggregated statistics in England (DfES 2006).

- The three-phased process for introducing remodelling is now completed and the NRT has presented case studies of schools where important gains have been made as a result of remodelling (www.tda.gov.uk). There are stories of changes in the composition of the school workforce that are enabling teachers to focus on teaching; the use of ICT (such as laptops and electronic whiteboards) to enhance lessons and to access learning resources; the use of time in creative ways to enable productive planning; changes in facilities so that staff are provided with places to work and to access drinks and food; and an approach to caring for staff so that their wider lives are given recognition as a means of enabling a work–life balance.

This fits the picture of what the TSW Project schools were able to achieve and resonates with the views of our co-authors and Project headteachers, each of whom have presented substantial evidence of gains. In particular, we note the pioneering work that was done on examining role boundaries and structures, on thinking through the strategic deployment of ICT and on how cultures and habits have been confronted and new ways of working have been developed. There have been small things, such as changing processes so that information gets to support staff in time for them to do their job, as well as bigger changes, such as the complete rethinking of student services and support. Much of this 'home improvement' has been the product of external direction, with the TSW Project and subsequent remodelling making explicit what needed to be done. Some changes, such as the legal requirement to provide teachers with time for PPA, have a more direct statutory origin. But many of these changes have been local – either the product of creative approaches in-house, or through the use of established forums, or through the adoption of bespoke change management teams. These changes did not happen overnight and a considerable amount of effort has gone into enabling staff to work in new ways and think differently about their work. Hence there have been particular local gains through experimentation, where entrenched practices caused by the externally driven 'have-to-do' culture (e.g. teachers typing up class lists at the weekend, or staying late to photocopy resources) have shifted back to an internally determined 'can-do' culture (e.g. how can teachers get on with teaching?). Here tasks might be abandoned altogether, but are usually just moved to other staff.

We must not underestimate the importance of what has been achieved locally. Much has been accomplished through the application of energy and commitment. As the TSW Project quite graphically showed, undertaking remodelling is hard work, much of it invisible and unquantifiable. Shifting the work–life balance of teachers has been a legitimate aim, but there are those in schools who have had to work harder to achieve change than they ever did before the reform process began. It is therefore something of an irony that a reform designed to deliver a fairer and a healthier work–life balance has had to be achieved through much out-of-hours work. We must also respect that an opportunity has been seized to sort out entrenched problems, to enable the profession to look after itself better and to care about the welfare of its staff. Finally, we must acknowledge that what has enabled and sustained change has been the traditionally embedded principles on which the majority of reforms have been implemented: do no harm to children and seek access to resources that can improve their learning experiences.

At the same time our responsibility as researchers is not to promote remodelling, or to provide victorious cases studies to encourage the implementation of the National Agreement. This book is not a ringbinder in which we seek to provide the recipes for good practice. Indeed, there are other ways in which the changes in schools can be read, not least through relating them to the bigger picture of educational restructuring. In addition, we must acknowledge that the means through which the changes have taken place have been on the basis of unfair arguments and fabricated characterizations of teachers. For example, teachers have not historically taken a register of students in the morning and afternoon as a means of maintaining provider capture – but because it was a way of facilitating pastoral care and tutor support. This does not mean that form periods have always worked well and could not be improved (not least by using ICT for the technical aspects of registration) but that the relationship between care and learning is central to teachers' professional identity in England. Hence we might ask: why has remodelling not provided investment for teachers to develop their pastoral skills in ways that could improve the services for children? This is not second-class work to the job of teaching and assessment; it is integral to it. Teachers could have been trained as counsellors and mentors, whilst the status of pastoral work and the organization of welfare could have been thought through in other ways. These might have focused on conceptualizations of what it is to be a teacher and what the act of teaching entails, rather than listing what teachers should not normally do.

Similarly, the action of teachers covering for absent colleagues (in house, or through supply) is not an example of demarcation boundaries being drawn in ways that are inefficient, but reflects a central tenet that teaching is a skilled process and that interventions into children's learning have to be designed by those who are appropriately trained. This is not substitute parenting, or 'easy work'. Lessons where teachers cover for absent colleagues may not have always lived up to high ideals, not least because teachers need time in the school day to prepare lessons. However, to replace teachers with non-teaching staff who 'supervise' suggests it is possible to separate the design of teaching from its delivery, and that learning will automatically result from reading a disembodied learning resource. We might ask why remodelling is not based on the training and supply of more teachers, combined with the allocation of more resources. If this was the case, schools could employ staff who have a degree, are trained to teach in ways which meet and exceed national standards and who understand how children learn and the strategies needed to enable learners to develop.

There was good teaching before 1988, just as there was innovation in schools before New Labour formed their first government in 1997. We know this because we were part of it. We also know that saying so can be dangerous, as we could be charged with romanticism and harking back to a 'golden age'. Such put-downs are the product of how people handle the strains of modernization, where we are told that the past is an unsafe place to travel back to. We would argue that how we characterize the past is essential to the success of current and planned reforms. We align ourselves with Popkewitz *et al.* (2001) who, building on Walter Benjamin, argue against the 'empty history' of 'boundless human progress' and instead present a case for 'a critical conversation' (p. 4). We realize the necessary dangers in doing this, particularly as we are reminded of Kostova's (2005) warning that 'as a historian, I have learned that, in fact, not everyone who reaches back into history can survive it. And it is not only reaching back that endangers us; sometimes history itself reaches inexorably forward for us with its shadowy claw' (p. ix).

The creativity that is such a strong feature of professional autonomy – knowing children with all the pitfalls and pleasures of human relationships, the excitement of developing and using resources to enable learning, and the witnessing of learning either in class or through project work – is also the key to school development. It is central to reform: the professionalism that Thatcherism and New Labour have criticized as being anti-modern is essentially the same culture that has delivered reform. Being in receipt of contradictory legal requirements and guidance on good practice takes some handling, particularly as the bidding culture demands not just relentless self-promotion but also the consequent management of multiple targets, income streams and reporting dates. The government and its agencies are not the sole fount of change ideas and developments – innovation can come from elsewhere, not least from classrooms and schools (see Hollins *et al.* 2006). We therefore need to share some restlessness with what we see going on. We would like to associate with what Fielding (2005) identifies as a form of 'claustrophobia' – where alternative places and spaces do not seem to feature and narratives that share concerns, or speak otherwise, are marginalized. The difficulty is that this could be read as undermining good people doing their best. Our contention is therefore that we speak with, and for, those who are 'creating a more fulfilling future' because this 'rests significantly on our knowledge and engagement with the past and with the establishment of continuities that contemporary culture denies' (pp. 61–2).

Our contribution is twofold: first, to challenge the anti-intellectualism within English education, through the advocacy and use of scholarship; and second, to bear witness to what is going on, story the underlying trends and answer back with counternarratives. In this way we would want to practise what Bourdieu (2003) identifies as 'scholarship with commitment' (p. 24), where we 'aim to restore politics' (p. 38) through thinking, dialogue, questioning and problem posing. We do this by returning to our original questions:

- What are the antecedents of the current waves of modernization and what directions is it taking in England and internationally?
- Does workforce modernization, in whatever form, offer meaningful ways forward for the teaching profession in England and in other countries?
- How is the leadership of change to take place with respect to educational modernization in England and elsewhere?
- What alternative approaches to remodelling might be developed with regard to the workforce labour market in England and other national contexts?

The antecedents and directions of modernization

There have been waves of modernization during the twentieth century when direct state interventions have been made in education in the name of the public, such as the 1944 and 1988 Education Acts. There have been periods of frenetic activity and of calm. Chitty (2004) notes that from 1944 to the late 1970s there were only three Education Acts worthy of note by Janet Finch in her 1984 book, but that the decades from 1979 to 2000 'saw the passing of over 30 separate Education Acts, together with large numbers of accompanying circulars, regulations and statutory instruments' (p. 33). Such rapid reform in the Thatcher–Major–Blair period has seen initiatives laid over each other, all of which have been presented with a combination of optimism ('this will make a difference') and urgency ('this is something we must do'). If, as seems to be the current trend, modernization is being downgraded to incremental change, whilst transformation is being singled out and upgraded as conceptual change, then we might ask what is being reconceptualized. Our task is to identify that professional practice in schools is located in wider contested debates about the purposes of education and, in particular, the security of publicly funded education. For example, some fundamental and accepted features are currently open to transformation:

- **Compulsory education:** Mundella's Act (1880) made education compulsory for ages 5–10, the 1944 Education Act extended this to age 15, and the 1972 *Raising of the School Leaving Age* reform raised it to 16 years of age. While it is widely assumed that education is essential, a case can be made that if parents can choose within a compulsory system then they should be allowed to choose to exit it. We might ask whether 55,000 children truanting every day means that they are already exercising this choice. Consequently current modernization may be leading to, either by design or default, a fundamental transformation which heralds the end of public education, or at best the creation of a 'safety net' system of education.

- **Free education:** in 1891 elementary education became free; this was extended by the 1944 Education Act to include secondary education. While it is widely assumed that parents can discharge their legal responsibilities to educate their children by accessing free state education, we might ask why some parents choose private schooling (which they subsidize by paying fees), or home tuition. Modernization may mean the end of free public education through privatized provision in the home, by faith group or through business.

- **Graduate profession**: teachers are licensed by the state and teaching is currently a graduate profession. While it is widely assumed that teaching should be done by qualified teachers we might ask whether the investment in teaching assistants – who are trained to 'supervise' and may be deployed locally to teach small groups and/or cover for absent teachers – is a means by which teaching is being deprofessionalized. Modernization may therefore signal the end of the need for qualified teachers to be graduates, such that the current shortages of teachers in some parts of England could be dealt with.

Remodelling of the school workforce has to be located within wider arguments about the purposes of education. Transformation is empty until it is filled with what is being transformed, how it is being done, by whom, for what reasons and in whose interests? What do we send children to school for? If schools should exist then we might want to ask whether education is a *public* good that all taxpayers should pay for and have access to. Or is it a *private* matter, where there is an opt-out clause for those who do not have children, or for parents who want to choose (i.e. buy) a different form of education?

We would want to argue that remodelling is part of a wider restructuring of education that is concerned with full-scale deregulation – for if education is seen as a *private* good, it is only a matter of time before the gains of the last hundred years are fully dismantled. While the *Every Child Matters* agenda has the potential to put the child at the centre of multi-agency provision – such that the site (buildings, grounds, equipment) that is currently called a school (or college or academy) becomes a place where access to education takes place alongside health and welfare provision (and even security, with a police station on site) – there is the possibility that the pedagogic relationships essential to these services will not develop. We would argue that doctors, nurses and social workers need to be trained if they are to integrate their expertise with that of teachers. We will also need to ensure that adults and children are indeed able to learn from, and within, the range of services provided. However we cannot detect this argument in play, for what seems to be unfolding at present are accusations of point scoring amongst professionals concerned about shifts in their territory. Indeed, there are debates about whether the most senior role incumbent of service provision – formerly known as a headteacher – needs to be a qualified teacher at all, or might simply be a chief executive who has generic leadership skills. It seems as if the previous strategic, procedural and organizational gains within local authorities are being rebuilt, but without accountability through directly elected local governance. Perhaps the chief executive role used within the NHS is being advanced as a model for local education, welfare and health provision? Our concern is, as Blackler (2006) argues, that New Labour has 'exaggerated expectations it held for performance management systems' (p. 8) – a point so graphically illustrated by the negative impact of performativity on current chief executives in the NHS.

Why do we raise such concerns? Remodelling is about creating a flexible, deployable workforce in a globalized economy. It is as simple and as complex as that. It is an example of what happens in the private sector when *making* more money with fewer people (downsizing), or cheaper people (outsourcing to other countries), meets *spending* less money with fewer people in the modernized public sector. The economy requires that its workers are capable of doing whatever jobs are advertised. What is important is the acquisition of transferable skills and the capacity to be endlessly trainable with regard to new procedures and equipment. The worker can then be deployed to do whatever needs doing, because the task to be done can be broken down into its component parts, itemized, sequenced and measured. The human factor (error, judgement, motivation, tiredness, illness) is minimized, or removed, through the standardization of procedures and/or through machines and computer software. Consequently we will not need to train teachers to teach because there will be no need for such skill or knowledge – indeed, such a claim is positioned as esoteric and ideological. If learning resources are provided online, anyone can access and use them. Children need not go to school because they can learn online in ways that are personal to them as learners; parental approval operates to ensure that they control the moral basis of learning such as faith-based learning; and learning can, like 'pay per view' television, be paid for as and when it is accessed. If we are fully in tune with lifelong learning then we might ask: why do we need to learn between the ages of five and sixteen? At most it could be argued that Mundella's Act was right to insist on compulsory education from five to ten, as this would enable basic and shared skills to be learned ready for the workplace. But beyond this age range it could be argued that schooling is unnecessary.

These are not arguments we agree with, although we know they are current within public and private discourse. For example, discussions about truancy are often rooted in deeper arguments concerning the failure of schools and teachers to make learning more interesting and relevant – as well as the failure of parents to discharge their particular responsibilities. However, these arguments are further underpinned by assertions about how the state should not be delivering public education because it always fails (Chubb and Moe 1990), about how the state is too big and cumbersome to do the job of service provision in the twenty-first century (Osborne and Gaebler 1992), and about how the primacy of the market is the only logical way to structure human association (Bobbitt 2002). Hence any discussion of remodelling should not just be about local gains, but also about wider purposes and questions – indeed, as Smyth (2006) so graphically argues, it will take much of our energy to put young people back into the debate as social subjects:

Turning around the current inhospitable policy situation with regard to schooling for a disturbingly large number of young people will not be easy.

There are some deeply entrenched interests that have a vice-like grip on continuing to control and progressively dismantle public education as we know it. Central to any reclamation will be the restoration of young people's trust in the social institution of schooling – something that is becoming increasingly and severely corroded at the moment. What this will require is courageous forms of leadership that fearlessly promote the importance of student ownership and student voice in respect of learning.   (p. 282)

We would argue that this is where conceptualizations of both modernization and transformation should be located. Teachers and schools will be required to face change and to work differently with their students – but society will also need to re-examine the case for public education and democratic renewal.

As our co-authors have shown, debates are taking place in English schools about remodelling, yet many key issues are being marginalized in the wider discussions – such as teacher motivation, how teacher identity is formed and how this identity is developed for and through work. Our international writers show how their own countries are wrestling with issues of change in professional practice, and how they are aiming to resist the importation of the English experiment. Indeed, modernization is being played out in a variety of forms in these countries, often with priorities at variance to those currently dominant in England. These writers have been mindful of the place of education within democratic development and are aware of the upheavals they have faced, or are currently facing, with regard to post-colonial systems (Berkhout, Fitzgerald, Smyth, Vidovich), or within an emerging European 'state' (Malet). The inclusion of their chapters shows that the validity of history cannot be 'managed away' through efficient systems, or 'visioned away' through futures-directed transformational leadership. What is vital to the debates is a recognition of the place of education within democratic development and an understanding of the ways in which powerful interests play the game either to concede or deny. The history of education within England illustrates this (Carr and Hartnett 1996; Chitty 2004; Fielding 2001a; Tomlinson 2005), revealing the significance of private interests (of parents, faith organizations, businesses and/or entrepreneurs) to the provision of public services. We would agree with Cuban (2004) that schools have been used in particular ways to further these private interests, from which there have been serious consequences:

In turning again and again to public schools for solutions to national problems, reformers picked a profoundly traditional institution – surely the type of institution least capable of correcting social, political, and economic woes. And because they expected the schools to be able to provide solutions, they criticized practitioners constantly for failing. The attempts to solve society's problems by changing the schools also allowed reformers to avoid direct action, thereby postponing solutions to the next generation. This familiar political strategy is designed to distort the full range of facts about schooling in order to convince voters that a serious social, political, or economic issue has to be solved by educators. This strategy has been used many times over the decades, not only by business leaders but also by U.S. presidents, state governors, and opinion elites. Public expectations that schools will conserve traditional values while at the same time providing solutions to broad national problems remains a painful contradiction facing those who support public schools and those who work in them.   (p. 174)

This contradiction is at the heart of remodelling. The reworking of professional identity – away from teaching and towards managing learning, predominantly through ICT and support staff – denies the reality of parents and children who want vibrant schools, staffed by trained teachers. In the same way the general public want hospitals to be staffed by trained doctors and nurses who they have direct access to, rather than to be treated by proxy (ICT and/or call centre). We would argue for a productive dependency where all can rely on high-quality schools (and hospitals, fire stations and police services) in their locality. Anything else just will not do, for these services cannot be secured safely through the trading and rationing system of the market.

So, our overall position on modernization is that the current wave of reform in English schools is bringing some short-term technical gains for those on the ground doing a difficult job. Those at local level who recognize the game in play are working hard to seize back control of the purposes of education, such that issues of teaching and learning are seen as the starting points of change and are recognized as the way forward for public education (Hollins *et al.* 2006).

Workforce and professionalism

A 'profession', as an identified group; a 'professional', as a member of such a group; 'professionalism', as the values underpinning that group; and 'professionality', as a practice exhibited by members of that group, are each constructed in time and space. Each generation inherits, reworks and leaves legacies in this regard. Inside and outside schools there are contested notions, practices and expectations about traits and behaviours (Gunter 2005d). These can be contrasted with unionism regarding conditions of service, combined with the need to get on with the job of teaching at 9 o'clock on a Monday morning. As McCulloch *et al.* (2000) argue, 'profession is a socially constructed, dynamic and contested term' (p. 6). What is being inherited in the current modernization of the school workforce are notions and practices of professional judgement, combined with an inherent sense of quality. These both drive the work ethic to ensure that what is done is 'right and proper', as well as handling the external direction of what is to be taught, when, by whom and to what standard. Both have something different to say about work–life balance.

Teachers are always teachers whether they are in the classroom or the supermarket, for their dispositions to practice are open to revelation through their interaction with life (Bourdieu 2000). Modernization sees the world as open to categorization – such that the person, rather like the Taylorist production-line worker, can be directed to do a job efficiently and effectively. He or she can clock in and clock off, or in a world of ICT the teacher can log in and log off. The TSW Project Evaluation found that 'work' was not a narrow statistical issue for teachers merely with regard to how many hours they put in, but involved a deeper set of issues concerning job satisfaction (Butt and Lance 2005a and b; Thomas *et al.* 2004). Teachers will work in the evenings, at weekends and in their vacations because they are deeply interested in their subject and their students. What they resent is undertaking work they have been *told* is necessary and urgent by those who are distant from the classroom. This has often been work that has humiliated them, or even caused breakdowns (see Gunter 2005a).

The new professionalism, as articulated in New Labour policy documents, has the potential to reach back and reconnect teachers with decision-making about both curriculum and pedagogy. However, the emphasis has been on bullet point lists of what teachers should *not* be doing, rather than on engaging the profession in a critical examination of what a defendable model of practice can and should be. It seems as if the power structures of schools and schooling have been reworked, so that teachers are sorted and sorted out (Gunter and Rayner 2007). Teachers are given other adults to manage, a laptop and external targets to meet. They are also differentiated – a process whereby a few are singled out for honours (Oscars, knighthoods and damehoods), whilst others are marked for retirement (Yarker 2005). On the one hand teachers are told they are to be 'new professionals' in order to meet the challenges of change (DfEE 1998), which they alone must face, while on the other hand they are no longer to be professionals but members of a much larger workforce.

It seems that arguments about teachers becoming technicians (Ball 1990b), within a process of deprofessionalization and proletarianization (Ozga and Lawn 1988), continue to resonate. Such analyses are shocking, but were previously ignored because they could be labelled (either rightly or wrongly) as extremist. We have also recognized that 'on the ground' implementation of policy has space for interpretation and requires judgement (Helsby 1999). Hence teachers could always modify and restrain the worst excesses of national policy through 'just doing the job', or by showing that teaching and learning required the expert skills and knowledge which policy and policymakers did not give sufficient credit for. As Grace (1995) has revealed, there are headteachers who endorse and manage the remodelling changes – but there are also those who try to keep pedagogy at the forefront, or who have resisted. Hence while successive governments have tried to make teaching and learning 'teacher-proof' this has not been sustainable in either the short or long term (McCulloch *et al.* 2000). However, there are two recent trends which could close down such spaces: first, the generation and use of fear as a policy strategy; and second, the removal of caring as central to teacher identity.

Sennett (1999) has identified a 'corrosion of character' with regard to work, highlighting how a person's relationship with work has been changed through the adoption of computerized machinery. It seems to us that we have moved from this deskilling, or deprofessionalization, argument about handing over work to machines and others, to a form of ordinary tyranny where we do things we do not agree with (Gunter 2005b). For example, we would concur with Arendt (2000) that there is a difference between labour, work and action – we labour to produce goods for survival (e.g. food), we work to produce goods that leave a legacy (e.g. institutions), but we take action with others to show who we are, to discuss and to initiate the new (e.g. democratic practices). Teaching is a public job: it happens in public, with the public – and as a consequence it should have opportunities for action. If teachers do not need to take action over teaching and learning anymore – because their job is to 'deliver', often through others – then they need not have care as a core feature of their identity. Indeed Forrester (2005, pp. 274–6) uses Acker's writings to distinguish between 'work' and 'non-work', and shows that practice related to performance ('doing your very best for the inspection regime') is of a higher status than caring ('doing your very best for the children'). She goes on to show that 'caring about', in relation to the leadership team's work and budget, is of higher status than teachers 'caring for' children. Hence the pastoral features of teaching can be done by others in ways that disconnect low-status caring from teaching – also supposedly increasing efficiency to secure targets and national standards.

Yarker (2005) provides an excellent example of the ongoing shift in identities, when, as a former teacher, he asks, 'How far is it proper for a teacher to stay silent or to be silenced and to disregard their personal views, in the implementation of education policy?' He details a letter from his daughter's school about how it intended to handle Workforce Reform, specifically by the use of Higher Level Teaching Assistants who would 'teach to their skills and experience, supported by their own designated teacher'. He goes on to say:

> I admired how the letter told it straight: 'to *teach* to their skills and experience'. But support-staff support: only teachers teach. I wrote back raising my concerns. I was replied to. An afternoon per week of planning, preparation and assessment time (PPA time) had enabled teachers to achieve real progress in dealing with their workload. Various options were being tested 'trying to ensure that the pupils continue to receive education from qualified teachers wherever possible. . . . However, regardless of my own personal views, I have been charged as Acting Headteacher with ensuring that a system of PPA is implemented for September 2005, it being a legal requirement'. Reading this, I was struck less by the submission to the force of the law than by the self-censorship. At no point in her letter had the Acting Headteacher in fact divulged her personal views. I still do not know what she thinks about Workforce Remodelling. But I think her silence is telling. (p. 170)

It seems that the person the teacher is, and is meant to be, is being elided – so the arguments that Noddings (2003) makes that the 'teacher as person is centrally important in teaching' (p. 244) becomes the myth and magic of teaching, which reform is trying to eradicate. Furthermore, we might expect that this headteacher had their union to call on for advice. However, as Stevenson (2006) argues, union representation of teachers and their concerns is being differently positioned as a result of the social partnership, and so there are those unions who are working within government policymaking, while the NUT remains outside. All is risky in the current climate, with teachers being polarized as either directly inside the modernization project or outside as an unmodernized trade unionist.

We would argue that the approach taken to remodelling has been focused too closely on organizational requirements and not closely enough on the nature of teaching and pedagogy. Consequently, reform has been about enabling local gains in handling a teaching workforce that is well trained, but either does not want to stay in teaching or does not want to progress to becoming headteachers (the General Teaching Council reported that only 4 per cent of teachers in England want to become headteachers in the next five years, and 34 per cent of heads plan to retire by 2011 (Smithers 2006)). Following Wilkinson (2005) we would agree that once teachers hand over their work to others, then those 'others' become professionalized and will demand more – in fact, they may expect the status that teachers have traditionally sought. Current evidence shows that varied local practices are emerging but, as Bach *et al.* (2006) show, teachers are co-opting TAs into 'the same professional norms as they applied within the classroom' (p. 20). The state is reworking who is to be known as a 'professional' and what the nature of 'professional work' is – such a reworking is perhaps the means by which education can continue in the welfarist tradition, but at a lesser cost.

Our argument is that we need to focus differently. Like Starratt (2003) we would argue for students to be put at the centre of schooling, and we agree that this also means that teachers and their work need to be up for debate and development. We would want to see teachers at the core of action about the nature of their own work and why it is distinctive. They also need to contribute fully to discussions about how they, and their practice, should develop. However, like all participation, this will take time – we therefore need a government that is less concerned with 'quick wins' and more concerned with investing in people, not just systems and buildings. There are numerous resources that can be drawn upon, not least the work of policy analysts and researchers who have examined the role of teachers (Ozga 2000a), the ways in which teachers can engage in productive pedagogies (Lingard *et al.* 2003) and the role of students as active participants in their own and others' learning (Fielding 2001b).

Teachers need the opportunity to take a long hard look at their practice; to examine research evidence about teaching, learning and assessment; and to be able to develop conceptually informed practice (Gunter 2001). Here the emphasis is not on data, or prepackaged notions of 'good practice', but on how teachers can use their judgement, their love of subject knowledge, their pedagogic expertise and their dedication to children and their learning. Before students can be given a voice their teachers need to have one – perhaps now the opportunity has arisen? While some spaces for dialogue have closed and there is a climate of fear-induced compliance (or resignation), there are local examples where voice remains and the professional cannot be silenced. Alternative narratives are in play, but they need to be heard and listened to. Teachers can retake control over their work and set the agenda – not least by working with students and parents in developing ideas about the type of education they both want and need. Perhaps the biggest brake on modernization is the unmodernized, particularly students and their parents – for while parents have been modernized as members of the general workforce through performativity, there remains the recognition amongst them that schools are not yet firms. As Yarker (2005) has so clearly shown, parents want *teachers* to teach their children: 'the politics of professionalism are partly about government actions that affect teachers but they are also about the ways in which teachers choose to respond and choose to publicly depict themselves' (McCulloch *et al.* 2000, p. 118).

Leadership of change

We have shown that we are in the midst of changes which have been referred to as 'modernization', but are now increasingly being labelled as 'transformation'. The process of reconceptualizing education as a means of transformation is interesting and we draw attention to how the labels of *Pathfinder* and *Test Bed* (see Appendices 1 and 2) are being used as metaphors to denote pioneering and problem resolution. There is a sense of excitement and optimism, combined with determination and goal achievement. New Labour has emphasized the importance of evidence-informed policy and practice, and so the commissioning of pilot projects with evaluation measurement is symbolic of a need to learn and develop. Furthermore, there are messages about how knowledge can be controlled and delivered, not least through the commissioning of private sector consultants as experts to define 'good practice', to deliver on reforms and to promote particular ways of constructing meaning about outcomes.

Of interest is how the label of 'remodelling' sets the agenda, for it assumes that there was once an existing model that had to be *re*modelled. It very much fits the cultural genre of modern life where bodies, gardens, personalities, relationships and houses are *made over* in order to improve the 'model'. This is not only to give visual appeal (stylish clothes, tasteful homes, sexy bodies) but also to change how people relate to each other (functional families, satisfying sex lives) and feel about themselves (emotionally stable with high esteem). Such transformations are presented as urgent, where death could be a likely consequence of inaction – either through poor physical and mental health and/or social isolation due to shame (e.g. dirty house, wrong lipstick) or relationship breakdown.

Makeovers can be viewed as surface remodelling (e.g. new clothes, new make-up, clean house, new garden plants), or can be more interventionist (e.g. surgery, therapy, conservatory). Gunter and Thomson (2006) have argued that remodelling of the school workforce in England has elements of both, with surface changes such as moving work around between members of the workforce – rather than examining the fundamental causes of overload (e.g. large-scale high-risk government reforms that schools have to implement if they want to survive the audit and accountability regime). Using Bourdieu's (1990) thinking tools, they show how the makeover genre has developed a logic of practice to control the power relationships between government and schools. Education policy texts, such as *teachers: meeting the challenge of change* (DfEE 1998) and *Time for Standards* (DfES 2002a), do the same job as the television expert:

- the ritual denunciation and demonisation of everything that has happened before, always via media – see the ways in which teachers and schools are continually berated for multiple deficiencies, young people in inner cities characterised as hood-ies, and those who favour some kind of social analysis as 'politically correct';
- the harnessing of new forms of 'expertise' to the task of reforming the object in question – be it standards of literacy, modes of assessment or the deployment of staff within schools;
- displays of willing acquiescence – agents of policy activity must be enthusiastic participants to this process, or risk being belittled in public;
- rituals of humiliation if the object of action fail to live up to expectations – the fate of allegedly failing, prior to salvation or damnation;
- continual monitoring and audit to ensure continued compliance – this has now moved schools to adopt an invidious form of self evaluation in which their statistical representation must be continually available for examination.

(Gunter and Thomson 2006, p. 12)

The danger of surface makeovers is that the person, or organization, can easily slip back into old ways of poor dress, bad diet and slack cleaning habits. Interventionist makeovers, where relapse is more difficult, are evident in the use of legal requirements (teachers must have planning, preparation and assessment time in school) and through shifts in culture – where it is difficult to resist what is regarded as good practice because to do so would declare the self to be 'unmodern' (teachers must no longer put up displays, even if they regard this as core to the pedagogic process). Thus teachers are part of a workforce, and old terms such as 'school staff' or 'teaching staff and non-teaching staff' are no longer appropriate. Teachers are workers who labour; they are no longer part of a profession which might claim to have a distinctive knowledge or set of practices. Indeed, teachers may no longer be the largest group of adults in schools, but are becoming a smaller proportion of those who work with children. Such delivery becomes unproblematic because those who teach are not now qualified in curriculum design, learning theory or values-based content, and so may not refuse packaged learning resources produced by private interests (see Jackson's (2006) reporting of how a religious group is promoting Intelligent Design through distributing learning resources). As Gunter and Thomson (2006) argue, the makeover reconstitutes class and gender in ways that give the illusion of transformation, although the women in programmes such as *What Not to Wear* remain firmly in their original space and place: 'the nirvana of the improved school is as remote to the majority of English schools as is a lifestyle on Sloane Square to the women who are addressed, undressed and redressed by Trinny and Susannah' (p. 12).

Similarly, we would argue that the new experts in government come mainly from the private sector. They have no accountability through governance, only through the market, for as long as someone buys their services then those services are acceptable. The workforce is not transformed with regard to social justice issues but instead remains, as the TSW Project shows, dominated by women on low pay (either as teachers, or as members of the support staff). Gunter *et al.* (2005) show that women dominate the TA role – a sizeable minority have a first degree but may not want to go on to train as teachers, whilst others have qualified teacher status but do not want to do teachers' work. While we might praise the development of a new route into teaching, we can see evidence of many highly qualified women doing teachers' work but not being paid fully for it and not getting appropriate recognition. For teachers the glass ceiling remains firmly in place because 'although women make up over two-thirds of the overall teaching population, they are significantly under-represented in senior posts' (Smithers 2006, p. 4). So, while New Labour has done a considerable amount of work to improve the status, pay and training of headteachers and senior managers, it is still the case that certain matters of equity are not being addressed. As Foster (1989) argues, it seems that there is little transformation going on in transformational leadership and change. Therefore when we seek to reconceptualize education in terms of its capacity to bring about 'transformation', we need to think about what it is we are aiming to change and whether we will deliver authentic changes for those who continue to experience social injustice.

Alternative narratives and strategies

We should also like to explore the location of children in the current educational reform agenda. It appears that reforms to education over the past 20 years have often been done in the name of parents (as consumers and taxpayers), but no policymaker has bothered to involve children – except as objects which elite adults (Secretary of State for Education, Private Sector Consultant, Headteacher) impact upon in order to meet targets (Gunter and Thomson 2006). While teachers in the 1980s and 1990s may have been willing to address how schools were organized with respect to their work, reform has subsequently ensured that schools are now increasingly organized around the work of external policy entrepreneurs (Kingdon 2003). The goals of national policymakers, in partnership with private consultancies and licensed headteachers, are central to the delivery of an efficient and effective standardized 'product'. This has stabilized and reinforced schools as places designed to deliver adult agendas, whilst teachers have subsequently been repositioned within this structural and cultural leviathan:

> The hardening of the policy regime and of educational attitudes has meant that, instead of schools changing their norms and ways of operating to accommodate the diversity of students, including the least advantaged, both the market arrangements under which schools now operate and the heavy compliance regimes force schools towards an impersonal homogeneity defined by impersonal and remote standards. Students and teachers are now expected to turn themselves into the kinds of people demanded by ostensible 'high performing' schools that are concerned with grades and test results and compliance with the managerial norms that now characterize education as an institution.
>
> (Angus 2006, pp. 369–70)

Careers and lives are tied up in such changes – but to challenge change can be read as undermining a life's work and dedication. We respect the commitment of teachers, but we also know that some teachers have been complicit in shoring up a schooling system that has undermined them and the children they teach. Bob Hewitt (Hewitt and Fitzsimons 2001) shows how he resisted a mode of lesson planning which he felt demeaned his professionalism and creativity, within a staff room of strategic compliers who adopted a 'just do it and they will go away' approach (see Gunter 2005a). We understand why people are complicit, and we have been complicit ourselves – for in the broad scheme of things complicity often does not seem to amount to much. After all, resigning from a job because of a new lesson planning process seems to be a little over the top! However, we all know that each of these minor, seemingly unconnected, events which we rather reluctantly comply with can add up to something much bigger – not least when they make statements about who we think we are and what we think our contribution to education should be.

We agree with Starratt (2003) that the student should be at the centre of learning, and that this focus fundamentally determines how teachers view their work:

> If we make the student the worker, then. . . the student now enters more actively into the learning process. Learning is the active engagement of the student, including all the sensitivities, points of view, talents, and imagination that he or she possesses, with the material under study. . . in the process of learning, and as a result of their active engagement with the material, students are asked to produce something that expresses their learning.   (p. 160)

Once we position the 'student as learner' at the centre of each teacher's concerns, then teachers can recapture the knowledge and pedagogic processes that have been denied them for the past 20 years. They can also engage with research evidence that has been accessible for some, but not widespread in its use (e.g. McGregor and Gunter 2006; Lingard *et al.* 2003).

Students can have a productive role in school improvement by telling adults what they think, or by being involved in evaluation processes (e.g. Flutter and Rudduck 2004; MacBeath 2000; Rudduck 2006; Rudduck and Flutter 2004). The danger lies in the strength of advocacy over conceptualization, or what Rudduck (2006) describes as ' "mile-wide" promotion with only "inch thick" understanding' (p. 133). The attractiveness of the student voice is that it can become integral to the makeover process, but it can also be used to put teachers in a deficit position. This could result in a gloss of consultation, without any authentic participation in the real issues that interest children themselves. We are aware of cases where students have become researchers (e.g. Fielding 2001b; Thomson and Gunter 2007; Thomson and Holdsworth 2003), and how this can be done with teacher consent and active participation. Nonetheless, students should not speak louder than teachers, or vice versa.

What we are advocating is what Fielding (2005) identifies as 'dialogic schools' based on evidence of what has been achieved so far and ideas about how things might develop further. Notably, if education (as distinct from training) is focused on the individual developing a sense of self within and through others, then schools are public places where we learn to be public and do public things. There are issues of trust, connection and humanity within this. We assume that leadership is not the labour of an elite adult, rather a relational process: 'it is a socially constructed relationship between people . . . it leads to the production and reproduction of various organizational practices, norms and structures' (Angus 2006, p. 372). This may not generate what adults want to hear but, as Smyth (2006) states, 'we need spaces of leadership from which young people can speak back regarding what they consider to be important and valuable about their learning' (p. 282). More than this, it means that students have to have greater control over their learning and have to take responsibility for the implementation of the type of education regime they want to see in place. It is one thing to moan about tests and homework, but quite another to be involved in a process of change and be expected to help make change work. There is no purity in student voice; they will bring to the table all the issues from the society in which they live. As Thomson and Gunter (2007) have shown, there is realpolitik in how this is negotiated and change secured. Indeed, Smyth (2006) is candid about the challenges:

> Turning around the current inhospitable situation with regard to schooling for a disturbingly large number of young people will not be easy. There are some deeply entrenched interests that have a vice-like grip on continuing to control and progressively dismantle public education as we know it. Central to any reclamation will be the restoration of young people's trust in the social institution of schooling – something that is becoming increasingly and severely corroded at the moment. What this will require is courageous forms of leadership that fearlessly promote the importance of student ownership and student voice in respect of learning. (p. 282)

Our argument is that this process is happening every day in certain English schools. Peter Hyman (2005), Blair's former speech writer at No. 10, gets close to it when he admits – having worked briefly in an inner-city school – that there 'is a chasm between Downing Street and the frontline' (p. 286). As such, the intention and requirement to deliver quickly cannot be realized. However, it is more than this: it is about how schools approach their work not as agencies of government but as agents of the governed. What teachers do is often invisible – their actions regularly get lost in the 'noise' of targets and data, largely because the schools where student voice is heard do well and often exceed the demands of performance. We would contend that more teachers want to work with children in this way and that such ways of working would raise retention rates in the profession. Indeed, many teachers who are currently trained and are practising elsewhere (like ourselves) could be tempted back to the classroom.

Ongoing debates. . .

We realize that in this book we have raised more issues than we have resolved. We have given voice to a range of people – both in and out of schools, in England and in other countries – who have a keen interest in the modernization and remodelling of the education workforce. We hope that the book has generated thinking and encouraged the conceptualization and planning of action. Small changes that are socially just and educationally defendable can happen in all schools and classrooms. They need not remain invisible. The secret to successful teaching and learning is how it develops and spreads, both as a 'matter of fact' process and by 'eureka' moments, although we are convinced of the need to view development differently. We do not see development in terms of fast food satisfaction or consumer gratification. Hence, our concluding thoughts are underpinned by an unrelenting defence of public education within our changing democracy – just as Bates (2003) challenges us to think about how, as diverse humans, we want to live and work together socially in ways that respect our individual and communal practices. Replacing traditional teacher professional cultures with that of the firm and market trading does not and cannot, in our view, produce an education system that engages with a diverse society. Not least because business cultures replicate and strengthen economic interests, and are anything but diverse! So our focus is on an agenda for dialogue and strategizing: first, What type of state schools do we want?; second, How do we want students to engage with learning?; third, How do we want to build a curriculum with (and for) them?; fourth, What type of adults do we want to support this learning?; and fifth, What role will the teacher have as the prime expert in teaching and learning?

While workforce reform is enabling gains at local level to be secured, the system in which these gains are happening is not secure. Remodelling can be read merely as the means of delivering the 'here and now', but it can also be seen as a means of problem solving in a system that is generating its own problems.

Critically, remodelling could become the way in which public education is to be dismantled – it therefore needs to be examined alongside the privatization of education, both as an 'individual' (student as target) and as an 'individualizing' (student as recipient of philanthropy) process. We do not believe that students and parents want this, but it is an issue that is unlikely to bring people onto the streets in the same way that the poll tax did. Instead, we argue for local gains which both create something different and pick away at the performance edifice. As Gewirtz (2002) concludes: 'consumers of politics can only choose between a limited range of options presented to them or they can reject those options. . . producers of politics, on the other hand, contribute to the creation of the agenda. They decide what the choices are' (pp. 181–2). We would like to repoliticize education as a public issue, not as a product to be traded. Serious damage has been done to teachers and to students (Smyth 2003), not least because 'young human capital [must] regard education as a preparation for the economy and not much else' (p. 8). What unites those who work in public educational institutions – in higher education, local authorities, colleges and schools – is the realization that we can make a difference to dialogue and strategy, not least through how we bear witness to inequalities and strive for social justice.

Appendix 1

The Transforming the School Workforce Pathfinder Project (TSW Project)

In Spring 2002, the DfES launched an initiative called the 'Transforming the School Workforce Pathfinder Project' (TSW Project). It was a pilot project in 32 schools with a further 9 comparator schools. The Project aimed, first, to secure significant reductions in the current weekly hours worked by teachers; and second, to increase the proportion of teachers' working week spent teaching or on tasks directly related to teaching. These aims were to be secured by supporting change in schools and providing resources to initiate new working practices:

- providing schools with consultancy support (School Workforce Advisers);
- training headteachers in change management;
- allocating funds for employing additional support staff;
- providing ICT hardware and software;
- funding the bursarial training of school managers;
- providing schools with capital build resources.

The Project in the 32 pilot schools and the training in change management was overseen by a team from the London Leadership Centre led by Dame Pat Collarbone. A team of 12 at the School of Education, University of Birmingham, under the leadership of Professor Hywel Thomas and Dr Helen Gunter, was contracted to evaluate these interventions.

The 32 pilot schools were selected by the DfES and included: 4 special, 16 primary, 12 secondary. All schools were visited twice, once at the beginning of the Project and once at the end. On both visits all teachers and support staff completed a substantial questionnaire which covered:

- information about the respondent: role, qualifications, personal details;
- amount of time spent on their work in the school day, evenings, weekends and vacation time;
- attitudes to job satisfaction and quality of life;
- attitudes to ICT and level of competence;
- attitudes to leadership of the school and the change process;
- views on the causes of and solutions to workload issues.

All members of staff completed the questionnaire, and the sample for interviews included a range of roles from across the workforce. In reporting the interview data the teaching staff have been categorized into senior managers (head-teacher, deputies and assistant headteachers); middle managers (heads of subject, faculty and year/house); and teachers. Support staff have been catego-rized into three groups: Support staff 1 = teaching assistants; Support staff 2 = technical staff such as ICT technicians or science technicians; Support staff 3 = bursar and administrative staff.

In comparing data from 2002 with 2003 we only used data on individuals who reported at both points, and we were able to link individual questionnaires because respondents put their names on when they completed them and then were coded. Staff turnover means that the number for whom we have data at both points is lower than the total number of responses in each of 2002 and 2003. In 2003, a total of 2,077 questionnaires were distributed and 1,578 were completed, a response rate of 76 per cent. In addition to this, interviews were held with a representative sample of the workforce and governors on both occa-sions with a total of 359 interviews in 2003. The departure of staff was monitored and information collected from exit questionnaires. Eight of the schools were selected as case studies (2 secondary, 1 special, 1 primary, 4 small primaries in a cluster), and two additional visits took place during the year to undertake inter-views with staff, governors and students, observe meetings and to debrief the staff who had completed a workload diary.

A total of 99 reports were produced. Each school received a bespoke confi-dential report including data for that school with a commentary at three stages: (a) immediately after the baseline data collection we reported on the question-naire data pertinent to change planning; (b) a few months after the baseline we reported in more detail on the questionnaire and interview data and provided a commentary; and, (c) an end-of-project report was sent to each school, and this included statistical and interview data on the changes and continuities for the school. The DfES received three reports at each of these stages containing aggregated data and commentary on the 32 schools, and requested reports were delivered during the Project on particular issues, e.g. bursars in the 32 schools.

Appendix 2

The ICT Test Bed Project

In Autumn 2002, the DfES launched the 'ICT Test Bed Pilot Project' which was designed both to evidence and demonstrate that effective use of ICT could make a significant contribution to the educational attainment, collaboration and workload agendas.

The Project took a holistic approach to ICT implementation in three Test Bed areas (three 'clusters' of schools and colleges in different local education authorities), concentrating not just on ICT hardware but also on areas such as:

- continuous professional development;
- assistance in the provision, identification and development of curriculum ICT resources;
- ensuring the most effective use of Management Information Systems;
- encouraging greater links between schools/colleges and parents and the wider community;
- encouraging schools to develop links with local post-16 education providers.

Particular emphasis was placed on supporting schools and colleges in their use of ICT to improve teaching and learning.

The effects of these activities was evaluated in the three local authority areas by a team from the School of Education, University of Birmingham, under the leadership of Professor Hywel Thomas and Dr Helen Gunter.

Visits to each school took place in October–November 2002, where interviews took place with a sample of the workforce, and a substantial questionnaire was administered. In total, 675 questionnaires were completed by teachers and 330 questionnaires were completed by support staff. The questionnaire and interviews included the following areas:

- views on the use of ICT;
- access to ICT in school and at home;
- knowledge of ICT applications;
- training experiences and knowledge;
- help in school and at home;
- frequency of use;
- use of specific applications in teaching and learning, and in administration;
- factors that affect use;

- student use and motivation in learning with ICT;
- workload and use of time, and in the use of ICT;
- job satisfaction and quality of life;
- views on the leadership and management of the school.

A total of 29 reports were produced. Each of the 28 schools received a bespoke confidential report based on the questionnaire and interview data. Each report provided data and a commentary on the readiness and capability of the work-force in regard to the current use and potential of ICT in teaching and learn-ing, and whole-school administration. The aim was to help the schools to undertake planning for investment in ICT based on evidence of current prac-tice and professional development needs. The DfES received a report which provided an overview of the data from the 28 schools in order to provide a base-line for measuring the impact of the projected investment. (From Thomas *et al.* (2003a))

Notes

Chapter 3 Workforce, workload and work–life balance: the initial impacts of modernization in English schools

1. The OECD has produced a detailed report on teacher demand and supply, and the strategies used to address shortages (Santiago 2002). For the English context a study by Smithers and Robinson (2003) for the DfES found that there are five factors that influence teachers' decisions to leave: workload, new challenge, the school situation, salary and personal circumstances.
2. 'Teaching Assistant' (TA) is the generic title preferred by the government for those in paid employment in support of teachers, including those with general roles, or those with specific responsibilities for a child, subject area or age group. In essence TAs can provide support for the pupil, the teacher, the curriculum and the school.
3. The definitions of staff included within each category of occupation recorded in Table 3.1 are as follows:

Deputy heads	= All leadership group except headteacher (deputy, assistant head, leadership group)
Class teachers	= Primary and special schools: this means all other teachers, excluding trainees. Secondary schools: this includes NQTs, main and upper-scale teachers
Heads of faculty	= Secondary schools: this includes management points, recruitment and retention points, advanced skills teachers

4. Thomas *et al.* (2004) suggest reasons for this, not least because the 'comparator' schools were not conventional 'controls' (as they had originally unsuccessfully applied to join the Project as pilot schools). Their general interest in the Project might mean they were already alert to the issue of workload and the means by which it might be tackled. The questionnaire sent to each member of staff would also have made the workload issue rather more prominent, possibly reinforced by the greater profile given to teacher workload by the signing of the National Agreement in January 2003 (DfES 2003a). See Thomas *et al.* (2004), p. 8.
5. See note 3.

Chapter 4 Challenging and changing role boundaries

1. The SENCO, in collaboration with the headteacher and governing body, plays a key role in determining the strategic development of the SEN policy and provision in the school in order to raise the achievement of children with SEN. (See DfES 2001a, *Special Educational Needs Code of Practice*, 5.30.)

2. Urban Primary School: the case study presented was one of four case studies undertaken as part of a doctoral research project examining the developing role of the primary SENCO (Szwed 2004). Questionnaire surveys were utilized to identify initial trends and then case-study schools chosen to form a purposive sample. Over a period of six months, research was undertaken in each case-study school. The research tools adopted consisted of an analysis of documentary evidence, interviews with the SENCO, Head and support staff, and diaries were also utilized to record SENCO workload and activity. For the purposes of this study, documentary references are left unreferenced in order to preserve the anonymity of the school.

Chapter 7 Networking change

1. Typically the external advisers employed by LAs are often focused on offering specialist support in areas of school improvement and raising standards. Many LAs have also developed their advisory teams such that they also fulfil inspection roles, often being labelled 'Advisory and Inspection Service'. Most LAs acknowledge that schools themselves are the main focus and agent for promoting and enabling improvement, with a commitment to collaborative working with schools and between schools and sharing good practice.

   The following is a list of 'change agents' often employed by LAs:

   - **Accredited advisers to help and support governing bodies** – Advisers who support governors with the performance management and appraisal of heads.
   - **Senior Education Advisers (SEAs)** – Advisers who monitor the standards of achievement and quality of education; who represent Director of Education (or similar) at headteacher appointments; who support headteachers in their first year of appointment; who support Acting headteachers; and carry out consultancy, information gathering and professional advice for LEA.
   - **School Improvement Advisers (SIAs)** – Advisers with responsibility for quality and standards, formal review, support for self-evaluation, INSET provision, curriculum advice, leadership and management, liaison with other agencies which support the work of schools, school governing bodies, provision of information to Council Education Committee (or similar) and project work on school improvement.
   - **School Improvement Partners (SIPs)** – Partners who analyse schools' strengths and areas for improvement, make judgement about a range of effective strategies for school improvement, interact with leaders in a variety of schools tailoring their challenge and support to the circumstances.

- **School advisers and consultants** – Advisers and consultants who support and advise on National Curriculum, National Strategies and individual subjects and phases.
- **Whole school management advisers** – Advisers who help to develop practice and procedures in schools.
- **Advisory teachers** – Advisers who support the professional development of teachers through training services (conferences, courses and workshops, consultancies, publications).
- **Special Needs Advisers** – Advisers to schools/teachers on aspects of special needs.

2. The SWAs were telephoned and notes taken of the dates, duration and purpose of the visits they had made to their allocated schools. Most SWAs were expected to advise two or three schools. They were asked the following questions to open up the issue for discussion:

- What attracted you to the position of School Workforce Adviser with the TSW Project?
- What do you think is the purpose of the School Workforce Adviser within the TSW Project?
- How do you think you will approach the role of being a School Workforce Adviser?
- How well do you think you have been prepared for your role as School Workforce Adviser?

Chapter 12 Remodelling schools and schooling, teachers and teaching: a New Zealand perspective

1. A caution here – in 2006 the eight universities in New Zealand have introduced a policy that all international doctoral students pay domestic fees. Those international students with children also pay domestic fees at their local school. This might be one factor in the decrease of 22 per cent enrolment in primary schools in 2003 (Education Review Office 2003).
2. This levy is estimated at $3.6 million per year (Deloitte New Zealand 2006) although $2.4 million is held in reserve against the collapse of education providers. This has occurred, in the main, in the tertiary education sector with a number of PTEs (private training establishments).
3. This is not to suggest that leadership, leaders and leading were not subject to the same level of control and regulation. There is not the space in this chapter to fully explore this argument.

Chapter 14 Navigating 'global' modernization policies in education: responses from Australia

1. The Commonwealth Department has been renamed numerous times since the late 1980s. From DEET, it became DEETYA and then DETYA, and then DEST.

Thus, different names and abbreviations are used when different periods are being referred to.

2. Prior to MCEETYA the ministerial council was called the Australian Education Council, but it was after it became MCEETYA that it became more policy proactive.

References

Alexiadou, N. and Ozga, J. (2002) 'Modernizing education governance in England and Scotland: devolution and control', *European Educational Research Journal*, 1, (4), 676–91.

ANC (1994) *A Policy Framework for Education and Training. Draft: for Discussion Purposes only*. Braamfontein: Education Department African National Congress.

Andres, A., Anstey, P., Broadfield, D., Farrar, M., Walsh, K., Whalley, M. and Wise, C. (2003) *Creative Waves: NCSL Discussion Paper on Future Schools*, National College of School Leadership (NCSL). Available at URL www.ncsl.org.uk/media/F7B/95/randd-futures-creative-waves.pdf, accessed 10 June 2006.

Angus, J. T. (1970) 'A new direction in teacher education in Ontario', address delivered to the Teacher Education Section, Ontario Education Association, March 24.

Angus, L. (2006) 'Educational leadership and the imperative of including student voices, student interests, and students' lives in the mainstream', *International Journal of Leadership in Education*, 9, (4), 369–79.

Appadurai, A. (1996) *Après le colonialisme. Les conséquences culturelles de la globalisation*, Paris: Payot.

Apple, M. W. (2001) *Educating the 'Right' Way: Markets, Standards, God and Inequality*. New York: Routledge Falmer.

Arendt, H. (2000) 'Labor, work, action', in P. Baehr (ed.), *The Portable Hannah Arendt*. London: Penguin Books, pp. 167–81.

Bach, S., Kessler, I. and Heron, P. (2006) 'Changing job boundaries and workforce reform: the case of teaching assistants', *Industrial Relations Journal*, 37, (1), 2–21.

Ball, S. J. (1990a) 'Introducing Monsieur Foucault', in S. Ball (ed.), *Foucault and Education. Disciplines and Knowledge*. London and New York: Routledge, pp. 1–10.

— (1990b) *Politics and Policymaking in Education: Explorations in Policy Sociology*. London: Routledge.

— (1997) 'Policy sociology and critical social research: a personal review of recent education policy and policy research', *British Educational Research Journal*, 23, (1), 257–74.

— (2003) 'The teacher's soul and the terrors of performativity', *Journal of Education Policy*, 18, (2), 215–28.

— (2006) 'New philanthropy, new networks and new governance in education', paper presented to the British Educational Research Association Annual Conference, University of Warwick, September 2006.

Baluteau, F. (1996) 'La prise de décision curriculaire en Grande-Bretagne et en France', in J. J. Paul and S. Tomamichel (eds), *Le Rôle des pouvoirs publics dans l'éducation, Revue d'éducation comparée*, 51, 67–94.

Barber, M. (2001) 'High expectations and standards for all, no matter what: creating a world class education service in England', in M.Fielding (ed.), *Taking Education Really Seriously*. London: RoutledgeFalmer.

— (2005) 'More money and smarter management can transform education – look at Britain', *How to Revive our Schools*, 23 September 2005, available at www.theage.com.au, accessed 5 December 2005.

Barrows, H. S. (1992) *The Tutorial Process*. Springfield, IL: Southern Illinois University School of Medicine.

Bartlett, L. (2004) 'Expanding teacher work roles: a resource for retention or a recipe for overwork?', *Journal of Education Policy*, 19, (5), 565–82.

Bates, R. (2003) 'Can we live together? The ethics of leadership in the learning community', paper presented to the Annual Conference of the British Educational Leadership, Management and Administration Society, Milton Keynes, October 2003.

Becta (1999) *Connecting Schools, Networking People 2000: ICT Planning, Purchasing and Good Practice for the National Grid for Learning*. Coventry: Becta.

— (2002) *Information sheet: ICT Co-ordination in Secondary Schools*. Coventry: Becta, www.becta.org.uk/technology/infosheets/html/ictcoordsecond.html

— (2003) *What the Research Says about Strategic Leadership and Management of ICT in Schools*. Coventry: Becta.

— (2004) *ICT: Essential Guides for School Governors 10. ICT and Whole-school Improvement*. Coventry: Becta, available at www.becta.org.uk/leadership/display. cfm?section=13

Becta/NCSL (2006) *Self-Review Framework*. Coventry: Becta, available at http:// schools.becta.org.uk/index.php?section=lv&rid=11966&PHPSESSID=33be550da 6b13325c9f6676b2a6bc5ca

Bennett, N. (1999) 'Middle management in secondary schools: introduction', *School Leadership and Management*, 19, (3), 289–92.

Bennett, N., Harvey, J. and Anderson, L. (2004) 'Control, autonomy and partnership in local education: views from six chief education officers', *Educational Management, Administration and Leadership*, 32, (4), 217–35.

Bennett, N., Wise, C., Woods, P. and Harvey, J. A. (2003) *Distributed Leadership. A Review of Literature*. Summary report. Nottingham: National College of School Leadership.

Bentley, T. and Miller, R. (2003) *Possible Futures*. Nottingham: National College of School Leadership.

Blackler, F. (2006) 'Chief executives and the modernization of the English National Health Service', *Leadership*, 2, (1), 5–30.

Blackmore, J. (1999) *Troubling Women: Feminism, Leadership and Educational Change*. Buckingham: Open University Press.

Blackmore, J. and Thomson, P. (2004) 'Just "good and bad news"? Disciplinary imaginaries of head teachers in Australian and English print media', *Journal of Education Policy*, 19,(3), 301–20.

Blair, T. (1997) *Foreword to Connecting the Learning Society (DfEE Consultation Document).* London: DfEE.

— (1999a) 'A message from the Prime Minister: Modernising Government White Paper', available at www.dfee.gov.uk/modgov/pmmg.html, accessed 19 November 1999.

— (1999b) *Speech to New Headteachers,* London: No. 10 Downing Street.

Blunkett, D. (2001) *The Challenges of Improving Schools: Lessons for Public Service Reform.* IPPR Seminar, 1 May 2001, London: DfES.

Bobbitt, P. (2002) *The Shield of Achilles.* London: Penguin Books.

Bosley, C. and Moon, S. (2003) *Review of Existing Literature on the Use of Information and Communication Technology within an Educational Context.* Derby: Centre for Guidance Studies, University of Derby.

Boston, J., Martin, J., Pallot, J. and Walsh, P. (1996) *Public Management: The New Zealand Model.* Auckland: Oxford University Press.

Bottery, M. (2006) 'Education and globalization: redefining the role of the educational professional', *Educational Review,* 58, (1), 95–113.

Bottery, M. and Wright, N. (2000) 'The directed profession: teachers and the state in the third millennium', *Journal of In-Service Education,* 26, (3), 475–87.

Bourdieu, P. (1990) *In Other Words: Essays towards a Reflexive Sociology,* trs. Matthew Adamson. Cambridge: Polity Press in association with Blackwell Publishers, Oxford.

— (2000) *Pascalian Meditations.* Cambridge: Polity Press.

— (2003) *Firing Back: Against the Tyranny of the Market.* London: Verso.

Bowers, H. (1950) *A Report on the Normal Schools of the Province of Ontario.* Toronto: Ontario Normal Schools Teachers' Association.

Bransford, J., Darlington-Hammond, L. and LePage, P. (2005) *Preparing Teachers for a Changing World: What Teachers should Learn and be Able to Do.* San Francisco: Jossey-Bass.

Brisard, E. and Malet, R. (2004) 'Evolution du professionnalisme enseignant et contextes culturels. Le cas du second degré en Angleterre, Ecosse et France', in *Recherche et Formation,* forthcoming

Britzman, D. P. (2003) *Practice Makes Practice: A Critical Study of Learning to Teach* (Rev. edn). Buffalo, NY: SUNY Press.

Broadfoot, P. (2000) 'Un nouveau mode de régulation dans un système décentralisé: l'Etat évaluateur, *Revue Française de Pédagogie,* 130, 43–56.

Brundrett, M., Fitzgerald, T. and Sommefeldt, D. (2006) 'The creation of national programmes of school leadership development in England and New Zealand: a comparative study', *International Studies in Educational Administration,* 34, (1), (in press).

Bryant, M. T. (2003) 'Cross-cultural perspectives on school leadership: themes from North American interviews', in N. Bennett, M. Crawford and M. Cartwright (eds), *Effective Educational Leadership.* London: Paul Chapman Publishing, pp. 216–28.

Buckingham, J. (2005) 'Up with the standard', *The Australian,* 31 January, p. 16, available at www.newstext.com.au, accessed 2 March 2006.

Burnett, N. (2005) *Leadership and SEN: Meeting the Challenge in Special and Mainstream Settings.* London: David Fulton.

Bush, L., Bell, L., Bolam, R., Glatter, R. and Ribbins, P. (1999) *Educational Management: Redefining Theory, Policy and Practice.* London: Paul Chapman Publishing.

Bush, T. and Glover, D. (2003) *School Leadership: Concepts and Evidence. A Review of the Literature. (Full Report).* Nottingham: National College of School Leadership.

Butt, G. and Gunter, H. M. (2005) 'The challenges of modernization in education', *Special Edition of Educational Review*, 57, (2).

Butt, G. and Lance, A. (2005a) 'Modernizing the roles of support staff: changing focus, changing function', *Educational Review*, 57, (2), 139–49.

— (2005b) 'Secondary teacher workload and job satisfaction: do successful strategies for change exist?', *Educational Management, Administration and Leadership*, 33, (4), 401–22.

Butt, G., Lance, A., Fielding, A., Gunter, H., Rayner, S. and Thomas, H. (2005a) 'Teacher job satisfaction: lessons from the TSW Pathfinder Project', *School Leadership and Management*, 25, (5), 455–71.

Butt, G., Lance, A. and Szwed, C. (2005b) 'Modernization, remodelling and change management in English Schools', Symposium at the British Educational Research Association, Glamorgan, September 2005.

Caldwell, B. J. (2004) 'A strategic view of efforts to lead the transformation of schools', *School Leadership and Management*, 24, (1), 81–99.

Caldwell, B. J. and Spinks, J. M. (1998) *Beyond the Self-managing School.* London: Falmer Press.

Calvert, M. (2000) ' "Winning half the battle". Managing change in pastoral care: a case study of changing personal social education provision in a secondary school context', unpublished PhD thesis, University of Sheffield.

Capper, P. and Munro, R. (1990) 'Professionals or workers?: changing teachers conditions of service', in S. Middleton, J. Codd and A. Jones (eds), *New Zealand Education Policy Today.* Wellington: Allen and Unwin.

Carr, W. and Hartnett, A. (1996) *Education and the Struggle for Democracy.* Buckingham: Open University Press.

Carrim, N. (2002) 'Teacher identity: tensions between roles', in K. Lewin, M. Samuel and Y. Sayed (eds), *Changing Patterns of Teacher Education in South Africa.* Sandown/ Cape Town: Heinemann, pp. 306–21.

Charles Sturt University (2006) 'About the Program [Ontario Campus]', available at www.csu.edu.au/campus/ontario/, accessed 21 October 2006.

Cheminais, R. (2005) *Every Child Matters: A New Role for SENCOs.* London: David Fulton.

Chia, R. and King, I. (2001) 'The language of organization theory', in R. Westwood and S. Linstead (eds), *The Language of Organization.* London, Thousand Oaks and New Delhi: Sage Publications.

Chitty, C. (2004) *Education Policy in Britain.* Basingstoke: Palgrave Macmillan.

Chubb, J. E. and Moe, T. M. (1990) *Politics, Markets and America's Schools.* Washington, DC: Brookings Institution.

Clark, M. (2002) 'Teaching assistants: their role in primary schools of the future', *Primary Practice*, 31, Summer, pp. 18–20.

Cochrane, A. (2004) 'Modernization, managerialism and the culture wars: reshaping the local welfare state in England', *Local Government Studies*, 30, (4), 481–96.

Codd, J. (2005a) 'Teachers as "managed professionals" in the global education industry: the New Zealand experience', *Educational Review*, 57, (2), 193–206.

Codd, J. (2005b) 'Education policy and the challenges of globalisation: commercialisation or citizenship?' in J. Codd and K. Sullivan (eds), *Education Policy Directions in Aotearoa New Zealand*. Melbourne: Thomson/Dunmore Press.

Cognition and Technology Group at Vanderbilt (1992) 'Technology and the design of generative learning environments', in T. M. Duffy and D. Jonassen (eds), *Constructivism and the Technology of Instruction: A Conversation*. Hillsdale, NJ: Lawrence Erlbaum Associates.

Cole, A. L. (2000a) 'Case studies of reform in Canadian preservice teacher education', *The Alberta Journal of Educational Research*, 40, (2), 192–5.

— (2000b) 'Academic freedom and the *publish or perish* paradox in schools of education', *Teacher Education Quarterly*, 27, (2), 33–48.

Collarbone, P. (2005a) 'Touching tomorrow: remodelling in English schools', *The Australian Economic Review*, 38, (1), 75–82.

— (2005b) 'Remodelling Leadership', North of England Education Conference speech, University of Manchester, 5–7 January 2005.

Cordingley, P. (2004) 'Teachers using evidence: using what we know about teaching and learning to re-conceptualize evidence-based practice', in G. Thomas and R. Pring (eds), *Evidence-Based Practice in Education*. Maidenhead: Open University Press, pp. 77–89.

Coulter, R. P. (1998) 'Educators for gender equity: organizing for change', *Canadian Woman Studies*, 17, (4), (Winter), 103–5.

Counsell, C. (2003) 'The forgotten games kit: putting historical thinking first in long, medium and short term planning', in T. Haydn and C. Counsell (eds), *History, ICT and Learning in the Secondary School*. London: RoutledgeFalmer.

Coutts, N., Drinkwater, R. and Simpson, M. (2001) 'Using information and communications technology in learning and teaching: a framework for reflection, planning and evaluation in school development', *Teacher Development*, 5, 225–39.

Cowne, E. (2003) *The SENCO Handbook: Working within a Whole School Approach* (4th edition). London: David Fulton.

Crawford, R. (1997) *Managing Information Technology in Secondary Schools*. London: Routledge.

Crook, C. (1994) *Computers and the Collaborative Experience of Learning*. Routledge, London.

— (1997) 'Children as computer users: the case of collaborative learning', *Computers and Education*, 30, 237–47.

Cuban, L. (2004) *The Blackboard and the Bottom Line*. Cambridge, MA: Harvard University Press.

Dalin, P. (1998) *School Development: Theories and Strategies*. London: Cassell.

D'Amato, L. (26 July 2006) 'WLU gets teachers college', *The [Kitchener-Waterloo] Record*. www.therecord.com/links/links_060731144128.html, accessed 21 October 2006.

Dawes, L. (1999) 'First connections: teachers and the National Grid for Learning', *Computers and Education*, 33, 235–52.

Dawkins, J. (1998) 'Strengthening Australia's schools: a consideration of the focus and content of schooling', White Paper. Canberra: Australian Government Publishing Service.

Day, C., Harris, A., Hadfield, M., Tolley, H. and Beresford, J. (2000) *Leading Schools in Times of Change*. Milton Keynes: Open University Press.

Dean, P. (2001) 'Blood on the tracks: an accusation and a proposal', *Journal of In-Service Education*, 27, (3), 491–9.

DEETYA (2000) *Teachers for the Twenty-First Century: Making the Difference*. Commonwealth of Australia, Canberra: Australian Government Publishing Service.

Deloitte New Zealand (2006) *Review of the Export Education Levy*. Wellington: Ministry of Education.

DES (1988) *Educational Reform Act: Local Management of Schools (Circular 7/88)*. London: DES.

DEST (2003) *Australia's Teachers: Australia's Future*, Report by the Committee for the Review of Teaching and Teacher Education (Dow Report), Commonwealth of Australia. Canberra: Australian Government Publishing Service.

— (2005) *An Evaluation of the Australian Government Quality Teacher Program 1999 to 2004*. Commonwealth of Australia. Canberra: Australian Government Publishing Service.

— (2006) *Teachers in Australian Schools: A Report from the 1999 National Survey*, Australian College of Education, available at: www.dest.gov.au.

DfEE (1997a) *Excellence in Schools*. CM3681. London: Her Majesty's Stationery Office.

— (1997b) *Connecting the Learning Society – National Grid for Learning (The Government's Consultation Paper)*. London: DfEE.

— (1998) *teachers: meeting the challenge of change*. London: DfEE.

— (1999) *Survey of Information and Communications Technology in Schools 1998*. London: DfEE.

— (2001) *£35 Million Technology Package to Help Schools Cut Bureaucracy – DfEE Press Release*. London: DfEE.

DfES (2000a) *The Ninth Report of the School Teachers' Review Body (STRB)*. London: STRB.

— (2000b) *Working with Teaching Assistants*. London: Her Majesty's Stationery Office.

— (2001a) *Special Educational Needs Code of Practice on the Identification and Assessment of Pupils with SEN*. London: DfES.

— (2001b) *Schools Achieving Success*. London: DfES.

— (2002a) *Time for Standards: Reforming the School Workforce*. London: DfES.

— (2002b) *IMPACT2: The Impact of Information and Communications Technologies on Pupil Learning and Attainment*, Becta for the Department for Education and Skills, National Grid for Learning Research and Evaluation Series Report No. 7. London: DfES.

— (2003a) *Raising Standards and Tackling Workload: A National Agreement*. London: DfES.

— (2003b) *ICT and Pedagogy: A Review of the Literature,* Becta for the Department for Education and Skills, National Grid for Learning Research and Evaluation Series Report No. 18. London: DfES.

— (2004a) *Every Child Matters: Change for Children.* London: HMSO.

— (2004b) *Raising Standards and Tackling Workload, Implementing the National Agreement, January 2004.* London: DfES.

— (2005a) *Higher Standards, Better Schools for All.* London: DfES.

— (2005b) *The Implementation Review Annual Report 2004–5: Reducing Bureaucracy in Schools – Progress Made, Challenges Ahead,* available at www.dfes.gov.uk/iru, accessed 14 March 2000.

— (2006) *School Workforce in England, January 2006 (revised).* London: DfES, available at www.dfes.gov.uk/rsgateway, accessed 12 September 2006.

Dibbon, D. (2004) *It's About Time!! A Report on the Impact of Workload on Teachers and Students.* Newfoundland: Memorial University of Newfoundland.

Dixon, A. (2003) 'Teaching assistants: whose definition?', *Forum,* 45, (1), Spring, 26–9.

Draper, I. (2005) 'Why reform the workforce? Effectively remodelling the school workforce requires a broader perspective than educational imperatives alone can provide', *Managing Schools Today,* 14, (3), 48–53.

Dubet, F. (2002) *Le Déclin de l'institution.* Paris: Seuil.

Dudley, J. and Vidovich, L. (1995) *The Politics of Education: Commonwealth Schools Policy 1973–95.* Melbourne: Australian Council for Educational Research.

Dyde, S. W. (1904–5) 'Should there be a faculty of education in the University?' *Queen's Quarterly,* 12, (1904–5), 167.

Dyer, C. and Rose, P. (2005) 'Decentralisation for educational development? An editorial introduction', *Compare,* 35, (2), 105–13.

Eason, B. (1999) *The Whimpering of the State.* Auckland: Auckland University Press.

Easton, C., Wilson, R. and Sharp, C. (2005) *National Remodelling Team: Evaluation Study (Year 2).* Slough: NFER.

Edelson, D. C., Gordin, D. N. and Pea, R. D. (1999) 'Addressing the challenges of inquiry-based learning through technology and curriculum design', *Journal of the Learning Sciences,* 8, 391–450.

Education Review Office (2003) *Foreign Fee Paying Students in New Zealand Schools.* Wellington: ERO.

European Commission (2002) *eEurope 2005: An Information Society for All.* Brussels: European Commission.

Evans, N. (1989) *The Role of the IT Co-ordinator.* Studley: Learning and Teaching Services.

Fairclough, N. (2000) *New Labour, New Language.* London: Routledge.

Farr, D. M. L. (1967) *Archives of Lakehead University, Senate Minutes.* Meeting Number 20, 12 December 1967, 30.

Farrell, C. and Morris, J. (2004) 'Resigned compliance: teacher attitudes towards performance-related pay in schools', *Educational Management Administration and Leadership,* 32, (1), 81–104.

Fergusson, R. (2000) 'Modernizing managerialism in education', in J. Clarke, S. Gewirtz and E. McLaughlin (eds), *New Managerialism, New Welfare?* London: Open University, pp. 202–21.

Fielding, M. (ed) (2001a) *Taking Education Really Seriously.* London: Routledge Falmer.
— (2001b) 'Students as radical agents of change', *Journal of Educational Change*, 2, (2), 123–41.
— (2005) 'Putting hands around the flame: reclaiming the radical tradition in state education', *Forum*, 47, (2 and 3), 61–9.
Firestone, W. (1989) 'Using reform: conceptualising district initiative', *Educational Evaluation and Policy Analysis*, 11, (2), 151–64.
Fiske, E. and Ladd, H. (2000) *When Schools Compete: A Cautionary Tale.* Washington, DC: Brookings Institution Press.
Fitzgerald, T. (2006) 'Walking between two worlds: indigenous women and educational leadership', *Educational Management Administration and Leadership*, 34, (2), 201–13.
Fitzgerald, T., Youngs, H. and Grootenboer, P. (2003) 'Bureaucratic control or professional autonomy?: performance management in NZ schools', *School Leadership and Management*, 23, (1), 91–105.
Fleming, W. G. (1971) *Ontario's Educative Society: Supporting Institutions and Services.* Toronto: University of Toronto Press.
Flutter, J. and Rudduck, J. (2004) *Consulting Pupils. What's in it for Schools?* London: RoutledgeFalmer.
Forrester, G. (2005) 'All in a day's work: primary teachers "performing" and "caring"', *Gender and Education*, 17, (3), 271–87.
Foster, W. (1989) 'Towards a critical practice of leadership', in J. Smyth (ed.), *Critical Perspectives on Educational Leadership.* London: Falmer Press, pp. 39–62.
Fox, B. (2003) *Successful ICT Leadership in Primary Schools.* Exeter: Learning Matters.
Freedman, T. (2005) *Managing ICT.* London: Hodder and Stoughton.
Friedland, M. (2002) *The University of Toronto: A History.* Toronto: University of Toronto Press.
Fullan, M. (2000) *The New Meaning of Educational Change* (Third edition). Toronto: Irwin.
— (2001) *Leading in a Culture of Change.* New York: Jossey Bass.
Fullan, M., Hill, P. and Crevola, C. (2006) *Breakthrough.* Toronto: Ontario Principals' Council.
Furlong, J. and Whitty, G. (1995) 'Re-defining partnership: revolution or reform in initial teacher education?', *Journal of Education for Teaching*, 22, (1), 35–55.
Gagnon, F., McAndrew, M. and Page, M. (eds) (1996) *Pluralisme, citoyenneté et éducation*, Paris: L'Harmattan.
Gardner, C. and Williamson, J. (2005) 'Teaching is the not the job it used to be', paper presented to the American Educational Research Association Conference, Montreal.
Gerschel, L. (2005) 'The special educational needs coordinator's role in managing teaching assistants: the Greenwich perspective', *Support for Learning*, 20, (2), 69–76.
Gewirtz, S. (2002) *The Managerial School.* London: Routledge.
Gewirtz, S., Ball, S.J. and Bowe, R. (1995) *Markets, Choice and Equity in Education.* Buckingham: Open University Press.
Giddens, A. (1991) *Modernity and Self-identity. Self and Society in the Late Modern Age.* Cambridge: Polity Press.

— (2000) *The Third Way and its Critics.* Cambridge: Polity Press.

Gidney, R. (1999) *From Hope to Harris: The Reshaping of Ontario's Schools.* Toronto: University of Toronto Press.

Gipson, S. (2003) *Issues of ICT, School Reform and Learning-Centred School Design,* International Practitioner Inquiry Report. Nottingham: National College for School Leadership.

Glassford, L. (2005) 'A triumph of politics over pedagogy? The case of the Ontario Teacher Qualifying Test, 2000–2005', *Canadian Journal of Educational Administration and Policy*, 45, November, available at www.umanitoba.ca/publications/cjeap/articles/glassford.htmlessed, accessed 21 October 2006.

Gleeson, D. and Husbands, C. (eds) (2001) *The Performing School.* London: RoutledgeFalmer.

Gleeson, D. and Husbands, C. (2003) 'Modernizing schooling through performance management: a critical appraisal', *Journal of Education Policy*, 18, (5), 499–511.

Goddard, G. and Ryall, A. (2002) 'Teaching assistants: issues for the primary school', *Primary Practice*, 30, 29–32.

Goodson, I. F. and Mangan, J. F. (1995) 'Subject cultures and the introduction of classroom computers', *British Educational Research Journal*, 21, (5), 613–29.

Government of New Zealand (1988) *Tomorrow's Schools: The Reform of Education Administration in New Zealand.* Wellington: Government Printer.

Grace, G. (1995) *School Leadership: Beyond Education Management.* London: Falmer.

Gray, C., Hagger-Vaughan, L., Pilkington, R. and Tomkins, S.-A. (2005) 'The pros and cons of interactive whiteboards in relation to Key Stage 3 strategy and framework', *Language Learning Journal*, 32, 38–45.

Gray, D., Reynolds, D. and Fitzgibbon, C. (1996) *Merging Traditions: The Future of Research on School Effectiveness and School Improvement.* London: Cassell.

Green, A. (1999) 'Education and globalization in Europe and East Asia: convergent and divergent trends', *Journal of Education Policy*, 14, (1), 55–71.

— (2002) *Education, Globalisation and the Nation State,* London: Macmillan.

Griffiths, M. (2003) *Action for Social Justice in Education.* Maidenhead: Open University Press.

Gronn, P. (2000) 'Distributed properties – a new architecture for leadership', *Educational Management Administration and Leadership*, 28, (3), 317–38.

— (2002) Distributed leadership as a unit of analysis', *The Leadership Quarterly*, 13, 423–51.

Gunter, H. M. (1997) *Rethinking Education: The Consequences of Jurassic Management.* London: Cassell.

— (2001) *Leaders and Leadership in Education.* London: Paul Chapman Publishing.

— (2004a) 'Labels and labelling in the field of educational leadership', *Discourse*, 25, (1), 21–42.

— (2004b) 'Remodelling the school workforce', paper presented at the School Leadership and Social Justice Seminar Society for Educational Studies, 4 November 2004.

— (2005a) *Leading Teachers.* London: Continuum.

— (2005b) 'Remodelling the school workforce in England: a study in tyranny', keynote address to the British Educational Leadership Management and Administration Society Annual Conference, Milton Keynes, September 2005.

— (2005c) 'Putting education back into leadership', *Forum*, 47, (2 and 3), 181–7.

— (2005d) 'Conceptualising research in educational leadership', *Educational Management, Administration and Leadership, Special Edition: Researching Leadership – A Review of Progress*, 33, (2), 165–80.

Gunter, H. M. and Rayner, S. (2005) 'The researcher, research and policy: the challenges of contract research in evaluating school workforce reform', paper presented at the American Educational Research Association Annual Meeting, Montreal, Canada, April 2005.

— (2007) Modernising the school workforce in England: challenging transformation and leadership?' *Leadership*, 3, (1), 47–64.

Gunter, H. M., Rayner, S., Butt, G., Fielding, A., Lance, A. and Thomas, H. (2007) 'Transforming the school workforce: perspectives on school reform in England', *Journal of Educational Change*, 25–39.

Gunter, H. M., Rayner, S., Thomas, H., Fielding, A., Butt, G. and Lance, A. (2005) 'Teachers, time and work: findings from the Evaluation of the Transforming the School Workforce Pathfinder Project', *School Leadership and Management*, 25, (5), 441–54.

Gunter, H. M. and Ribbins, P. (2003) 'Challenging orthodoxy in school leadership studies: knowers, knowing and knowledge?', *School Leadership and Management*, 23, (2), 129–47.

Gunter, H. M. and Thomson, P. (2006) 'The makeover: a new logic of practice in policy making?', paper presented to the ECER (European Conference for Educational Research), University of Geneva, Geneva, September 2006.

Hall, E. with Altman, M., Nkomo, N., Peltzer, K. and Zuma, K. (2005) *Potential Attrition in Education. The Impact of Job Satisfaction, Morale, Workload and HIV/AIDS.* Cape Town: HSRC Press. Report presented to the ELRC and prepared by a research consortium of the Human Sciences Research Council and the Medical Research Council of South Africa.

Hallinger, P. and Snodvings, K. (2005) *Adding Value to School Leadership and Management.* Nottingham: NCSL.

Hammersley-Fletcher, L. and Lowe, M. (2005) 'Remodelling schools – experiences from within "change teams"', paper presented to the British Educational Leadership Management and Administration Society Annual Conference, Milton Keynes, September 2005.

Hargreaves, A. (1994) *Changing Teachers, Changing Times: Teachers' Work and Culture in the Post Modern Age.* London: Cassell.

Hargreaves, D. and Hopkins, D. (1991) *The Empowered School: The Management and Practice of Development Planning.* London: Cassell.

Harrison, M. (1998) *Co-ordinating Information and Communications Technology across the Primary School: A Book for the Primary IT Co-ordinator.* London: Falmer Press.

Hartle, F. (2005) *Shaping up to the Future. A Guide to Roles, Structures and Career Development in Secondary Schools.* Summary report. Nottingham: NCSL.

Hastings, S. (2002) 'Workload', *Times Educational Supplement*, pp. 15–18.

Hay McBer Group (2001) *Identifying the Skills, Knowledge, Attributes and Competencies for First-time Principals: Shaping the Next Generation of Principals: Report to the Ministry of Education*. London: Hay Acquisitions Inc.

Hayes, D. (2003) *A Student Teacher's Guide to Primary School Placement. Learning to Survive and Prosper*. London: RoutledgeFalmer.

Heap, R., Millar, W. and Smyth, E. M. (2005) 'Introduction', *Learning to Practice*. Ottawa: University of Ottawa Press, pp. 1–10.

Helsby, G. (1999) *Changing Teachers' Work*. Buckingham: Open University Press.

Henry, M., Lingard, B., Rizvi, F. and Taylor, S. (2001) *The OECD, Globalization and Education Policy*. London: Pergamon.

Herring, S. (ed.) (1996) *Computer Mediated Communication: Linguistic Social and Cross-cultural Perspectives*. Amsterdam: John Benjamins.

Hewitt, B. and Fitzsimons, C. (2001) 'I quit', *Education, The Guardian*, 9 January 2001, pp. 2–3.

HMCIC (2004) *Report of HMCIC 2003–2004*. London: The Stationery Office.

HMI/OfSTED (2002) *Teaching Assistants in Primary Schools: An Evaluation of the Quality and Impact of their Work*. London: OfSTED HMI 434.

HMI for Education and Training in Wales (2005) *Raising Standards and Tackling Workload in Schools in Wales*. Cardiff: Estyn Publication Section.

Hodgins, T. A. (1971) 'University education for elementary school teachers of Ontario 1950–1970 (a case study)', PhD thesis, Syracuse University.

Hollins, K., Gunter, H. and Thomson, P. (2006) 'Living improvement: a case study of a secondary school in England', *Improving Schools*, 9, (2), 141–52.

Holly, P. and Southworth, G. (1989) *The Developing School*. London: Falmer.

Hopkins, D. and Jackson, D. (2003) 'Building the capacity for leading and learning', in A. Harris, C. Day, M. Hadfield, A. Hargreaves and C. Chapman (eds), *Effective Leadership for School Improvement*. London: RoutledgeFalmer, pp. 84–104.

Horne, M. (2001) 'Teacher knows best', *The Guardian*, 4 September 2001.

Hoyle, E. (1999) 'The two faces of micropolitics', *School Leadership and Management*, 18, (1), 213–22.

— (2001) 'Teaching: prestige, status and esteem', *Educational Management and Administration*, 29, (2), 139–52.

Hunter, I. (1996) 'Assembling the school', in A. Barry, T. Osborne and N. Rose. *Foucault and Political Reason. Liberalism, Neo-liberalism and Rationalities of Government*. London: University College London Press, pp. 143–65.

Huxham, C. and Vangon, S. (2000) 'What makes partnerships work?', in S. Osborne, *Public Private Partnerships: Theory and Practice in International Perspective*. London: Routledge, pp. 294–310.

Hyman, P. (2005) *1 out of 10, from Downing Street Vision to Classroom Reality*. London: Vintage.

IFIP (1972) *Aims and Objectives of Teacher Education*. Geneva: IFIP.

IRU (2003) *Implementation Review Unit*. London: DfES.

Istance, D. (2005) *Work on Schooling for Tomorrow: Trends, Themes and Scenarios to Inform Leadership Issues*. Nottingham: NCSL.

Jackson, D. (2000) 'School improvement and the planned growth of leadership capacity', BERA, Cardiff, September 2000.

Jackson, N. (2006) 'Does creationism have a place in the classroom?', *The Independent/Education*, 12 October 2006.

Jansen, D. J. (2002) 'Image-ining teachers: policy images and teacher identity in South African classrooms', in K. Lewin, M. Samuel and Y. Sayed (eds), *Changing Patterns of Teacher Education in South Africa*. Sandown/Cape Town: Heinemann, pp. 118–29.

— (n.d.) Rethinking education policy making in South Africa: symbols of change, signals of conflict', in A. Kraak and M. Young, *Education in Retrospect. Policy and implementation since 1990*. Pretoria: Human Sciences Research Council in association with the Institute of Education, University of London, pp. 41–57.

John, P. (2005) 'The sacred and the profane: subject sub-culture, pedagogical practice and teachers' perceptions of the classroom use of ICT', *Educational Review*, 57, (4), 471–90.

John, P. and La Velle, L. (2004) 'Devices and desires: subject subcultures, pedagogic identity and the challenge of information communication technology', *Technology, Pedagogy and Education*, 13, (3), 307–26.

John, P. and Sutherland, R. (2005) 'Affordance, opportunity and the pedagogical implications of ICT', *Educational Review*, 57, (4), 405–13.

Jones, A. (2004) *A Review of the Research Literature on Barriers to the Uptake of ICT by Teachers*. Coventry: Becta.

Kelly, R. (2006) 'Action on SEN bureaucracy: progress or confusion?', *SENCO Update*, 73, 1, 1.

Kennewell, S. (2001) 'Is there really a lack of pedagogy for ICT?', *The ITTE Newsletter*.

Kennewell, S. and Selwood, I. (1997) 'The professional development needs of secondary school IT co-ordinators', *Journal of Information Technology for Teacher Education*, 6, (3), 339–56.

Kingdon, J. (2003) *Agendas, Alternatives and Public Policies*. New York: Addison-Wesley Educational Publishers Inc.

Kitchen, J., Thompson, S., Foster, J. and Smyth, E. (2006) 'Promoting equity, diversity and social justice: a UTS school-wide initiative'. A UTS–OISE/UT collaborative project available at www.uts.utoronto.ca/projectsandpublications/newprojects2005-2006.html, accessed 21 October 2006.

Knowles, M. (1970) 'Andragogy: an emerging technology for adult learning', in M. Tight (ed.), *Education for Adults: Adult Learning in Education*. London: Croom Helm.

Kolb, D. A. (1984) *Experiential Learning: Experience as the Source of Learning and Development*. Englewood Cliffs, NJ: Prentice-Hall.

Kosnick, C., Brown, R. and Beck, C. (2003) *Report for the Preservice Admissions Committee: An Examination of the Effectiveness of the Admissions Process of the Teacher Certification Program*. Toronto: OISE/UT.

Kostova, E. (2005) *The Historian*. London: Little, Brown.

Kraak, A. and Young, M. (n.d.) *Education in Retrospect. Policy and Implementation since 1990*. Pretoria: Human Sciences Research Council in association with the Institute of Education, University of London.

Lakehead University (1969) Senate Minutes. Meeting No. 33, 22 March 1969. Proposed agreement between the Minister of Education and Lakehead University, regarding the matter of Teacher Education.

Lambert, L. (2000) *Building Leadership Capacity in Schools.* South Australian Secondary Principals Association.

Lance, A. (2004) 'It needn't fall about our ears', *Primary Practice*, Spring, 2, 2–3.

Lang, D. and Eastman, J. (2002) *Mergers in Higher Education: Lessons from Theory and Practice.* Toronto: University of Toronto Press.

Larsen, M. (2005) 'A critical analysis of teacher evaluation policy trends', *Australian Journal of Education*, 49, (3), 292–403.

Lave, J. and Wenger, E. (1991) *Situated Learning: Legitimate Peripheral Participation.* Cambridge: Cambridge University Press.

Lawn, M. (1996) *Modern Times? Work, Professionalism and Citizenship in Teaching.* London: Falmer Press.

Layton, L. (2005) 'Special educational needs coordinators and leadership: a role too far?', *Support for Learning*, 20, (2), 34–52.

Leadbeater, C. (2004) *Learning about Personalisation: How Can We Put the Learner at the Heart of the Education System?* London: DfES, in partnership with DEMOS and the NCSL.

Leask, M. and Pachler, N. (eds) (1999) *Learning to Teach Using ICT in Secondary Schools.* London: Routledge.

Leithwood, K. (1994) 'Leadership for school restructuring', *Educational Administration Quarterly*, 30, (4), 498–518.

Lessard, C. (2000) 'Evolution du métier d'enseignant et nouvelle régulation de l'éducation', *Recherche et Formation*, 35, 91–116.

Levin, B. (1998) 'An epidemic of education policy: What we can learn from each other?' *Comparative Education*, 34, (2), 131–41.

Lewin, K., Samuel, M. and Sayed, Y. (2002) *Changing Patterns of Teacher Education in South Africa.* Sandown/Cape Town: Heinemann.

Lingard, B., Hayes, D. and Mills, M. (2003) 'Teachers and productive pedagogies: contextualizing, conceptualizing and utilizing', *Pedagogy, Culture and Society*, 11, (3), 399–424.

Lingard, B., Hayes, D., Mills, M. and Christie, P. (2003) *Leading Learning.* Maidenhead: Open University Press.

Louden, W. (2000) 'Standards for standards: the development of Australian professional standards for teaching', *Australian Journal of Education*, 44, (2), 118–34.

Lynch, K. (1989) *The Hidden Curriculum: Reproduction in Education, an Appraisal.* London: Falmer Press.

Mabilon-Bonfils, B. and Saadoun, L. (2001) *Sociologie politique de l'école*, Paris: Presses Universitaries. de France.

MacBeath, J. (2000) *Schools should Speak for Themselves.* London: Falmer.

— (2005) 'Leadership as distributed: a matter of practice', *School Leadership and Management*, 25, (4), 349–66.

MacBeath, J. and Galton, M. with Steward, S., Page, C. and Edwards, J. (2004) *A life in secondary teaching: finding time for learning.* A report commissioned by the

National Union of Teachers concerning the workloads in secondary schools. Cambridge: University of Cambridge.

MacGilchrist, B., Mortimer, P., Savage, J. and Beresford, C. (1995) *Planning Matters: The Impact of Development Planning in Primary Schools.* London: Paul Chapman.

McAuley, D. (1990) *25 Years of Teacher Education at Brock University.* Vanwell, Canada: St Catharine's.

McCarthy, J. R. (1970) 'From teachers' colleges to faculties of education', in W. Rees (ed.), *Teacher Education: A Search for New Relationships.* Toronto: Ontario Institute for Studies in Education.

McCulloch, G., Helsby, G. and Knight, P. (2000) *The Politics of Professionalism.* London: Continuum.

McGregor, D. and Gunter, B. (2006) 'Invigorating pedagogic change. Suggestions from findings of the development of secondary science teachers' practice and cognisance of the learning process', *European Journal of Teacher Education,* 29, (1), 23–48.

McMullan, T. (2002) *Wired to Learn: What's Holding up the School of the Future?* London: Adam Smith Research Institute, ASI Research Ltd, UK.

Malet, E. and Brisard, E. (2005a) *Modernisation de l'école et contextes culturels. Dès politiques aux pratiques en France et en Grande-Bretagne.* Paris: L'Harmattan.

— (2005b) Travailler ensemble dans le secondaire en France et en Angleterre. *Recherche et Formation,* 49, 17–34.

Marginson, S. and Rhoades, G. (2002) 'Beyond national states, markets and systems of higher education: a glonacal agency heuristic', *Higher Education,* 43, (3), 281–309.

Marquand, D. (2004) *Decline of the Public.* Cambridge: Polity Press.

Martinez, K. (2004) 'Mentoring new teachers: promise and problems in times of teacher shortage', *Australian Journal of Education,* 48, 1, 95–108.

Mattson, E. and Harley, K. (2002) 'Teacher identities and strategic mimicry in the policy/practice gap', in K. Lewin, M. Samuel and Y. Sayed (eds), *Changing Patterns of Teacher Education in South Africa.* Sandown/Cape Town: Heinemann.

Mayer, R. E. and Anderson, R. B. (1991) 'Animations need narrations: an experimental test of a dual-coding hypothesis', *Journal of Educational Psychology,* 83, 444–52.

Menter, I., Mahony, P. and Hextall, I. (2004) 'Ne'er the twain shall meet?: modernizing the teaching profession in Scotland and England', *Journal of Education Policy,* 19, (2), 195–214.

Menter, I., McMahon, M., Forde, C., Hall, J., McPhee, A., Patrick, F. and Devlin, A. (2006) *Teacher Working Time Research. Final Report to the Scottish Negotiating Committee for Teachers.* Glasgow: Faculty of Education, University of Glasgow.

Miliband, D. (2003) '21st century teaching', speech at the launch of the TTA corporate plan, 7 April 2003.

Mills, J. and Mills, R. W. (eds) (1995) *Primary School People. Getting to Know your Colleagues.* London: Routledge.

Minister's Committee on the Training of Elementary School Teachers (C. R. MacLeod, Chair) (1966) *Report.* Toronto: Ministry of Education.

Ministry of Education, NZ (1991) *The National Curriculum Framework of New Zealand: A Discussion Document.* Wellington: Ministry of Education.

— (1993) *Education Priorities for New Zealand*. Wellington: Ministry of Education.

— (1997) *Performance Management Systems*. Wellington: Learning Media.

— (1999) *Professional Standards: Criteria for Quality Teaching*. Wellington: Government Printer.

— (2002a) *Code of Practice for the Pastoral Care of International Students*. Wellington: Ministry of Education.

— (2002b) *Recruitment and Retention in New Zealand Secondary Schools*. Wellington: Ministry of Education.

— (2003) 'Education priorities for New Zealand', available at www.beehive.govt.nz/ mallard/priorities, accessed 17 March 2006.

— (2005) *Making a Bigger Difference for All Students: Schooling Strategy 2005–2010*. Wellington: Government Printer.

Mori (2002) *Teachers on Teaching, A Survey of the Teaching Profession*, Research study conducted for the General Teaching Council (with PR21 and the *Guardian*). London: Mori.

Morris, E. (2001) 'Professionalism and trust – the future of teachers and teaching. A speech to the Social Market Foundation', 12 November 2001. Available at www.dfes.gov.uk/speeches, accessed 20 January 2003.

— (2006) 'What use is research if it sits on the shelf?', *Education Guardian*, 26 September 2006, p. 4.

Mortimore, P. and Whitty, G. (1997) *Can School Improvement Overcome the Effects of Disadvantage?* London: Institute of Education.

Moyles, J. and Suschitzky, W. (1997) *Jills of All Trades . . . ? Classroom Assistants in KS1 Classes*. London: ATL.

Murphy, J. and Hallinger, P. (1992) 'The principalship in an era of transformation', *Journal of Educational Administration*, 30, (3), 77–88.

Najjar, L. J. (1996) 'Multimedia information and learning', *Journal of Educational Multimedia and Hypermedia*, 5, 129–51.

Narsee, H. (2005) 'The common and contested meanings of education districts in South Africa', University of Pretoria, PhD.

NASUWT (2003) *Administrative and Clerical Tasks*. Birmingham: NASUWT, available at www.nasuwt.org.uk/templates?internal.asp?nodeid=69806&11=-1&12=69806], accessed 5 October 2006.

NCC (1990) *Technology Non-Statutory Guidance: Information Technology Capacity York:* NCC.

NCET/NAACE (1997) *Implementing IT: Resource Pack*. Coventry, NCET/NAACE.

NEPI (1993) *The National Educational Policy Investigation. The Framework Report and Final Report Summaries*. Cape Town: Oxford University Press. A project of the Natural Education Co-ordinating Committee.

Newman, J. (2000) 'Beyond the new public management? Modernizing public services', in J. Clarke, S. Gewirtz and E. Mclaughlin (eds), *New Managerialism, New Welfare*. London: Open University Press and Sage, pp. 45–61.

New Zealand Treasury (1987) *Government Management: Brief to the Incoming Government* (2 vols). Wellington: Government Printer.

Noddings, N. (2003) 'Is teaching a practice?', *Journal of Philosophy of Education*, 37, (2), 241–51.

Norris, C. (2000) 'Post-modernism: a guide for the perplexed', in G. Browning, A. Halcli and F. Webster (eds), *Understanding Contemporary Society: Theories of the Present.* London, Thousand Oaks and New Delhi: Sage Publications.

North, R. (1990) *Managing Information Technology: The Role of the IT Co-ordinator.* Londonderry: University of Ulster.

Novoa, A. (2002) 'La raison et la responsabilité: vers une science du gouvernement des âmes', in R. Hofstetter and B. Scheuwly (eds), *Sciences de l'Education 19è–20è siècles.* Berne: Peter Lang.

Novoa, A. and Popkewitz, T. (2001) 'Conversation', *Recherche et Formation*, 38, 119–29.

NRT (2003) *Touching Tomorrow.* Nottingham: NCSL.

Obin, J.-P. (2002) *Enseigner, un métier pour demain.* Report to the National Ministry of Education. Paris: Ministre de l'Education Nationale.

OECD (2003) 'Learning for tomorrow's world: programme for international student achievement', available at www.minedu.govt.nz, accessed 17 March 2006.

— (2004) 'Policy brief: lifelong learning', available at www.oecd.org/dataoecd/17/11/29478789.pdf, accessed 10 June 2006.

Office for Manpower Economics (2006) *School Teachers' Review Board: Teachers' Workloads Diary Survey.* London: British Market Research Bureau Social Research.

OfSTED (2002) *ICT in Schools, the Effect of Government Initiatives: Pupil's Achievement Progress Report.* Rothwell, Northants: OfSTED.

— (2004a) *Remodelling the School Workforce, Phase 1.* London: HMI 2298.

— (2004b) *ICT in Schools. The Impact of Government Initiatives Five Years On.* London: Her Majesty's Stationery Office.

— (2004c) *2004 Report. ICT in Schools – the Impact of Government Initiatives. Primary Schools.* London: Her Majesty's Stationery Office.

— (2005) *Embedding ICT in Schools – a Dual Evaluation Exercise.* London: Her Majesty's Stationery Office.

Olsen, P. (2002) *Towards a European Administrative Space? Advanced Research on the Europeanisation of the Nation-State.* Oslo: ARENA, University of Oslo, Working Paper, 26.

Olson, J. (2000) 'Trojan horse or teachers's pet? Computers and the culture of schools', *Journal of Curriculum Studies*, 32, (1), 1–9.

Olssen, M., Codd, J. and O'Neill, A. M. (2004) *Education Policy: Globalization, Citizenship and Democracy.* London, Thousand Oaks and New Delhi: Sage Publications.

Ontario Conference on Education (1961) *The Quest for Excellence in Education.* Peterborough: Newson.

Ontario Legislative Assembly (1961) *Debates and Proceedings*, 2 February 1961, p. 835.

— (1966) *Debates and Proceedings*, 28 March, 1966, p. 2009e

Ontario Ministry of Education (2004) 'Teacher excellence – unlocking student potential through continuing professional development', available at www.edu.gov.on.ca/eng/general/elemsec/partnership/potential.html, accessed 22 October 2006.

Osborne, D. and Gaebler, T. A. (1992) *Reinventing Government: How the Entrepreneurial Spirit is Transforming the Public Sector.* New York: Perseus.

Osborne, S. (2000) *Public Private Partnerships: Theory and Practice in International Perspective.* London: Routledge.

Ozga, J. (2000a) *Policy Research in Educational Settings*, Buckingham: Open University Press.

— (2000b) 'Education: new labour, new teachers', in G. Clarke, S. Gerwitz and E. McLaughlin (eds), *New Managerialism, New Welfare?* London, Thousand Oaks and New Delhi: Open University in association with Sage Publications, pp. 222–35.

— (2002) 'Education governance in the United Kingdom: the modernization project', *European Educational Research Journal*, 1, (2), 331–41.

— (2005) 'Modernizing the education workforce: a perspective from Scotland', *Educational Review*, 57, (2), 207–19.

Ozga, J. and Lawn, M. (1988) 'Schoolwork: interpreting the labour process of teaching', *British Journal of Sociology of Education*, 9, (3), 323–36.

Paivio, A. (1991) *Images in Mind: The Evolution of a Theory*. Hemel Hempstead: Harvester Wheatsheaf.

Pakenham, W. H. (1922) 'The university and the training of teachers', in *The Eighth Conference of the Canadian Universities*. Winnipeg: University of Manitoba.

Palinscar, A. S. and Brown, A. L. (1984) 'Reciprocal teaching of comprehension fostering and comprehension monitoring activities', *Cognition and Instruction*, 2, 117–75.

Parker, B. (2002) 'Roles and responsibilities, institutional landscapes and curriculum mindscapes: a partial view of teacher education policy in South Africa: 1990–2000', in K. Lewin, M. Samuel and Y. Sayed (eds), *Changing Patterns of Teacher Education in South Africa*. Sandown/Cape Town: Heinemann. pp. 16–44.

Passey, D., Rogers, C., Machell, J., McHugh, G. and Allaway, D. (2003) *The Motivational Effect of ICT on Pupils: Emerging Findings 1*. London: DfES/0794/2003.

Pelgrum, W. J. and Anderson, R. A. (eds) (1999) *ICT and the Emerging Paradigm for Lifelong Learning: A Worldwide Educational Assessment of Infrastructure, Goals and Practices*. Amsterdam: International Association for the Evaluation of Educational Achievement.

Peters, M. and Marshall, J. (2004) 'The politics of curriculum: autonomous choosers and enterprise', in A.-M. O'Neill, J. Clark and R. Openshaw (eds), *Reshaping Culture, Knowledge and Learning?: Policy and Content in the New Zealand Curriculum*. Palmerston North: Dunmore Press.

Phillips, C. E. (1977) *College of Education Toronto: Memories of OCE*. Toronto: Faculty of Education, University of Toronto.

Phurutse, M. C. (2005) *Factors Affecting Teaching and Learning in South African Public Schools*. Cape Town: HSRC Press. Report presented to the ELRC and prepared by a research consortium of the Human Sciences Research Council and the Medical Research Council of South Africa.

Pilkington, R. M. and Gray, C. (2004) 'Embedding ICT in the modern goreign language curriculum: pedagogy into practice', in *Research Proceedings of the ALT-C 2004 Conference on 'Blue Skies and Pragmatism: Learning Technologies for the Next Decade', 14–16 September*. University of Exeter: Association for Learning Technology, pp. 271–83.

Pilkington, R. M. and Parker-Jones, C. H. (1996) 'Interacting with computer-based simulation: the role of dialogue', *Computers and Education*, 27, 1–14.

Pilkington, R. M. and Walker, S. A. (2003) 'Using CMC to develop argumentation skills in children with a literacy deficit', in J. Adriessen, M. Baker and D. Suthers (eds), *Arguing to Learn: Confronting Cognitions in Computer-Supported Collaborative Learning Environments.* Amsterdam: Kluwer Academic, pp. 144–75.

PIU (2001) *Strengthening Leadership.* London: PIU, available at www.number-10.gov. uk/su/leadership, accessed 23 March 2004.

Popkewitz, T. (ed.) (1993) *Changing Patterns of Power: Social Regulation and Teacher Education Reform in Eight Countries.* Albany, NY: SUNY Press.

— (1998) *Struggling for the Soul. The Politics of Schooling and the Construction of the Teacher.* New York: Teachers' College Press.

Popkewitz, T. S., Pereyra, M. A. and Franklin, B. M. (2001) 'History, the problem of knowledge, and the new cultural history of schooling', in T. W. Popkewitz, B. M. Franklin and M. A. Pereyra (eds), *Cultural History and Education.* New York: RoutledgeFalmer, pp. 3–42.

Preece, J. (2000) *Online Communities: Designing Usability, Supporting Sociability.* Chichester: John Wiley and Sons.

Preston, C. (2004) *Learning to Use ICT in Classrooms. Part One: A Summary of the Evaluation of English NOF ICT Teacher Training Programme 1999–2003.* Oxford: MirandaNet.

PwC (2001) *Teacher Workload Study.* London: DfES.

Quicke, J. (2003) 'Teaching assistants: students or servants?', *Forum*, 45, (2), Summer, 71–4.

Ranson, S. (2003) 'Public accountability in the age of neo-liberal governance', *Journal of Education Policy*, 18, (5), 459–80.

Rayner, S. and Gunter, H. M. (2005a) 'Rethinking leadership: perspectives on remodelling practice', *Educational Review*, 57, (2), 1–11.

— (2005b) 'The entrepreneurial role in school leadership: lessons from the UK Transforming the School Workforce Project', paper presented at the Commonwealth Council for Educational Administration and Management Symposium, 'Educational Leadership and Entrepreneurship across the Commonwealth', at the American Educational Research Association Annual Meeting, Montreal, Canada, April 2005.

Rayner, S., Gunter, H. M., Thomas, H., Butt, G. and Lance, A. (2005) Transforming the school workforce: remodelling experiences in the special school', *Management in Education*, 19, (5), 22–8.

Reynolds, D. (1992) 'School effectiveness and school improvement: an updated review of the British literature', in D. Reynolds and P. Cuttance (eds), *School Effectiveness: Research, Policy and Practice.* London: Cassell.

Reynolds, D., Treharne, D. and Tripp, H. (2003) 'ICT: the hopes and the reality', *British Journal of Educational Technology*, 34, 151–67.

Rice, S. (2005) 'You don't bring me flowers any more: a fresh look at the vexed issue of teacher status', *Australian Journal of Education*, 49, (2), 182–96.

Riley, K. (1998) *Whose School is it anyway?* London: Falmer.

Robertson, S. (2000) *A Class Act. Changing Teachers' Work, the State, and Globalisation.* London/New York: Falmer Press.

Robertson, S. and Dale, R. (2002) 'Local states of emergency: the contradictions of neo-liberal governance in education in New Zealand', *British Journal of Sociology*, 23, (3), 463–82.

Rolheiser, C. and Evans, M. (2004) 'Teaching for depth in teacher education', in K. Leithwood, P. McAdie, N. Bascia and A. Rodrigue (eds), *Teaching for Deep Understanding: Towards the Ontario Curriculum We Need*. Toronto: OISE/UT/ ETFO, pp. 128–34.

Rosenshine, B. and Meister, C. (1994) 'Reciprocal teaching: a review of the research', *Educational Research*, 64, 479–530.

Royal Commission on the University of Toronto (1906) *Report*. Toronto: Cameron.

RSA, (1992) *Education Renewal Strategy*. Pretoria: Department of National Education.

— (1996) *South African Schools Act*, Act No. 84 of 1996.

Rudduck, J. (2006) 'The past, the papers and the project', *Educational Review*, 58, (2), 131–43.

Rudduck, J. and Flutter, J. (2004) *How to Improve your School*. London: Continuum.

Sachs, J. (2003) *The Activist Teaching Profession*. Buckingham: Open University Press.

Santiago, P. (2002) *Teacher Demand and Supply: Improving Teaching Quality and Addressing Teacher Shortages*. OECD Education Working Paper No. 1. Paris: OECD.

Savery, J. R. and Duffy, T. M. (1996) 'Problem based learning: an instructional model and its constructivist framework', in B. Wilson (ed.), *Constructivist Learning Environments: Case Studies in Instructional Design*. Englewood Cliffs, NJ: Educational Technology Publications.

Sayed, Y. and Soudien, C. (2005) 'Decentralisation and the construction of inclusion education policy in South Africa', *Compare*, 35, (2), 115–25.

Scardamalia, M. and Bereiter, C. (1991) Higher levels of agency for children in knowledge building: a challenge for the design of new knowledge media', *The Journal of the Learning Sciences*, 1, 37–68.

Schnapper, D. (2000) *Qu'est-ce que la citoyenneté?* Paris: Gallimard.

Schön, D. A. (1983) *The Reflective Practitioner: How Professionals Think in Action*. New York: Basic Books.

Scrimshaw, P. (2004) *Enabling Teachers to Make Successful Use of ICT*. Coventry: Becta.

Sebba, J. (2004) 'Developing evidence-informed policy and practice in education', in G. Thomas and R. Pring (eds), *Evidence-Based Practice in Education*. Maidenhead: Open University Press, pp. 34–43.

Secondary Teachers' Collective Agreement 2004–2007, available at www.ppta.org.nz, accessed 14 March 2006.

Selwood, I. and Drenoyianni, H. (1997) 'Administration, management and IT in education', in A. Fung, A. Visscher, B. Z. Barta and D. Teather (eds), *Information Technology in Educational Management for the Schools of the Future*. London: Chapman and Hall.

Selwood, I. and Kennewell, S. (1999) 'Coordinating information technology in secondary schools', in A. Jimoyiaannis (ed.), *Panhellenic Conference: Information Technology and Education*. Ioannina: Association of IT Teachers of Greece.

Selwood, I. and Pilkington, R. (2005) 'Teacher workload: using ICT to release time to teach', *Educational Review*, 57, (2), 162–74.

Sennett, R. (1999) *The Corrosion of Character.* New York: Norton.

Sheppard, B. (2003) 'Leadership, organizational learning and the successful integration of information and communication technology in teaching and learning, *International Electronic Journal for Leadership in Learning,* 7, (14). www.ucalgary.ca/~iejll/volume7/sheppard.htm, accesed 7 October 2006.

Shuttleworth, V. (2000) *The Special Educational Needs Coordinator. Maximising your Potential.* London: Pearson.

Silverman, B. G. (1995) 'Computer supported collaborative learning', *Computers and Education,* 25, 81–91.

Simkins, T. (2005) 'Leadership in action: "What Works" or "What Makes Sense"?', *Educational Management Administration and Leadership,* 33, (1), 9–28.

Singh, M., Kenway, J. and Apple, M. (2005) 'Globalizing education: perspectives from above and below', in M. W. Apple, J. Kenway and M. Singh (eds), *Globalizing Education: Policies, Pedagogies and Politics.* New York: Peter Lang.

Smit, B. (2000) How primary school teachers experience education policy change in South Africa', *Perspectives in Education,* 19, (3), 67–83.

Smith, M. (2006) 'Leadership matters', speech at the Bradford and Ripon and Leeds Diocesan Education Conference, 15 March 2006.

Smith, H., Higgins, S., Wall, K. and Miller, J. (2005) 'Interactive whiteboards: boon or bandwagon?' *Journal of Computer Assisted Learning,* 21, (2), 91–102.

Smithers, A. and Robinson, P. (2003) *Factors Affecting Teachers' Decisions to Leave the Profession,* Research report RR 430. London: DfES.

Smithers, R. (2006) 'Schools facing heads crisis, warns survey', *The Guardian,* 5 September 2006, p. 4.

Smyth, E. M. (2003) "It should be the centre . . . of professional training in education": the Faculty of Education at the University of Toronto: 1871–1996', *Tidskrift: Journal of Research in Teacher Education,* 3–4, 135–54.

Smyth, J. (ed.) (1993) *A Socially Critical View of the Self-managing School.* London: Falmer Press.

— (2003) 'Undamaging "damaged" teachers: an antidote to the "self managing school"', *Delta,* 55, (1 and 2), 15–42.

— (2005) 'Modernizing the Australian education workplace: a case of failure to deliver for teachers of young disadvantaged adolescents', *Educational Review,* 57 (2), 221–33.

— (2006) 'Educational leadership that fosters "student voice"', *International Journal of Leadership in Education,* 9, (4), 279–84.

Smyth, J., Dow, A., Hattam, R., Reid, A. and Shacklock, G. (2000) *Teachers' Work in a Globalizing Economy.* London: Falmer.

Somekh, B., Underwood, J., Convery, A., Dillon, G., Harber-Stuart, T., Jarvis, J., Lewin, C., Mathers, D., Twining, P. and Woodrow, D. (2006) *Evaluation of the ICT Test Bed Project. Annual Report 2006.* Coventry: Becta.

Southworth, G. (2002) *Distributed Leadership in Action: A Study of Current Practice in Schools.* Nottingham: National College of School Leadership.

Spillane, J. P., Halverson, R. and Diamond, J. B. (2001) 'Investigating school leadership practice: a distributed perspective', *Educational Researcher,* April, 23–8.

Stamp, R. (1982) *The Schools of Ontario.* Toronto: University of Toronto Press.

Starkey, H. (2000) 'Citizenship education in France and Britain: evolving theories and practices', *The Curriculum Journal,* 11, (1), 39–54.

Starratt, R. J. (2003) *Centering Educational Administration.* Mahwah, NJ: Lawrence Erlbaum Associates.

Steed, M. (1992) 'STELLA, a simulation construction kit: cognitive process and educational implications', *Journal of Computers in Mathematics and Science Teaching,* 11, 39–52.

Stevenson, H. (2006) 'Another case of a wolf dressed as a sheep? Teachers, workforce remodelling and the new professionalism', paper presented at BELMAS Annual Conference, Birmingham, October 2006.

Stevenson Committee (1997) *Information and Communications Technology in UK Schools – an Independent Enquiry (The Stevenson Report).* London: Pearson, available at rubble. ultralab.anglia.ac.uk/stevenson/contents.html, accesed 26 September 2006.

Stoll, L. and Myers, K. (1998) *Changing our Schools: Linking School Effectiveness and School Improvement.* Buckingham: Open University Press.

STRB (2004) *School Teacher Review Body – Teachers Workload Survey.* London: STRB.

Stronach, I., Corbin, B., McNamara, O., Stark, S. and Warne, T. (2002) 'Towards an uncertain politics of professionalism: teacher and nurse identities in flux', *Journal of Education Policy,* 17, (1), 109–38.

Szwed, C. (2004) 'The developing role of the primary special educational needs coordinator'. EdD thesis, University of Birmingham.

Tabberer. R. (2004) 'Teachernet', available at www.teachernet.gov.uk, accessed 27 September 2005.

Tagg, B. (ed.) (1999) *Taking the Pain out of School Management.* Baldock: Tagg Oram Partnership.

Teacher Registration Board (1994) *Advice and Guidance Programmes for Teachers.* Wellington: TRB.

Thélot, C. (1993) *L'Evaluation du système éducatif.* Paris: Nathan.

Thomas, H., Butt, G., Fielding, A., Foster, J., Gunter, H., Lance, A., Lock, R., Pilkington, R., Potts, E., Powers, S., Rayner, S., Rutherford, D., Selwood, I. and Soares, A. (2003a) *Baseline Evaluation of the ICT Test Bed Project.* Report to the DfES. Birmingham: School of Education, University of Birmingham.

— (2003b) *Baseline Evaluation of the ICT Test Bed Project (28 Individual Reports to Schools).* Birmingham: School of Education, University of Birmingham.

Thomas, H., Butt, G., Fielding, A., Foster, J., Gunter, H., Lance, A., Pilkington, R., Potts, E., Powers, S., Rayner, S., Rutherford, D., Selwood, I. and Szwed, C. (2004) *The Evaluation of the Transforming the School Workforce Pathfinder Project.* Research Report 541. London: DfES,

Thomas, S. (2005) 'Taking teachers out of the education: construction of teachers in education policy documents over a ten year period', *The Australian Educational Researcher,* 32, (3), 45–62.

Thompson, L. A. (1986) 'Breaking away in teacher education: the development of a concurrent teacher education program at York University 1968–1980', PhD thesis, University of Toronto.

Thomson, P. and Gunter, H. M. (2006) 'From "consulting pupils" to "pupils as researchers": a situated case narrative', *British Educational Research Journal*, 32, (6), in press.

Thomson, P. and Gunter, H. M. (2007) 'Researching bullying with students: a lens on everyday life in an innovative school', *International Journal of Inclusive Education*, in press.

Thomson, P. and Holdsworth (2003) 'Theorising change in the educational field: re-readings of student participation projects', *International Journal of Leadership in Education*, 6, (4), 371–91.

Thrupp, M. (2001) 'School-level education policy under New Labour and New Zealand Labour: a comparative update', *British Journal of Educational Studies*, 49, (2), 187–212.

— (2005) 'Importing England's "Third Way" education policy: a cautionary note', in J. Codd and K. Sullivan (eds), *Education Policy Directions in Aotearoa New Zealand*. Melbourne: Thomson/Dunmore Press.

Tilley, D. (2003) 'Doing it my way', *Primary Practice*, 33, Spring, 36–8.

Tomlinson, S. (2005) *Education in a post-welfare society* (Second edition). Maidenhead: Open University Press.

Tooley, J. (1995) 'Markets or democracy for education? A reply to Stewart Ranson', *British Journal of Educational Studies*, 43, (1), 21–34.

TOPILOT (1996) *The TOPILOT Project, EU 4th framework Telematics Applications Programme (TAP)*. Sheffield: University of Sheffield, EFECOT, EDM, National Institute for Curriculum Development. Available at www.efecot.net/projects/topilot/intro.htm, accessed 10 June 2006.

Townsley, E. (2001) '"The Sixties" trope', *Theory, Culture and Society*, 18, (6), 99–123.

TTA (1998a) *The National Curriculum for Initial Teacher Training – Annex B (ICT)*. London: DfEE.

— (1998b) *New Opportunities Fund. The Use of ICT in Subject Teaching Lottery-funded Training. Expected Outcomes*. London: DfEE.

University of Toronto (2003) 'A Green Paper for public discussion describing the characteristics of the best (public) research universities', available at www.utoronto.ca/plan2003/greenB.htm#s13, accessed 21 October 2006.

van Haecht, P. (1998) 'Les politiques éducatives, figure exemplaire des politiques publiques?', *Education et Sociétés*, 1, 15–25.

van Joolingen, W. R. and de Jong, T. (1991) 'Supporting hypothesis generation by learners exploring an interactive computer simulation', *Instructional Science*, 20, 389–404.

Vidovich, L. (2001) 'That chameleon "quality": the multiple and contradictory discourses of "quality" policy in Australian higher education', *Discourse: Studies in the Cultural Politics of Education*, 22, (2), 249–61.

Voogt, J. and Pelgrum, H. (2005) 'ICT and curriculum change', *Human Technology*, 1, (2), 157–75.

Vygotsky, L. S. (1978) *Mind in Society: The Development of Higher Psychological Processes*, Cambridge, MA: Harvard University Press.

Waghid, Y. (2004a) Democratic citizenship and higher education in South Africa:

preparing students for the world of work', *Kwartalnik Pedagogiczny*, 1–2(191–192), 293–312.

— (2004b) 'Compassion, citizenship and education in South Africa: an opportunity for transformation', *International Review of Education*, 50, (5–6), 525–42.

Walsh, K. (2002) *Leading and Managing the Future School – Developing Organisational and Management Structure in Secondary Schools*, National College for School Leadership, available at www.ncsl.org.uk/media/F7B/95/randd-fs-kwalsh.pdf, accessed 10 June 2006.

Warnock, M. (2006) Select Committee focus on SEN training: *SENCO Update*, 72, 2. London: Optimus Publishing.

Watson, D. M. (2001) 'Pedagogy before technology: re-thinking the relationship between ICT and teaching', *Education and Information Technologies*, 6, (4), 251–66.

Watson, L. (2005) 'Quality teaching and schooling leadership', National Institute for Quality Teaching and School Leadership, available at www.niqtsl.edu.au, accessed 20 March 2006.

Wegerif, R. and Dawes, L. (1998) 'Encouraging exploratory talk around computers', in M. Monteith (ed.), *IT for Learning Enhancement*. Exeter: Intellect Books.

Weiner, G. and D. Kallos (2000) 'Positively women: professionalism and practice in teaching and teacher education', paper presented to the symposium 'Teacher Education in Europe: Current Tendencies in a Comparative Perspective'. American Education Research Association, New Orleans, April 24–8.

Welch, A. R (1998) 'The cult of efficiency: comparative reflections on the reality and the rhetoric', *Comparative Education*, 34, (2), 157–75.

Wenger, E. (1990) 'Towards a theory of cultural transparency: elements of a discourse of the visible and the invisible', PhD thesis, University of California.

Westwood, R. and Linstead, S. (eds) (2001) *The Language of Organization*. London, Thousand Oaks and New Delhi: Sage Publications.

White, J., Ferguson, P., Hay, P., Dixon, M. and Moss, J. (2003) 'Ownership and identity: developing and implementing teacher professional standards in Australia', www.austcolled.com.au/dbing, Australian College of Educators, Unicorn Online. Refereed Article No. 32.

Whitty, G. (2000) 'Teacher professionalism in new times', *Journal of In-Service Education*, 26, (2), 281–95.

Whitty, G., Power, S. and Halpin, D. (1997) *Devolution and Choice in Education: The School, the State and the Market*. Buckingham: Open University Press.

Wild, P. and Walker, J. (2001) 'The commercially developed SIMS from a humble beginning', in A. Visscher, P. Wild and A. C. W. Fung (eds), *Information Technology in Educational Management: Synthesis of Experience, Research and Future Perspectives on Computer-assisted School Information Systems*. London: Kluwer.

Wilkinson, G. (2005) 'Workforce remodelling and formal knowledge: the erosion of teachers' professional jurisdiction in English schools', *School Leadership and Management*, 25, (5), 421–39.

Wilson, R., Easton, C., Smith, P. and Sharp, C. (2005) *National Remodelling Team: Evaluation and Impact Study (Year 1)*. Slough: NFER.

Woods, P., Woods, G. and Gunter, H. (2007) 'Academy schools and entrepreneurialism in education', *Journal of Education Policy*, in press.

Woodward, W. (2003) 'A third of teachers plan to quit', *Guardian*, 7 January 2003, p. 1.

Woolgar, S. (1991) 'Configuring the user: the case of usability trials', in J. Law (ed.), *A Sociology of Monsters: Essays on Power, Technology and Domination*. London: Routledge.

Yarker, P. (2005) 'On not being a teacher: the professional and personal costs of workforce remodelling', *Forum*, 47, (2 and 3), 169–74.

Young, J. and Hall, C. J. (2004) 'Oceans apart? Teaching and teacher preparation in Canada and the UK', *Canadian Journal of Educational Administration and Policy*, 32, (1), 2–6.

Index